Along the tracks of Cobb and Co.

The Great Northern Road

History speaking for itself ...

Research and compilation by Hazel Johnson

Author's Note

"The old stage coach has been pushed off the roads by the motor, but the ghosts of the romantic past will ever linger." (The Sydney Mail, 1921) From the horse and sulky, or the stage coach and galloping horses ... to mail planes ... to the motor buggy ...

Courtesy of John Elliott, writer/photographer

Journey through a broad spectrum of change, along some of the tracks of Cobb and Co.

As a proud Australian with a deep love for history, I believe exploring Cobb and Co. highlights a significant chapter of our nation's past. The people behind Cobb and Co., along with those who helped shape modern Australia, have my deepest admiration. Their hard work, resilience, and problem-solving abilities are reflected throughout this book's excerpts.

My research has reinforced a powerful truth—those who came before us were not so different from people today. They were visionary entrepreneurs, creative thinkers, and innovators. They tackled the daily grind, no matter the weather, much like our vegetable farmers and dairy workers today. They also had a sharp wit, as shown in anecdotes like:

"At an unnamed change station, the boss would flick off the covering of the food and say, What would you like—lamb, mutton, or ram!"

You may ask, What Makes This Book Different? This series aims to share the positive history of Cobb and Co. and the postal service, showcasing their contribution to modern Australia. To achieve this, I have woven together fragments of historical accounts spanning the 1800s to mid-1900s—allowing *history to speak for itself*. Through original texts, readers may feel as though they are sitting on the box seat next to the driver, jolting along the tracks of Cobb and Co. At times, the authentic words of the past carry far greater meaning than reinterpretations. My goal has been to preserve the integrity of each excerpt, ensuring the emotional depth and historical significance remain intact. The inspiration for Book 1 'Along the Tracks of Cobb and Co. – The Great Northern Road' (Tenterfield to Warwick) came from the recreation of a Cobb and Co. coach and the establishment of the *Cobb and Co. Coach & Collectables Museum* in Liston, New South Wales. This being the legacy of old-timer John Charles Burton, Junior, as a nod to the past, honoring Australia's pioneering spirit.

While this book explores Cobb and Co.'s legacy, it does not delve into the rich cultural history of Australia's First Peoples or their interactions during the period of colonisation.

Spelling, punctuation, and grammar remain faithful to historical sources, enhancing the story's authenticity and illustrating the evolution of language. Additionally, the progression of photography, from its early limitations to improved quality, is evident throughout the book.

Acknowledgement of Country

We acknowledge the Traditional Custodians of the land
on which the Cobb and Co. stage coaches travelled.
We pay our respect to Elders past, present and emerging,
and extend our deep respect to all Aboriginal and Torres Strait Islander Peoples.

TITLES

Book 1
Along the tracks of Cobb and Co. —The Great Northern Road
(Tenterfield to Warwick)

Book 2
Along the tracks of Cobb and Co. —The Western Run
(Brisbane, Toowoomba, Roma & Charleville)

Book 3
Along the tracks of Cobb and Co. —The New South Wales Headquarters
(In & Around Bathurst)

Book 4
Along the tracks of Cobb and Co. —Back to the Beginning
(Victoria & the Goldfields)

Book 5
Along the tracks of Cobb and Co. —Cobb's Coach Drivers

Book 6
Along the tracks of Cobb and Co. —The Roaring Days !
(Amusing Anecdotes & Tales of Grit and Graft)

Book 7
Along the tracks of Cobb and Co. —Queensland
(Brisbane & Beyond) (Release date ... late 2025)

Print | Audiobooks | eBooks
Copyright by Hazel T. Johnson

First Edition 2021, Reprinted July 2022 & May 2023, Second Edition April 2024, Third Edition July 2025

Content mainly courtesy of Trove (The National Library of Australia) and their many partners including State Library of New South Wales, State Library of Queensland, State Library of Western Australia, and State Library of Victoria, as well as The Sovereign Hills Museums. Photographs taken before 1955 and maps created before 1955 are out of copyright (Australian Copyright Council). Special thanks to the other contributors of photos and/or information, to assist in the telling of part of the story of Cobb and Co. in Australia. Spelling, punctuation and grammar are as per historical sources. Every attempt has been made to ensure the correct use and acknowledgement of all sources. The information in this book is by no means exhaustive. Corrections and/or contributions welcome for the next edition. Book cover image: Driving along the track - Courtesy The Sovereign Hill Museums Association Limited, Ballarat, Victoria.

Available from www.cobbandcotracks.au or local outlets

Further contact: email dvhtjohnson@gmail.com; Mobile phone +61 417984455

ISBN 978-0-6459759-8-7

This book was printed by:
IngramSpark

Typeset in Garamond

Contents

2	**Author's Note**
6	**Chapter One:** The Great Northern Road, Sydney to Brisbane ca. 1846
24	**Chapter Two:** The beginnings of the Australian Postal Service 1800-1849
36	**Chapter Three:** 'American Telegraph Line of Coaches' comes to Australia 1850s
42	**Chapter Four:** Communication & Cobb and Co. 1860s
50	**Chapter Five:** Cobb and Co.'s mail conveyancing 1870s
68	**Chapter Six:** Along the mail routes 1880s & 1890s
80	**Chapter Seven:** The changing landscape 1900-1920s
102	**Chapter Eight:** Early motoring 1900s onwards
112	**Chapter Nine:** Liston, N.S.W., & district on the Great Northern Road ... Just a snippet
160	**Chapter Ten:** Cobb & Co. Coach and Collectables Museum, Liston, N.S.W.
166	**Appendices**
174	**Reference List**

Chapter One

The Great Northern Road
Sydney to Brisbane
ca. 1846

THE DAYS OF COBB & CO.
By G. M. Smith

To travel out a thousand miles
You'd book yourself in town;
They'd guarantee to pull you through
When you paid your money down;
They travelled then by rough bush tracks,
Through mountains, bog and snow,
And deliver you well up to time,
Would good old Cobb and Co.

(The Days of Cobb & Co., 'Watchman',
Cunnamulla, 4 Mar 1904, p.4)

The great firm of Cobb and Co. embodies a romance older than Queensland itself—the rhythmic trot, trot, clicketty-clack of iron-shod hooves and wheels echoed through history, carrying the dreams and destinies of those who rode its coaches. Brave men and horses made the bush ring as they traversed the Great Northern Road, a rugged inland pathway linking Sydney to Brisbane.

Cobb and Co. coaches rattled along the tracks, carrying passengers, parcels, and mail through settlements, such as Armidale, Glenn Innes, Tenterfield, Maryland, Warwick, and beyond. Early maps reveal a coaching route through Tenterfield, Boonoo Boonoo, Wilson's Downfall, Amosfield, the future site of Liston, Maryland, and Warwick (Queensland). See *Appendix A: Map Reference List*.

Maps of the County of Buller and County of Ruby mark an 'old mail track' along The Seven Mile or Herding Yard Creek, from Maryland to Liston. See *Appendix F: Map of Parish of Wylie & Appendix G: Map of Parish of Ruby*.

TABLE OF DISTANCES ON NORTHERN DISTRICT ROADS

- Sydney to Maitland – 112 miles
- Maitland to Singleton – 70 miles
- Singleton to Muswell Brook – 30 miles
- Muswell Brook to Murrurundi – 40 miles
- Murrurundi to Cowrindi (Loders) – 25 miles
- Loder's to Tamworth – 42 miles
- Tamworth to Bendemere – 27 miles
- Bendemere to Rocky River – 31 miles
- Rocky River to Armidale – 14 miles
- Armidale to Falconer – 25 miles
- Falconer to Stonehenge – 20 miles
- Stonehenge to Glen Innes – 8 miles
- Glen Innes to Dundee – 15 miles
- Dundee to Balivie – 23 miles
- Balivie to Tenterfield – 22 miles
- Tenterfield to Maryland – 48 miles
- Maryland to Warwick – 30 miles
- Warwick to Eton Vale – 40 miles
- Eton Vale to Drayton – 8 miles

Total Distance – 590 miles
(Land Carriage Companies for the Northern, Southern, and Western Interior, 24 Jun 1854, p.4)

The Maryland Hotel—A change station

The Maryland Hotel served as a changing station along the Warwick–Tenterfield run. "In 1866, George Fagg, formerly of the Court House Hotel in Tenterfield, advertised: George Fagg … Begs respectfully to call attention to travellers and the public to the fact that he has completed the erection of a commodious hotel at Maryland, situated on the main line of road between Warwick and Tenterfield, which will be opened on Easter Monday, the 2nd April next. The want of accommodation at this place for travellers passing between the two colonies has long been felt, and the proprietor is determined to entertain his customers in a manner equal to any town hotel, having had several years experience in that particular business at Tenterfield. A large well grassed paddock is attached to the premises and stabling will be well attended to." (Advertising, 28 Mar 1866, p.4)

By 1867, there appeared to be a significant change at the hotel. "Mr. James Arbouin – At the residence of Mr. George Fagg, Maryland Hotel, Maryland, on Thursday next, at 11 o'clock prompt: Household Furniture, Bar Fittings, Wines and Spirits, Plated Ware, Crockery, Cooking Utensils, etc. Also: Stack of Hay, Cart and Set of Harness, Buggy and Harness, and the Unexpired Term of License of the Maryland Hotel." (Tenterfield, 26 Feb 1867, p.2) However, Fagg remained connected to the establishment, as public records from 1870 listed him as a licensee in the Tenterfield District. "Return of Publicans' Licenses … Fagg George … Tenterfield District. Maryland … Maryland Hotel." (From Government Gazette, 26 Oct 1870, p.288)

The Maryland Hotel became the third Cobb and Co. changing station on the Warwick-Tenterfield run, offering a break to passengers. Cobb and Co. began servicing this route at the start of 1870.

By 1872, a marked tree just north of the hotel "serves as an indicator of the demarcation line between New South Wales and Queensland. The road from Warwick to Maryland spans twenty-seven miles and is reported to be in excellent condition, reflecting great credit on the road trustees for its upkeep." (The Tin Country, 4 May 1872, p.6)

1866 Tenders for Conveyance of Mails

- James Shield, Brisbane and Moggill, once a week, £45 ;
- Cobb and Co., Brisbane and Ipswich, twice a day, £691 ;
- Chas. J. West, Brisbane and Maryborough, once a fortnight, £200 ;
- Cobb and Co., Helidon and Toowoomba, twice a day, £548 ;
- Cobb and Co., Condamine and Roma, twice a week, £831 ;
- Patrick Layden, Taroom and Roma, once a fortnight, £140 ;
- Cobb and Co., Toowoomba and Warwick, three times a week, £683 ;
- James Fox, Warwick and Maryland, twice a week, £85. (Government Notifications, 15 Dec 1866, p.7)

1870 Cobb and Co. Mail Services

£5058 19s. 8d. per annum,
- Brisbane, Stewart's Ferry, Yandina, One-mile creek, and Gympie ; twice a week ; coach ; two years
- Brisbane, Rocky Waterholes, Oxley, Goodna, and Ipswich ; twice a day, except Sundays, and expresses when required ; coach ; two years
- Dalby and Condamine, via Kogan and Wombo ; twice a week ; coach ; two years
- Condamine and Roma via Morabie, Wallumbilla and Blythedale ; twice a week ; coach ; two years
- Warwick, Maryland (N.S.W.), and Tenterfield (N.S.W.) ; twice a week ; coach ; two years
- Brisbane and Pimpama, via Eight-mile Plains, Logan Reserve, Waterford, and Benleigh ; twice a week ; coach ; one year
- Allora Railway Station and Warwick ; once every day, Sundays excepted ; coach ; one year.
(Mail Contracts, 11 Dec 1869, p.2)

The Great Northern Road—A vital mail route

In 1871, a newspaper described the route from Glen Innes to Tenterfield as "the greatest and most important mail road in the colony—the connecting line between Sydney and Brisbane, Queensland … being the Great Northern Road." (The Tenterfield Road, 27 Jan 1871, p.3)

As travel increased, government funding became essential. Back in 1870, "a grant of £15 per mile" was allocated for the road from Tenterfield to the Queensland border. (Tenterfield, 21 May 1870, p.2)

By 1872, concerns about inadequate funding were voiced. Alderman Whereat, writing to The Star,"The road from Glen Innes to Tenterfield has been gradually reduced from £50 to £25 and £15 per mile, and now to £7 per mile. The road also from Tenterfield to Maryland is placed at the same rate. Surely the Government must forget that this road is the Main Northern Road, and that at the present time, when tin land has been so extensively taken up, there is more than five times the traffic along the whole of this road than formerly … Do they not place the principal obstacle in the way of our advancement by allowing at present one of the chief roads in the colony to be in a disgraceful state of repair?" (Tenterfield, 31 Aug 1872, p.6) The route between Tenterfield and Ruby Creek also continued to challenge travelers, with reports describing it as "one of the worst roads in the district." (Quartpot and Ruby Creeks Revisited, 9 Nov 1872, p.2)

Late in 1872, funding was allocated for repairs to the Great Northern Road. "1873:—1. For the formation and repair of the road from Maryland to Tenterfield, a sum not exceeding £2260. 2. For the formation and repair from Tenterfield to the Clarence, a sum not exceeding £5600." (Epitome of News, 23 Nov 1872, p.2) Later it was reported that the money was never spent.

Along the tracks—Tenterfield to Warwick

Tenterfield to Sugarloaf

In the year 1872 Tenterfield was described as: "The town of Tenterfield is distant from Sydney 431 miles, from Grafton 130 miles. It is the most northerly town in the colony. From the 'Elbow,' or 'Lawrence,' on the Clarence River, it is distant 120 miles. Supplies from Sydney are generally conveyed by steamer to the Elbow and by teams through Tabulam and Fairfield to Tenterfield, the time of transit being about three weeks.

The township is pleasantly situated, and when the cultivation paddocks are green must afford a cheering view. At this season, however, everything looks parched—the want of rain, which has not fallen for over two months, being a serious drawback to the numerous free selectors and farmers. A creek called the Tenterfield, a tributary of the 'Sovereign,' flows north and south on the west side of the town. The buildings all stand well up above flood mark, as the country slopes well up from the banks of the creek.

Entering the township from the north, on the right, a pretty view is obtainable, the hills forming a very pretty background —one of them, of peculiar form, is called 'The Doctor's Nose.' The main street is rather narrow, but still wide enough for the requirements of the traffic. The Main or Rouse Street is graced on each side for nearly a mile with substantial structures, and the knots of people standing around the Post Office, waiting for the delivery of the mail which had just arrived as I entered the town, would lead one to believe that business is on the increase.

From the numerous hotels, parties are continually coming from or going to the mines, drays loading or unloading at every store, and on the whole, a smart business aspect is noticeable through the town. Tenterfield has lately been proclaimed a municipality. The present mayor is Mr. Wellburn. Three neat places of worship have been erected—the Roman Catholic, a stone structure, being the most substantial. The Church of England is a brick building with a very neat exterior. The Wesleyan is a weatherboard. The hospital is built half a mile north of the town. It is nicely situated and under the management of a local committee. At the time of my visit, there were no patients—a healthy sign.

The telegraph station, a neat brick building, is situated in one of the cross streets, a little out of the way, but still not too far for convenience. The station is under the charge of Mr. Tucker, who has two operators—Mr. Quirk and Mr. Martin. The opening up of tin country around the district has much increased the telegraphic business, and from morning till night Mr. Tucker and his assistants are as busy as bees ... See *Appendix B: Telegraphic Communication*

The Joint Stock is the only bank with a branch in town. Mr. Trollope is the manager, and of late has had his hands full of business, making it necessary to augment his staff. Some substantial stores and hotels can be found in the town, Mr. C. A. Lee's store (a stone building) being the largest. Several others are worthy of note, and all are doing a good trade.

Of the hotels, the largest and most commodious is the 'Tenterfield,' kept by Mr. Farrell. The stabling in this establishment is particularly good, the best I have seen out of Sydney. Mr. Robert Laird's Golden Fleece Hotel is most patronized by the mining community, as Mr. Farrell's by the commercial. The Royal and other hotels come in for a fair share of business. Mails for Sydney are made up twice a week—on Sunday and Thursday nights—taking in transmission to Sydney four days." (Tenterfield to Stanthorpe, 20 Jul 1872, p.5)

After leaving Tenterfield, the journey to Warwick via Maryland led through a landscape of established cattle stations and growing townships. "Thirteen miles on the road, a small station of Mr. Banbury's—the Boonoo Boonoo—was passed on the left of the road. Seven miles from that, the Bookookoorara—a cattle station belonging to Mr. Rutland—had its fences along the way. Four miles past the station, or twenty-four miles from Tenterfield, a halting place was afforded in Mr. Jenner's public house, named the 'Half-way.'

The tin discovery had been to this house a boon in its way. Numbers of speculators, miners, and others now, from daylight to midnight, sought refreshment and, in many cases, lodging for the night. So great had been the rush that Mr. Jenner found his old slab mansion too small for his visitors and was at present building a large weatherboard hotel, which would meet the increasing demand. A 'shake-down' [makeshift sleeping arrangements] at Jenner's had once been a byword, but I fancied the new building tacked on to the old would do away with the term, as I inspected the new building and found bedrooms laid out to accommodate a dozen at least." (Tenterfield to Stanthorpe, 17 Jul 1872, p.9) In November of 1872 "Mrs. Jenner informed us she had made up over 50 beds on the previous night, and had to provide for as many breakfasts that morning ; and she added that the Circus had been there, and had just left for Stanthorpe." (Quartpot and Ruby Creeks Revisited, 9 Nov 1872, p.2)

"I found one store opened opposite Jenner, by Mr. Juergens. The tin dishes, sluicing forks, horse gear &c., displayed outside would lead one to suppose that the storekeeper was fully aware of the likely wants, and that he was willing to supply them. This gentleman as yet has no opposition, but in time no doubt a small township will spring up around this place as it stands close to many selections which will shortly be at work ... the inhabitants, now numbering, I should guess close on five hundred ...

I might add that a rifle would be useful, as the marksman can find kangaroos or wallabies in plenty to try his skill on. On every flat, scores of 'tripods' may be seen hopping along gracefully over the sward. Kangaroo hunters would find a fine field for sport close to the Queensland border. My sporting friends need not fear a fruitless day's chase, only one drawback exists, the country is a very rocky one. The country around is badly timbered, peppermint, gum, box, stringybark, honey suckle, and dogwood are plentiful enough, but stunted, affording but little opportunity to the builder. One misses the ironbark sadly when slabs are required either for mining or building purposes ...

The first block of country I crossed on my way from Jenners was the Border Consols, a private company, managed by Mr. M. Kay, for Mr. Trockmorton—80 acres ...

I examined the wash and found it thickly impregnated with ruby tin ...

The custom of this and the adjoining selections is to send their tin down by drays to Warwick, a distance of sixty miles. The carriage to that town, on the average, is £3 per ton. From Warwick it goes by rail to Ipswich. From Ipswich by water it is transported to Brisbane, and there transhipped for Sydney ... The next selection to the east is one of 20 acres, named the Star of Tenterfield, under the management of Mr. Lyndsay." (Tenterfield to Stanthorpe, 17 Jul 1872, p.9) See *Appendix C: Rail Development*.

The cost of travel remained high as tin mining surged. "Eight shillings per night for your horse" was an expense many had to bear. Those venturing further toward Warwick encountered Wilson's Downfall and Sugarloaf Creek area, where pioneering miners established claims. "On the Sugarloaf (Creek) Mr. Laird purchased 160 acres for 1300 pounds; on the junction of Sugar Loaf and Thirteen Mile Creeks, is the Ruby Tin Company; Thirteen Mile Creek is Amos and party." (Tenterfield to Stanthorpe, 17 Jul 1872, p.9)

"Wilson's Downfall, or Four Mile Creek ... to all appearance is a rugged spot ... I cannot explain how strange it appears to the visitor to be enabled to place one foot in New South Wales the other in Queensland, it is a favourite joke at this point, and when parties pass a flask being at hand, the welfare of both the colonies is often drunk with honours." (Tenterfield to Stanthorpe, 17 Jul 1872, p.9)

By 1874, Sugarloaf township had started to take shape. "Around the Sugarloaf quite a township has sprung up since my last visit, graced by a police station, lock-up, Queensland properties, and several new stores—quite a brisk little place, with a contented population." (The Tourist, 27 Jun 1874, p.816)

WARWICK, MARYLAND TO STANTHORPE/QUART POT CREEK

"In the early times the road from Maryland to Warwick came by Turner's Gap. When Perrott was in charge of Maryland he found an easier and shorter road through what is now called Parrot's Gap ... 1849 ... At that time I was hut-keeper for two shepherds on Maryland, seven miles from the head station ... Joseph Rigby, senr." (The Early Days, 10 Jul 1902, p.6)

On the reverse route from Warwick to Maryland then onto Stanthorpe "travellers found a relatively good road to Maryland, covering approximately twenty-eight miles. The journey extended another fourteen miles to reach the key selections on Quart-pot Creek. "For a stranger to travel, is to follow the road until reaching the station of Mr. Jones, the overseer of Maryland, where directions can be obtained for finding with greater facility the required localities." (The Maryland Tin Discoveries, 19 Mar 1872, p.3) At various times "Cobb and Co.'s jostling coach, which, from the anti-Macadam condition of the road, rolled and pitched to such an extent as to produce sickness in one case, an unexpected contingency which compelled the unfortunate passenger to lay up for a day at a roadside hotel." (The Iron Road to Stanthorpe, 18 Oct 1879, p.2)

"It was a cold winter's morning in 1871 when, as a schoolboy, I hopped into the coach with a male guardian, not related to me, at the front of the Commercial Hotel, Warwick, on our way to occupy a tin selection at what is now Stanthorpe. I fancy Host Dinte presided at the hotel then, with a smart young fellow named Arthur, who seemed to be his right-hand man in everything. At the word go, the bugle was sounded by the driver as a signal for the Post Office people in Albion-street to have the mails ready for him.

The Post and Telegraph Office in those days was in a nice stone building opposite Mr. Flitcroft's coach factory ; next door to it was the Court House, and at the back of this building were the police cells, etc. Two prominent officers then were Harris and King. I can still hear the strong voice of the latter as he called out 'Silence in the court!' when the schoolboys used to sneak in to have a look at the judge and barristers with their wigs on. The present postmaster at Toowoomba is a son of the late sub-inspector, and the well-known police officers of later years. Tom, Walter, Willie, and Nat, were sons of the late Sergeant King.

The road to Stanthorpe was a busy scene of swaggies humping bluey, spring carts, bullock and horse teams, all loaded, and horsemen heading for the Tin Eldorado. As the coach crawled up the Maryland Gap, we passed many people I knew by sight, and on the top of the Gap was a snug place, where I remember the stock were branded MA over 44. After this, the N.S. Wales boundary soon barred the way, where slip rails had to be taken down to get into a Maryland paddock.

The large trees on either side of the slip rails had initials cut into the bark as high as anyone could reach by standing on their saddles.

Maryland Station came into view; it seemed quite a township. A Mr. Fagg kept a nice place there, and other names I remember were Flint, Hart, Hardy, and Butler.

On arriving at Quart Pot, the place was a maze of tents, with quite a number of buildings in the course of erection for hotels, stores, and dwellings. The only old house there was the Quart Pot Hotel, built on a selection belonging to Maryland Station. Hotels were selling drink from temporary bars, and sly grog shops were rampant, while the old Quart Pot Hotel, near the then nice running creek, was simply deluged with custom. There were one or two large, deep waterholes near the hotel. Now I see they are as dry as the streets nearby, and a stranger would never imagine that enthusiastic young fellows used to dive to the bottom with the buckets and place as much tin wash in them as possible before coming to the top for breath, yet I have seen it done.

We were met by the third member of the party, who had a dray with two horses, loaded up with supplies, blankets, but no tent. Spare my days, but the perishing cold winter nights are impressed upon my mental chart as Siberia, never to be forgotten on this planet. Eventually, we pulled up at what I imagine was near the head of Cannon Creek. Further down the creek was an outstation, with sheep yards; still lower down, over the edge and below the rocky gorge, were Bugden and party, who were getting fair tin under the management of a Frenchman. Where this creek ran into Quart Pot Creek, a man named McGlew was washing out fabulous quantities of tin by using Californian pumps. Unfortunately for our party, we were out of the tin area, so abandoned the ground—40 acres. Had it been held, the total cost would have been about £8; now I notice the railway line built to the soldiers' settlement runs across the end of this block, so it will, in all probability, be a returned soldier's orchard in a few months' time. May he have better luck than we had when I used to shoot at the kangaroos, emus, and Crimson Lowry parrots. At that time, had anyone suggested that I would live to see railway trains running past the spot, I would have seriously considered he had an attack of white ants in the top storey.

Rations were always obtained by making to Quart Pot, and it was no trouble to get these on a Sunday. Prominent business men I remember were Tevlin and Farley. Between times on these occasions,

I was a spectator of the fights which used to take place up the ridge, not far from where the railway station is now—Sunday being the recognized day for settling disputes by the noble art ...

On my way from our camp to what is now Stanthorpe, I used to walk past the fair-sized cave, now called 'Thunderbolt's,' in which were the remains of a saddle and broken bridle bit. Possibly these belonged to Thunderbolt, who still reigned supreme in these parts and the northern districts of N.S. Wales. This spot was a convenient one for him to lie in wait until the clouds rolled by, where he could keep in touch with his relative, who lived at Maryland. However, I was more interested in the rock wallabies that were to be seen here than troubled about the gallant Fred.

Now it is a pleasant change to see the up-to-date residences hereabouts, where one can order bacon and eggs for breakfast instead of dining on rock wallaby or stewed Lowry parrots. The growing of fruit as a commercial product was not even thought of at Stanthorpe, although the owner of Glentanner, near Dalveen, had some splendid stone fruits and vines in bearing, which were from the fine garden of Glengallan Station. The principal products of the district were stream tin, wool, stock, tallow, and hides, and these continued to hold their place up to the time the railway was opened to Stanthorpe in 1881. In 1889 the Rev. Father Davadi was very enthusiastic in his efforts to interest people in the capabilities of Stanthorpe as a fruit-growing district, and proved it in his own garden. In this he was ably supported by the Fletcher family, of Ballandean. This genial priest always compared Stanthorpe, as regards soil and climate, to his native country, Italy, where apples grew to perfection, and he was certain they would do well at Stanthorpe. If he could have a look at the network of orchards there now he would see every word of his verified.

As the tin worked out, the healthy, invigorating climate of this district attracted invalids suffering from all the ills that mankind picks up, and medical men begun to recommend it for chest trouble ; now it is a recognised sanitorium for everything in the way of sickness. Naturally, many of the invalids were experienced in the cultivation of fruit, vegetables and flowers. These people at once saw the possibilities of the Stanthorpe country for orchards, and, after regaining their health, launched out by establishing orchards, and now we see all around the result of their efforts and experience, followed closely by others, until we find the Stanthorpe district, orchards a valuable asset of the State.

The latest figures available for 1919 show that Stanthorpe, and 11 miles on either side of it, returned railway revenue for that period amounting to £29,000, and that in the same year, over 87,000 fruit trees came into the district. The expansion is still going on by leaps and bounds, making it a producing district in harmony with the ideas of our best thinkers. For 1918, 72,177 bushels of apples were produced, and in the same period the grapes gathered were 147,395 lbs. Apart from these figures there is the vegetable crop, for which separate statistics are not available, but this crop bulks largely in the prosperity of the district.

For such a nice comfortable lot of dwellings, with their cheery surroundings, it would be very hard to beat this very fine district, with its bracing, pure mountain air. Its educational requirements have kept step. Now its schools rank in the front row, and their efforts are all helping in the direction we like to think our State is progressing, that is, an educated, virile, self-contained and prosperous part of what is to be the Australian nation." (A Retrospect, 31 May 1920, p.6)

Branch off the Great Northern Road–Sugarloaf to Stanthorpe

1874, from Wilson's Downfall, "the drive to Stanthorpe (eight miles) is over a sandy rough road dotted here and there with boulders that would capsize a vehicle without much warning if anything like pace was attempted. Along the line there are any number of public houses—so many that I lost count, and must defer giving the correct return until my next visit, when I shall carry a stick and notch as I go along. Of one fact I am certain, that did I refresh at all along the way, my course might well be unsteady before I reached Stanthorpe, that is assuming my draught to be stronger than lemonade.

Stanthorpe looks a little better or brisker than it was eighteen months ago, a period when I in my correspondence noted it as about the dullest place I had met in my travels. Things seem a little brisker, and

> the sheets a little dirtier than they were at that time; the latter I suppose must be taken as a sign of prosperity, as it gives evidence of increased population ...

The Chinese quarter forms nearly half the town ... The new rush signs are disappearing, giving way to those of more permanent settlement. Some nice wooden churches, a good hospital (the latter was badly required) is, I am happy to say, in the hands of a good medical man. The stores are, like the hotels, numerous enough indeed, I fancy in trade there is rather too much opposition.

A smelting works is in course of erection in the heart of the town—a praiseworthy venture of Mr. Ransome. A short distance out, at Mount Marlay, furnaces are or have been in operation, but in consequence of the quality of the bricks not being up to the standard, or from some defect in construction, a stoppage for a while had to be made. I saw two very fine mineral collections—one at the Commissioner's office, the other with Mr. Cane, at the Joint Stock Bank; the latter embraces nearly all the mineral products around not only the district but the colonies of Queensland and New South Wales, and reflects great credit on its collector." (The Tourist, 27 Jun 1874, p.816)

As noted in 1872 "our Main North Road, does not touch upon Stanthorpe." (A Trip to the Tin Mines, 3 Dec 1872, p.3) However, "between Stanthorpe and Warwick, Cobb and Co. run a line of coaches daily—the best and the quickest travelling one I have met with … On the way there are four changes—first, Maryland, for lunch. The road is fearfully rough for thirty miles, passing over what might be termed a barren tract, very thinly settled upon. Maryland, spite of its pretty name, I consider as mean a looking place as one could possibly fancy. It consists of two hotels, a mile space between them, and a few huts; also, some place that looks like a station homestead." (The Tourist, 27 Jun 1874, p.816)

By 1889, as settlement expanded, maintaining an extensive road network became increasingly difficult. "It was found impossible to extend the elaborate system of roads in the same proportion to the territory as heretofore, and the Government had to limit itself to 'great roads' or main lines of communication with the most distant parts. The chief of these as they now stand are the Northern Road, length 405 miles from Morpeth to Maryland in New England." (History of New South Wales, 5 Oct 1889, p.8)

Despite the ongoing challenges of road maintenance and travel costs, the Great Northern Road remained a vital inland link between Sydney and Brisbane. However, travelers had to be ever mindful of unexpected hazards—such as a 'white cow' ...

Accident To Tenterfield Mail Coach

"A sensational accident happened to the Tenterfield Casino mail coach one night last week. Six miles this side of Tabulam, the five horses that drew the cumbersome vehicle shied at a white cow lying on the road, the sudden swerve causing the coach to heel over into a dry watercourse.

> Driver Flannagan was thrown clear and gamely stuck to the reins, thus preventing a bolt. Rev. D. D. Carruthers, who was a passenger, had the ball of the little finger torn off down to the bone;

Mr. S. French, of Kyogle, had a deep cut in his head which necessitated half-a-dozen stitches; Mrs. French had an arm dislocated; while her baby, although considerably bruised, had a miraculous escape, for a press account says that it 'fell right underneath the coach with a bar across its legs.'

The three men lifted the coach up and enabled the child to be rescued by its mother. Subsequently, five men were unable to lift the coach even after it had been unloaded. The accident occurred at 9:15 p.m., and it was 5 a.m. the next day before the injuries of the passengers were properly dressed.

The coach was totally disabled. The side was smashed in, the lamps smashed, the big leather spring was jolted out of gear, and the king-bolt snapped off short. Messrs. Morrissey and O'Keeffe, contractors, paid all expenses incurred by the passengers and provided for their conveyance to their destinations." (Local and General News, 11 Jan 1907, p.9)

Queensland railway expansion

As the demand for improved transportation increased, attention in 1875 shifted toward railway expansion. "A Stanthorpe correspondent writes:—As the agitation for railway extension to the border of New South Wales, through Stanthorpe, from Warwick, is now a subject of interest." (Stanthorpe, 31 Jul 1875, p.3)

By 1878, the well-trodden paths of Cobb and Co.'s coaches had defined the route from Tenterfield to Maryland. "In fact, it is an open question, whether the road from Tenterfield to Maryland is even marked out. Travellers get along by the track of Cobb and Co.'s coach." (Country News, 19 Oct 1878, p.633) The coach journey continued to test even the hardiest of travelers.

Meanwhile the "gold mining, which was being carried on in various places in the neighbourhood, has all been suspended, and the tin mining at Maryland and around Stanthorpe and the neighbourhood is at such a low ebb that Tenterfield can reap little or no benefit from it just now … Everybody is wishing and waiting for the Queensland railway to be extended to Stanthorpe, in the hope and belief that this will give the people of this portion of New England a better and more certain market in which to sell their produce and purchase their stores; wishing and waiting, too, for the drought to break up, so that the land may again, yield its accustomed harvests …

How very much alike people all over Australia seem to be, after all! Here, in Tenterfield, in two hours, I was as much at home with the residents I met as though they had been residents of Brisbane or Ipswich, and I was talking trade and politics, and public works and the land question with them—

forgetting half the time that I was in another colony.
And these people of Tenterfield are more of Queensland than of New South Wales.

They regard Warwick as of far more importance to them than Glen Innes or Armidale, and Brisbane as their commercial capital when the railway is once open to the border. And Governments are very much alike also. At Tenterfield is a telegraph office, which is a repeating station for Queensland, consequently all telegraphic messages between the two colonies have to be repeated here." (Tenterfield, 2 Mar 1878, p.21)

It was only in 1881 that the railway finally reached Stanthorpe. "A special train left Brisbane at half-past seven o'clock this morning to convey the Colonial Secretary, the Mayor and Corporation, and a few others invited to take part in the ceremony of opening the extension of the Southern and Western Railway from Cherry Gully to Stanthorpe. The train is expected to reach Stanthorpe at about a quarter-past four this afternoon and the opening, ceremony will take place immediately afterwards. The banquet will come off at seven and a ball will follow. When bed will be reached is problematical ; possibly it will be, in the case of many, anticipated by breakfast." (Opening of the Stanthorpe Railway, 3 May 1881, p.2)

By 1886, Tenterfield was experiencing an economic boom. "Tenterfield is in a very flourishing state at present, and additional impetus will be given to business by the commencement of the new Tenterfield-Border railway." (Tenterfield, 10 Apr 1886, p.2)

Australia's postal and transport history reflects how pioneering efforts paved the way for modern road and rail systems, particularly along the Great Northern Road. It highlights the resilience of early transport networks including Cobb and Co., the growth of settlements, the necessity of infrastructure funding, and the challenges faced by travelers and communities.

1859 Cobb & Co. coach on the Sydney road (Watercolour) – Courtesy National Library of Australia

ca. 1870 Tenterfield, view of town from Glen Innes Road – Courtesy State Library of New South Wales

1913 Royal Mail – Courtesy Bruce Robertson, Tenterfield

1886 Opening of the Tenterfield Railway – Courtesy Tenterfield Information Centre

ca. 1912 Buggy and Lismore Mail Coach in High Street, Tenterfield, NSW – Courtesy State Library of New South Wales

1887 Mail coach at Royal Hotel, Wallangarra, en route to Tenterfield – Courtesy State Library of Queensland

Carnarvon Bridge, Stanthorpe, Clinton's Folly, a causeway is to the left of the bridge – Courtesy State Library of Queensland

1872 The Roll-up Tree, Maryland Street, Stanthorpe (looking south) – Courtesy State Library of Queensland

ca. 1882 Stanthorpe settlement showing a church and some settler's cottages – Courtesy State Library of Queensland

ca. 1880 Laying of the railway line at Stanthorpe (looking from Marley) – Courtesy State Library of Queensland

The opening of the extension of the Southern Railway Line at Stanthorpe, 3 May 1881 – Courtesy State Library of Queensland

ca. 1868 Palmerin Street, Warwick – Courtesy State Library of Queensland

ca. 1871 Anderson's General Store, corner of Palmerin & Albert Streets, Warwick; Adjacent store, Warwick's first tinsmith & galvanised iron worker – Courtesy State Library of Queensland

ca. 1860 View of timber buildings lining East Street, Ipswich – Courtesy State Library of Queensland

1864 Charlotte Street, Brisbane, during the flood – Courtesy State Library of Queensland

ca. 1895 Stagecoach on the riverbank, Town Reach of the Brisbane River
(Hardcastle Family Album) – Courtesy State Library of Queensland

ca. 1872 Queen Street, Brisbane (William Boag) – Courtesy State Library of Queensland

Rooftop view along Stanley Street, South Brisbane, during the 1887 floods – Courtesy State Library of Queensland

1893 Flooding at the Breakfast Creek Hotel, Brisbane – Courtesy State Library of Queensland

1924 Last Cobb and Co. coach – Courtesy Laidley Pioneer Village and Museum

Chapter Two

The beginnings of the Australian Postal Service 1800-1849

THE GOOD OLD DAYS.
By Arthur Gordon

What memories the old hands retain of the bus,
The great changes they actually saw.
What books we could write of that gallant old push
When life in itself was quite raw ;
For we cannot but praise these grand pioneers,
Their practical and old-fashioned ways.
Still life was worthwhile in those rollickin' years,
'Way back in the good old days.

(On the Track, 17 Apr 1944, p.3)

"The establishment of the Australian Postal Service marked a significant milestone in the country's communication history. The journey began in 1809 when Colonel William Paterson, then Lieutenant-Governor of the colony, issued an order to address the 'complaints having been made … that numerous frauds had been committed by individuals repairing on board ships on their arrival at this port and impersonating others, by which they have obtained possession of letters and parcels'." (Communications Across the Generations, Read 1971, p.171)

Sydney—First post office

On April 25, 1809 saw Paterson establish an office under the direction of Mr. Issac Nichols. "Post offices were originally private offices used for postal purposes. Thus the first post office, that is, the first place used for postal purposes in Australia, was the house of Mr Isaac Nichols, assistant to the Naval Offices in High-street, now Lower George street, Sydney. When Isaac Nichols died in 1819, Mr. George Panton was appointed, and being a wharfinger, he carried out his postal duties in a small apartment on the King's wharf.

It was not till 1825 that a regular postal service was established, and the Governor in Council was empowered to appoint postmasters. Mr. James Raymond, grandfather of Mr. E. Denny Day, was the first regular postmaster of Australia. Under his regime a post office was established at Moreton Bay under a deputy postmaster, in 1834." (Brisbane, 4 Nov 1916, p.12)

North to settle Morton Bay

As the colony expanded with "settlement in the territory now called Queensland began in September, 1824 … Morton Bay became the third penal station on the east coast of Australia … to relieve overcrowding" [at Port Macquarie] … it was recommended "Redcliffe Point as the best place to start the penal settlement … Murray reported the place unsuitable … Oxley himself advised removal to a site on the left bank of the Brisbane River about fourteen miles from the south. This suggestion was adopted, and the removal began in December." (Geographic History of Queensland, 1895, pp.7-9)

Thus, the penal settlement was moved from Redcliffe to Edenglassie, the original name given to Brisbane.

Governor Brisbane arrived in Moreton Bay on November 25, 1824, marking the beginnings of the settlement of Brisbane town. The Queensland's half-century publication from December 8, 1909, noted: "Nov 4.—Penal Settlement removed from Redcliffe to Edenglassie—the first name given to Brisbane … Nov 25.—Governor Brisbane arrived in Moreton Bay." (Queensland's … notable events, 8 Dec 1909, p.23)

"The penal settlements are for the purpose of receiving and trying to reclaim convicts who have committed crimes after transportation. According to the nature of the offence are they punished. Those guilty of the least are sent to Port Macquarie, those of a graver nature to Morton Bay, and those of the deepest dye to Norfolk Island … These unfortunate individuals are engaged in clearing the country, in the first place, for the immediate wants of the settlement, and when that is accomplished they go in order to prepare it for free settlers …

At the time of Macquarie's visit there were 300 convicts at the Brisbane station, employed in growing maize in the localities now known as New Farm and Bulimba. All work was done by spades, hoes, and mattocks. The convicts were marched out in the morning in gangs, under the overseers and soldiers, and marched home and locked up in the barracks at night. The female convicts were kept for some years at a factory on the locality still known as Eagle Farm, about six miles from Brisbane, where they were employed in clearing and cultivation … It is but just to remember that in the penal days many a good man was sent out for crimes that today would be punished by a small fine or a caution in the police court, and many were sent out for crimes of which they were entirely innocent." (Geographic History of Queensland, 1895, pp.7-9)

"Governor Brisbane left the colony to return to England on the 1st December, 1825, after having administered the government for four years." (Governor Brisbane, 25 Jan 1879, p.133) 1826 "Dec. 19.—Death of Governor Brisbane." (Queensland's … notable events, 8 Dec 1909, p.23)

In 1828, Charles Fraser, the Colonial Botanist, arrived in Brisbane in the Lucy Ann, after a passage of twenty-three days from Sydney. He "came up to layout the site of the present Brisbane Botanic Gardens. He was accompanied by the famous botanist, Allan Cunningham. Fraser's narrative states that he was sent to establish a public garden, to collect the vegetable product of the country, to make observations on their uses and importance, especially the forest trees ; to report on the nature of the soil, and to what extent it is fitted for grazing or agriculture." (Geographic History of Queensland, 1895, pp.9-10)

To further illustrate Brisbane's growth, "A historical map of Brisbane City circa 1844 includes a detailed legend marking significant locations including the old post office: Andrew Petrie, Handel, cattle drover, Savory (the only baker), Bensteads, sawyers, T. Richardson (the only general store), Convict Barracks, W. Kent (druggist shop), Fitzpatrick (the first Chief Constable), The Lock-up, The Constable's place (only two in all), Slade's Post Office (old), Slade's Pineapple Garden, Church of England, The Hospital, Mort, milkman, Wright's Hotel, General Cemetery, Tread and Windmill, Edmonton's Paddock, Old R. Jones, Dr. Simpson (the first Commissioner), Old Major Prior, The Gaol, Skyring's Beehives (soft goods shop), Hayes, milkman, Brothers Fraser (first houses), Catholic Church, McLean's Blacksmith's Shop, Edmonston's butcher, Bow's Hotel, Taylor Shappart, Montifeur (a financier), W. Pickering, Sergeant Jones, Soldiers' Barracks, Officer de Winton, Commission Stores, Queen's Wharf, Captain Wickham's office, Commissioner T. Kent, Commissioner's Garden, Captain Coley, Government Gardens, Father Hanley (the only priest), Saw Pits, Queen Street, The Boat House and Boatman's House, The First Tombstone (two graves). (Description supplied with photograph.) The Postmaster in 1844 was George M. Slade."

Moreton Bay evolved into the city of Brisbane

The first "post office was established at Moreton Bay under a deputy postmaster, in 1834. As Moreton Bay was then and for eight years after a non-free settlement, it is certain that the postal arrangements were in the hands of the military authorities, and highly probable that they were carried out ... in or near the Commissariat office in William-street ...

After Moreton Bay was thrown open to free settlement in 1842 ... Mr. William Whyte was appointed clerk of the bench and postmaster, a position which he held till his death on February 18, 1844. During his tenure of office Mr. H. N. Wade prepared the plan of North and South Brisbane ... On this plan 'Post 0' is written on the block at the corner of Queen and George streets, now known as Wilkinson's Corner.

Mr Whyte's successor was Mr. George Miller Slade, formerly paymaster 60th Rifles, who died in 1848. In his time Gerler made" a map which "shows, according to the reproduction in the Jubilee History of Queensland published by H J Diddams and Co, in 1909, 'Slate's Pine Apple Garden' as occupying the block marked 'Post 0' in Wade's map, and a little lower down Queen-street 'Slate's Post Office (Old)' is shown in a building which also contained the lockup and the constables' quarters. Next to the constables' quarters a cottage is shown as the shop of W. Kent, druggist, and next to Kent's shop the convict barracks. 'Slate' is of course 'Slade.' The inference is that both Mr. Whyte and Mr. Slade transacted postal business in the office of the clerk of petty sessions. On Mr. Slade's death Mr. W. A. Brown was appointed C.P.S. and Post-master ...

It may be assumed that the post office continued to be in the clerk of petty sessions' office. Mr. W. A. Brown was C.P.S. and postmaster until 1852, when the increase of business led to the separation of the duties of C.P.S. and postmaster, and the appointment of the first regular postmaster in Capt. Barney ...

Capt Barney had to find other premises for the post office, and took a small wooden building in Queen street, which he used as a dwelling-house and post office ... It remained the post office until 1872, when it was replaced by the present post office ... F. W. S. Cumbrae Stewart." (Brisbane's First Post Office, 4 Nov 1916, p.12)

As Brisbane grew, buildings were leased at Moreton Bay. "His Excellency the Governor directs it to be notified, that the undermentioned Buildings, or parts of Buildings, will be let by Public Auction, at Brisbane, on or about the 20th of May next. Each lot will be let separately, for one year, and the day of letting will be notified, at Brisbane, after the arrival of the Steamer in May. Lots: Nos. 1, 2, and 3. Three Rooms on the ground floor of the right wing of the Prisoners' Barrack. 4. A Building, consisting of four rooms, in the continuation of the same wing, and opening into the Court Yard of the Barrack. 5. A House (lately used as a Public Office,) situated between the Military Barrack and the House occupied by the Rev. Mr. Handt. 6. A part (lately occupied by Mr. Marriott,) of the Range of Buildings, situate between the Post Office and the Prisoners' Barrack. 7. The remainder of the same range, with the exception of the Prisoners' Cells, on the part of the range situate between the Cells and the Prisoners' Barrack. 8. The Buildings known by the name of the Barn Range, with the exception of the part of the same used as a Slaughter House. By His Excellency's Command—Deas Thomson." (Lease of Buildings at Moreton Bay, 12 Apr 1842, p.551)

In the same year, letter carriers required uniforms. "The under-mentioned Articles of Clothing being required for the Public Service, persons disposed to provide the same are invited to transmit their Offers, in writing, to the Colonial Secretary's Office, by Twelve o'Clock on Monday the 2nd May next, endorsed 'Tenders for Letter Carriers' Uniform.'

Thirteen Red Coats with the V. R. Button. Thirteen Black Beaver Hats with Gold Bands. Samples must accompany the Tenders, and Patterns for the Coats may be seen at the General Post Office. Persons tendering are requested to attend at the Colonial Secretary's Office on the day appointed for opening the Offers." (Sale of Town Allotments, 22 Apr 1842, p.3)

News along the tracks—Ipswich

Ipswich traces its origins to 1826, "Limestone (Ipswich) named by Logan." (Queensland's ... notable events, 8 Dec 1909, p.23)

By 1846, the "first steamer, the Experiment, ran between Brisbane and Ipswich." (Queensland's ... notable events, 8 Dec 1909, p.24) Passengers could enjoy conveniences on board, as advertisements stated, "Refreshments provided on board at moderate charges ... Cabin Passage, 6s. ; Steerage, 4s." (Classified Advertising, 12 Sep 1846, p.1)

In 1848, the "first mails despatched to Ipswich by steamer". On November 28 a "Post office box at South Brisbane was established." (Queensland's ... notable events, 8 Dec 1909, p.24) By 1861, records indicate that the Ipswich Post Office offered "town delivery daily" and "an iron letter receiver is fixed in Brisbane-street ... cleared daily." (Ipswich Post Office, 8 Mar 1861, p.2)

As Ipswich developed, replies to advertisements for skilled tradespeople were received via the post office. In 1849, an advertisement sought an apprentice "To the General Watch, Clock, and Jewellery Business. N.B.—Must be a respectable lad, of religious education and industrious habits. A premium required. Term: five years. Address: A. B. C., Post-office, Ipswich."

Postal communication encountered occasional setbacks. In December 1849, a notice announced: "the Private Post Bag from Warwick to Canning Downs, containing the Brisbane post for the undermentioned persons of the 11th inst, having been accidentally lost, correspondents will please write again. George F. Leslie, Patrick Leslie, William Leith Hay, Canning Downs, 21st Dec, 1849." (Classified Advertising, 12 Jan 1850, p.1)

By 1899, the Observer reported: "Plans are just being completed for the erection of new post and telegraph offices at Ipswich." (The Ipswich Post-Office, 23 May 1899, p.4) In September 1899, approval was given for the construction. "Ipswich—Post Office Tender. The Governor-in-Council has approved the acceptance of the tender of Mr. Midson for the erection of a new post and telegraph office in Ipswich, including stables, fencing, gates, together with front walls, and a tower of double-pressed brick with stone detailing. The price for the contract is £8,568, and the work is to be completed within twelve months." (Ipswich Post Office Tender, 22 Sep 1899)

Timeline of the Darling Downs

Discovery (1827)

- June 5, 1827 – "Darling Downs discovered by Allan Cunningham." (Queensland's ... notable events, 8 Dec 1909, p.23)
- "On his return southward passed about 15 miles west of Tenterfield." (Tenterfield, 1949, p.6)

Squatters and pastoral runs (1839-1842)

- 1839-1842 – "The first squatter on the Darling Downs, and therefore the first in Queensland territory, was Patrick Leslie ... Walter Leslie followed his brother with 5,600 sheep, 10 saddle horses, 2 bullock teams and drays, and a team of horses and dray. Their assistants were twenty-two ticket-of-leave convicts, said by Leslie in a letter of 1878 *to be good and game as ever existed, and equal to any forty I have ever seen since.*" (Geographic History of Queensland, 1895, p.32)
- Others followed including "Sibley and King on Clifton, Hodgson and Elliot on Eaton Vale, Hughes and Isaacs on Gowrie, John Campbell on Westbrook, Scougall on Jimbour, Charles Coxen on Myall Creek (now Dalby), Irving on Warra, and Dennis on Jondaryan." (Geographic History of Queensland, 1895, p.33)

First transport to the Downs (1840)

- August 12, 1840 – "First pack bullocks took supplies to the Downs from Brisbane." (Queensland's ... notable events, 8 Dec 1909, p.24)
- October 19, 1840 – First dray taken through Cunningham's Gap." (Queensland's ... notable events, 8 Dec 1909, p.24)

Pastoral stations and infrastructure (1845-1849)

- May 1845 – "Rosenthal, Aberdeen Company; Canning Downs, W. and G. Leslie; Maryland, M. Marsh." (Geographic History of Queensland, 1895, p.35)

- 1845 – "A post office was established at The Swamp now Drayton. Rea, p.181 states Drayton was allegedly named from Dray Town—and in 1846, one at Limestone (now Ipswich) and a mail service established between Ipswich, and the Darling Downs, extended the following year from Drayton through Warwick to Armidale." (Coaching in Australia, 1917, p.49) By 1864 – "The erection of a new post-office at Toowoomba is to be shortly commenced." (Miscellaneous, 16 Jul 1864, p.4)

- June 30, 1846 – "First census taken, population including Darling Downs, 2258." (Queensland's ... notable events, 8 Dec 1909, p.24)

- April 1847 – "Discovery of a road over the range to Southern end of Downs." (Queensland's ... notable events, 8 Dec 1909, p.24)

- January 1849 – "Surveyor Burnett laid out town of Drayton." (Queensland's ... notable events, 8 Dec 1909, p.24)

- September 8, 1849 – "Wanted to purchase, 30 good Rams, Wool fine and thickly set on the carcase, average weight of wool, three pounds each sheep. Any person having Rams of this description for sale will please communicate with X Y Z, Post Office, Drayton." (Classified Advertising, 8 Sep 1849, p.1)

Darling Downs—'Billy' the Ram

By 1883, significant progress had been made in sheep breeding across the Darling Downs, with certain flocks gaining notable recognition. "From the earliest date of settlement the Darling Downs possessed some superior flocks, notably those of Rosenthal and Canning Downs. To the late Mr. Frederic Bracker, of Warroo, is due much of the credit of laying the foundation of several of the best flocks now in the colony. Whilst recognising to the fullest extent the value of fineness, Mr. Bracker would appear to have avoided the mistake, too common at that early period, of sacrificing quantity or weight to more fineness of staple. Hence in all the flocks in which the blood of his sheep is traceable, or in which his mature judgment had been employed in selection, we find density and weight a decided characteristic—profitable clips, in short. To the late Mr. John Deuchar, of Glengallan, however, may be said to belong the credit of first bringing the fine wools of Queensland prominently before the world, and of stimulating that healthy spirit of emulation that has resulted so successfully in establishing so many fine flocks on the Downs ... the late Mr. John Deuchar, in 1855, selected 100 ewes, and so started his stud flock ...

> *one of the best rams then known on the Downs, and was long and widely known by his familiar name 'Billy.'*

This ram was unapproachable at every showyard at which he put in an appearance. He is described by those who remember him well as a fine deep-set animal, with a superb aristocratic head, and covered with a magnificent fleece. Billy was coupled, in 1855, with the 100 ewes above referred to, and the progeny were the origin of this now celebrated flock." (Our Pure Merino Stud Flocks, 7 Apr 1883, p.551)

News along the tracks—Warwick

In 1848 "A post office was established at Warwick ... Mr. W. A. Brown, C.P.S., was appointed postmaster." (Coaching in Australia, 1917, p.49)

Warwick's development is demonstrated by this chronology of its key milestones: "Genesis of Warwick (By 'Gooragooby,' Dalveen.) For the information of inquiring ones the writer is submitting a rough chronology of Warwick:—Police station formed, 1849; first court house, 1849; St. Mark's schoolroom, 1858; old Presbyterian church, 1859; A. J. S. Bank, 1861; first Town Hall, 1862; second court house (Albion-street), 1862; telegraph office, 1862; Helene-street bridge, 1863; East Warwick school, 1864; Warwick Argus established, 1864; first St. Mary's Roman Catholic Church, 1864; School of Arts established, 1865; New South Wales Bank, 1866; Examiner established, 1867; Governor Bowen's second visit, 1867; Eastern Downs Society, 1867; St. Mark's Church, 1868; recreation squares fenced, 1868; Governor Blackall visit, 1869; railway opened to Hendon, 1869; new Presbyterian church, 1870; post and telegraph offices (Albion-street), 1870; Lord Normanby's visit, 1871; railway opened, 1871; Caledonian Society, 1871; first Masonic Hall, 1871; second Town Hall, 1873; Victoria bridge, 1873; St. Patrick's Day sports, 1874; and Central School, 1875 ... reminds me of a past record flood ... rescue from their home at Albert-street East ... five members of the Fallon Family." (Echoes of the Past, 30 Mar 1935, p.9)

Beyond infrastructure, Warwick was also home to pioneering families whose contributions shaped the region. "By the death on January 15 of Mrs. Mary Aspinall, the Warwick district lost one of its oldest pioneers … In 1858, she married the late Mr. John Aspinall, and went to live at Maryland Gap, on the road from Warwick to Stanthorpe, then known as Quart Pot Creek, where her husband, a mail contractor, had built a house to serve as a mail station. For twelve years Mrs. Aspinall lived there and looked after the station, while Mr. Aspinall carried the mails on horseback between Ipswich, Tenterfield, and Armidale. Then they bought the Golden Fleece Hotel at Quart Pot Creek, which they kept for two years, at the end of which time the Cobb and Co. coaches took over the mail contract." (Obituary—Mrs Mary Aspinall, 30 Jan 1926, p.15)

News along the tracks—Quart Pot Creek, Maryland

In 1856, the region witnessed an unusual theft. "Thomas Toe was indicted for stealing a silver watch from John Glanville at Quart Pot Creek, in the police district of Warwick, on the 9th December last. It appeared from the evidence that prosecutor and prisoner were together at Ross's public house near Maryland on the night in question, and that prosecutor took his watch out, holding it by the ribbon, when prisoner seized the watch in one hand and with the other cut the ribbon with a knife and made off.

Next morning, Glanville asked him for the watch, when he said that some person had since taken it from him. Chief Constable Gordon apprehended the prisoner, and in consequence of some conversation had with him that evening, he accompanied him to an uninhabited hut near, where prisoner raked the watch out of some ashes in the fireplace and gave it up. In defence, prisoner said that he had never intended to steal the watch; that prosecutor was exhibiting it in the public house and, at his request, gave it into his hands, when he took it away to take care of it, as they were all drinking; that he secreted it in the fireplace of the empty hut and subsequently gave it up to the Chief Constable. The jury, after half an hour's deliberation, found the prisoner guilty, and he was sentenced to two years' hard labour in Parramatta gaol." (Domestic Intelligence, 24 May 1856, p.2)

While theft, loss and the riding of horses often caused disruptions. In 1859, a reward notice declared: "Twenty Pounds Reward. LOST, from Ballindeen run, a CHESTNUT MARE, branded EM on the off shoulder, ML (conjoined) on the near rump, with three head of increase not branded, and last seen near Glenlyon, near Tenterfield. Twenty pounds will be paid for the mare if stolen upon conviction of the thief or thieves; or, if strayed, five pounds will be paid on her being delivered to Mr. Philip Sullivan, Tenterfield; or Bartholomew Ross, Quart Pot Creek, Maryland." (Advertising, 10 Sep 1859, p.1)

Following this on December 20, 1859, another theft occurred: "Stolen on the night of the 20th December last, from the 'Golden Fleece Inn,' Quart Pot Creek, Maryland, a bay mare, Bridle, and Saddle. The mare was branded TF (conjoined) on the near shoulder, small snip on nose, switch tail saddle, colonial bag leather, with a hole cut in the pommel in place of a D; new bridle. The mare was taken when in hobbles, and the bridle taken out of the tap-room at the break of day. She is supposed to have been taken towards the McIntyre Brook. I hereby offer a reward of Five Pounds for the recovery of the mare, bridle, and saddle; and Ten Pounds on the apprehension of the thief." (Advertising, 7 Jan 1860, p.1)

In early 1860, tragedy struck Maryland. "MELANCHOLY AND FATAL ACCIDENT—Our Warwick correspondent, writing under date the 12th, says:—From what we are able to gather, it appears that on Sunday last, a man named George Crosby left Mr. Ross's public house, Quart Pot Creek, under the influence of liquor. He had left but a few minutes when his horse returned with the saddle and bridle on, but minus the rider. A search was at once made, and the rider was found a short distance off, lying on the road in a most fearful state. He was at once conveyed back to the Inn and received every possible attention, but the poor fellow lingered about an hour when death put an end to his sufferings." (Local and Domestic, 19 Jan 1860, p.3)

Maryland continued to grow as a settlement. "Maryland—Post Office at established." (Index Page, 31 Dec 1859, p.IX)

News along the tracks—Tenterfield

In 1849, just across the border in New South Wales "the first Post Office and mail service in Tenterfield were established on 1st January … The Post Office was situated in the Station Store, a convict built brick building, across Tenterfield Creek, from the northern end of Rouse Street, and nearly two miles from the present Post Office." (Tenterfield, 1949, p.2)

By 1870, "the rate upon letters from Queensland to any of the other colonies is sixpence, and correspondents have to pay just as much for a letter from Warwick to Tenterfield as they have for one from Warwick—or any other town in Queensland—to any part of England. The distance from Warwick, our nearest border town, to Tenterfield in New South Wales is about eighty miles, yet it costs as much to send a letter between those two points as it does to forward one sixteen thousand miles ... In Queensland, small as our population may be compared to New South Wales or Victoria, our postal lines now extend more than 9,000 miles. During the year 1868, more than two million letters and nearly a million and a half newspapers were received and dispatched, not to mention book packets. The total income of the General Post Office for 1868 was £1,493, while expenditure reached approximately £47,000, leaving a deficit of about £25,000 against the Postmaster General. It would be absurd to expect a post office department to be self-paying in a colony like ours—or, indeed, in any colony." (The Courier, 28 Jan 1870, p.2)

Local post office news

1869 FLOODS "We have had some very heavy rain since my last report, followed by such a flood that, for the short time it lasted—a few hours—we had not seen one like it in the past five years. The mails for Tenterfield and Inverell had to return and were only able to proceed the following day. The rain has done a great deal of good for both squatters and farmers. Though very heavy, it soon subsided." (Country News, 4 Dec 1869, p.3)

1920 RAIN "has been falling every day since the last issue, with registrations at the local post office as follows: Friday at 9 a.m., 37 points; Saturday, 47 points; Monday, 8 points. On Friday night, the electric light failed temporarily in Tenterfield and was out for about 20 minutes. No issues were found at the powerhouse or with the mains outside. It is thought that someone was tampering with the mains, causing a short that tripped the breakers." (Tenterfield, 24 Sep 1920, p.6)

1920 "ANZAC DAY was observed here yesterday. Prior to the united service of the churches, crowds gathered at the Post Office and marched to the Memorial Hall, where a service was held, headed by the Boy Scouts, the military, and the Border Caledonian Pipe Band. In the absence of the Mayor (Alderman S. Armstrong), the Deputy Mayor (Alderman Lance Walker) opened the service. The Rev. Mr. May, of the Anglican Church, Rev. Mr. Wesley Booth (Methodist), and Rev. Mr. Paul (Presbyterian) gave very fine addresses. The names of Tenterfield's dead heroes, 64 in all, were read, while the crowd stood with bared heads." (Tenterfield, 27 Apr 1920, p.18)

1926 POST OFFICE DESTROYED "On Wednesday night, the home of Mr. P. Wright, Wyeera, Ten Mile, Clifton Road, near Tenterfield, was destroyed by fire. The outbreak occurred around midnight when one of the inmates was awakened by the crackling noise of flames. The rest of the household woke just in time to gather a few clothes and escape from the burning building. The house, a weatherboard structure, served as the receiving station for mail in that district and was fitted with a public telephone. The building was completely destroyed, and very little of the contents were saved." (A Post Office Destroyed, 28 Dec 1926, p.4)

Other businesses

Tenterfield's economic growth was largely pastoral with "About 500 acres of land cultivated." (Tenterfield, 1949, p.14). An 1856 impoundment record reflected its agricultural foundations. "Impounded at Tenterfield, on the 18th of January, 1856, by order of Mr. King:—One red and white poley bullock:, branded VI off rump, 2 near rump. One red heifer, DD off rump, 5 off thigh, bit off near ear 8. One strawberry bullock, WW near side, C near rump, bit off near ear. IH One strawberry poley cow, O off rump. One brindle cow, M-M near side. One yellow sided cow, TW near side." (Impounded at Tenterfield, 15 Feb 1856, p.540)

In 1891, a meat-chilling venture sought to modernise the industry. "The Tenterfield people ... propose to kill fat cattle and deliver the chilled meat in Sydney at 30s per carcase. The prospectus, as published in the papers, does not specify what additional charge beyond 5s per head will be made by the company—such as the retention of offal, fat, etc. However, it does highlight Tenterfield's suitability for the venture, citing its proximity to key fattening regions, including the Clarence, and its potential role as the "probable junction of the Tenterfield-Casino railway." (Echoes and Opinions, 12 May 1891, p.2)

These milestones highlight how postal networks, businesses, and infrastructure shaped Queensland's development, paving the way for modern advancements.

ca. 1883 Post Office in Maryland Street, Stanthorpe – Courtesy State Library Queensland

1884 Brisbane Post Office building in Queen Street – Courtesy State Library of Queensland

ca. 1870 Post Office, Molesworth & Logan Streets, Tenterfield – Courtesy State Library of New South Wales

ca. 1885 The first Sydney Post Office, George Street – Courtesy State Library of New South Wales ca. 1880 Post Office, Margaret Street, Toowoomba – Courtesy State Library of Queensland

ca. 1875 Post Office, Albion Street, Warwick – Courtesy State Library of Queensland ca. 1859 Canning Downs station homestead – Courtesy State Library of Queensland

ca. 1865 Canning Downs station homestead, Warwick district (when Davidson lived there) – Courtesy State Library of Queensland

Walter Leslie – Courtesy State Library of Queensland

Patrick Leslie – Courtesy State Library of Queensland

1858 Portrait of Freeman Cobb –
Courtesy National Library of Australia

ca. 1835 Allan Cunningham – On permanent
loan to National Portrait Gallery, Canberra

Chapter Three

'American Telegraph Line of Coaches'
comes to Australia
1850s

GLENGALLAN.
By W.W., Brisbane

Where the bold mountains lift their rugged heads,
Keeping still guard o'er Millar's happy vale,
And lonely Sturt his sullen shadow sheds,
Braving the Christmas sun and wintry gale,—
And lowing herds adown the peaceful dale,
Answer the bleatings of the timid ewe,
Luring her sportive young with plaintive wail—
Behold! Glengallan bursts upon the view,
To weary wanderers a beacon kind and true.

(Original Poetry, 31 Oct 1846, p.4)

"During a good many years of life in Australia, it has been my fortune to travel much, both by sea and land. I have experienced the dirt and discomfort of the steamer ... Railway and road, bush and river, horseback and on foot, in dray and in buggy ... by coach and by boat ... Each method of travelling has its delights, each its annoyances, its comforts and its discomforts. None has more of each, or less of each, according to the circumstances and temperament, than has that throne of John, that place of proud pre-eminence, the seat of 'Philip Cobb's Box'... But why Cobb? As Betsy Prig said to Mrs. 'Arris; *there ain't no Cobb. Cobb's dead, defunct, gone out, has passed in his checks, so far as Australia is concerned.* Is he, and has he? ... He may be anybody, Robertson & Wagner, Crawford, Chaplin, Quick, or who not; yet he is Cobb after all ... Who is Cobb? ... a man who certainly did well for Australia ... consider the wear and tear of horse flesh over the roads, or rather no roads, of those days ... these were the days that made the name of the line a household word throughout the length and breadth of many lands ... the good rough and tumble old times when it was a favor to get a place at all in Cobb's coaches, and the highest honor mortal man could aspire to, was to obtain a seat on 'Cobb's Box' ... Furious driving, I grant you, a reckless disregard, sometimes, of their own and their passengers' necks ... There was no time then to be shilly-shallying on the edge of a swamp, no use hesitating at taking a header down a steep gully with a broken boulder or slimy bottom.

It was a shake of reins, a crack of the stinging whipcord, a heigh ho! houp la! a mad plunge, a creaking of springs, a straining of harness, a flying of mud and gravel, and a get out on the other side at full gallop, for you know, Her Majesty's mails must not be delayed."
(Cobb & Co., 5 May 1875, p.4)

Cobb and Co. commenced in Australia

"When gold was discovered in Victoria, in 1851, and up to the middle of 1853, the only means of conveyance to the then existing gold fields, was by paying a carrier so much for head for the carrying of the passengers' swags and tools, the men walking, and, of course, camping out at night." (The Contributor, 25 Nov 1908, p.1405) During 1852 and early 1853 "British or English style coaches ran in the colonies in Australia with little success, as the coaches were too rigid and heavy for the bush tracks." (An Historical Magazine, 4 Mar 1911, p.19)

"About the middle of 1853 a change came over this mode of transit." (The Contributor, 25 Nov 1908, p.1405) In mid-1853 "Freeman Cobb came to Melbourne ... with George Mowton, to form a branch of Adam and Co, famed in the United States as express carriers." (Death of the Founder of Cobb and Co., 28 Sep 1878, p.3) "Hauling their waggons through the mud ... they gave it up." (Old Coaching Days, 10 Jun 1922, p.7) "They advised their principals in the United States [Adams and Co.] against the carrying business, but told them that there was a good opening for a real up-to-date line of coaches to the diggings, and a certainty, if established, of getting the mail contracts, as those then in existence were only an apology for coaches, and the mails often days behind ... the United States companies turned down the coaching proposition." (A [?] Drive, 31 July 1937, p.4)

Following this "George Francis Train ... says: *I told Freeman Cobb, who was then with Adams and Co., that I wanted him to start a line of coaches between Melbourne and the gold-mines, a distance of about sixty miles. I advanced the money for the enterprise, and a line was established, the first in Australia ... These were the first coaches seen in that continent."* (My Life of Many States and Foreign Lands, 1902, pp.133-134) Cobb and Co. was established and commenced running January 1854: "AMERICAN TELEGRAPH LINE OF COACHES. Daily Communication between Melbourne, Forest Creek and Bendigo—Cobb and Co. beg to announce to the public that they have determined to run a line of well-appointed Coaches between the above places, starting from the Criterion Hotel every morning, (Sunday excepted) at 6 o'clock, and from Forest Creek, daily, at the same hour. The vehicles intended to run are the new American coaches, recently imported, and acknowledged to be the easiest conveyances in the colony. The first coach will start from the Criterion, on Monday, January 30th, and every attention will be given to ensure punctuality COBB and CO., Proprietors Feb 3" (Advertising, 31 Jan 1854, p.3)

Freeman Cobb "was a young American destined to impress his personality so deeply upon the coaching business during his brief career in Victoria that his name has survived as a synonym of the 'coaching days' while those of most of his associates and successors have been forgotten." (Story of Cobb and Co., 20 May 1922, p.5) The other partners in Cobb and Co. at that time being "John Lamber, James Swanton, and John Murray Peck." (Old Coaching Days, 10 Jun 1922, p.7) Note. The many proprietors who ran 'under the style' of Cobb and Co. are listed in 'Along the tracks of Cobb and Co. - Back to the Beginning'.

By 1856, Freeman Cobb prepared to leave Australia. "Thursday, 22nd May. Sale of Handsome Furniture, & Symons and Perry have received in instructions from Freeman Cobb, Esq. (who is leaving the colony per Royal Charter) to sell by auction, at the Telegraph Coach Office, 23 Bourke-street east, on Thursday, 22nd inst., at twelve o'clock," (Advertising, 19 May 1856, p.2)

While "a complimentary dinner is to be given to this gentleman on his departure from the colony … Mr. Cobb has conferred great benefits on the country by his energetic and successful efforts to establish communication with the interior, and we sincerely trust that a large party of good colonists will meet him, and show that they appreciate his services. We are authorised to state that the dinner will take place at the Criterion Hotel, on Friday, the 33rd inst., and that tickets can be paid on application to the following parties:— Messrs. Rogers, Warfield, Lord, and Co.; Messrs. Fisher, Ricards, and Co.; H. Flint, Esq., Bourke-street; and Lachlan Mackinnon, Esq., Argus office. Argus." (Advertising, 23 May 1856, p.3)

As the firm of Cobb and Co. expanded, "the coaches of this line spread from the Great centre like a network over the colony." (Local and General, 19 Sep 1859, p.3) Always seeking new opportunities, "ever on the look-out for fresh fields." (Local and Provincial, 14 Jun 1862, p.2) Cobb and Co. ventured into the Lachlan goldfields in New South Wales in 1862 when gold escorts were required "for the conveyance of the gold ... between the Lachlan gold-fields and Bathurst via Orange, in connection with the escort which leaves Bathurst weekly for the Mint," (Advertising, 21 Mar 1862, p.2) before advancing into Queensland.

Cobb and Co. arrived in Queensland

After expanding into New South Wales "Cobb and Co. obtained their first footing in Queensland in 1865 (12 years after James Rutherford's first visit to Brisbane). The firm secured the mail coach contract for the Brisbane to Ipswich run at £691 a year—twice a day service. Hiram Barnes, the first driver and partner, took charge of the ribbons, and soon 16 coaches, constructed at Bathurst, were sent to Brisbane and were on the roads in Queensland. In rapid succession followed coach services to the Gympie goldfields, Kilkivan, Maryborough, and many other important centres, and extending, as the various railways pushed out their railheads.

Cobb and Co.'s acted as excellent feeders to and from the railway system for passengers and mails. One outstanding feature of their career in the northern State was the remarkable continuity of the service, once opened. Heat waves and dust and droughts ; rain, mud and floods made little difference." (Cobb and Company's Coaches, 10 Apr 1925, p.28)

Later in 1865, it was "satisfactory to know that the tender of Messrs. Cobb and Co. has been accepted for the conveyance of mails between Ipswich and Toowoomba. Their contract will commence on the 1st of January next." (Telegraphic, 21 Oct 1865, p.4)

Proclamation of the state of Queensland

THE AUSTRALIAN COLONIES

A "rare 1859 map of Australia" illustrates a brief but significant period in the nation's territorial development. "This fascinating map shows Australia as it appeared in the early months of 1859, featuring a peculiar combination of interim intercolonial boundaries. It is one of the only maps to show this arrangement, for it existed for a mere matter of months." See *Appendix D: 1859 Map of The Australian Colonies*.

THE NEW COLONY OF QUEENSLAND

The movement for separation gained momentum over several years. "The agitation in favour of separation continued. In 1856 the Brisbane committee sent the Rev. Wm. Ridley overland to the Clarence and Richmond for signatures to a petition, assuming that those districts would be included in the new colony." (Geographic History of Queensland, 1895, pp.14-15). Ultimately, separation was granted, and on 10th December 1859, Governor Denison of New South Wales formally "proclaimed the new colony of Queensland" and introduced its first political divisions—sixteen electorates returning twenty-six representatives. "The southern boundary was fixed, not south of the Clarence, but along the McPherson Range, precisely where it had been located by proclamation in the Sydney Gazette on 10th May, 1842, in a definition of the boundaries of Morton Bay. Queensland was born with a population of 28,056 people. The statistical record of 1860 shows 1,236 births, 478 deaths, and 278 marriages." (Geographic History of Queensland, 1895, pp.14-15)

THE PROCLAMATION OF QUEENSLAND. Official recognition of Queensland's establishment came through an Order in Council: "By an Order in Council published in the London Gazette, her Majesty has been pleased to erect Moreton Bay into a separate colony, under the name of Queensland." (Proclamation of Queensland, 8 Aug 1859, p.5)

With its creation, territorial adjustments followed—"Rosenthal and Canning Downs were cut off from Maryland to become a portion of the new colony of Queensland." (Echoes of the Past, 24 Jun 1933, p.7) On April 20, 1877, "the land on Rosenthal and Canning Downs South runs were thrown open ... The number of applications lodged amounted to 54, of which 31 were for 80-acre homesteads, and the remainder conditional purchases. Twenty-three selections were applied for on Rosenthal, and 31 on Canning Downs South. The rent and survey fees payable amounted to £1172 7s. The total area applied for was upwards of 17,000 acres, and comparatively few of the applications overlap." (Warwick, 24 Apr 1877, p.2)

Rosenthal happenings

- "IMPOUNDED, at the Warwick Pound, on the 23rd July, from the run of Mr. J. Deuchar, Rosenthal:—A chestnut mare, branded like PF near shoulder, blaze down forehead, long tail. A bay foal, unbranded, white streak down forehead—belonging to the above mare. If not released on or before the 15th of August, will be sold." (Classified Advertising, 10 Aug 1850, p.1)

- "2000 EWE SHEEP Deliverable at Rosenthal Station, Darling Downs, near Warwick. Mr. Mort is instructed to sell by public auction, at his rooms, Pitt Street, On Tuesday, 29th March, At 11 o'clock. 2000 fine-woolled ewes of mixed ages, which are warranted sound and never to have been diseased. The wool of this well-known stock obtains the very highest prices in the home markets. Forms on application to the Auctioneer." (Advertising, 19 Feb 1853, p.1)

- "MARRIED, At Rosenthal, on the 27th ult., by the Rev. Thos. Kingsford, of Warwick, Thomas Craig, eldest son of Mr. Wm. Craig, Wright, Warwick, to Bridget Ryan, of Rosenthal." (Family Notices, 10 Mar 1855, p.2)

- "A FLOUR MILL is now in the course of being constructed at Warwick, and when completed will be worked by water power. The grinding stones and machinery have been purchased from the proprietor of the Rosenthal station, and it is expected that they will soon be in working order." (Local and Domestic, 3 Feb 1857, p.3)

- "SNAKE IN CANARY CAGE. Yesterday morning, Mr. S. J. Nunn of Rosenthal Road, upon examining his large canary cage, which contained a dozen canaries, looked particularly for one that was nesting in a box about six by three inches and three inches deep, situated near the top of the cage. Instead of the canary, however, he was astonished to see a snake's head lying over the edge of the box. The snake was curled up beneath the soft and feathery substances of the nest, with only its head showing. Upon counting the canaries, two birds were missing. The difficulty then was how to kill the snake. It was impossible to get inside the cage, and care had to be taken to prevent the birds from escaping. Mr. Nunn got a long piece of iron and pushed the snake out of the nest onto the floor of the cage, where it wriggled about and resisted capture. A pea rifle was brought out, and the snake was dispatched with three bullets to the head. Upon opening the body, the two full-grown canaries were found inside, having been swallowed whole—one going down head first and the other tail first. The marvel is how a brown snake, measuring 4 feet 3 inches long, got into the cage. The cage was carefully examined, and no way of entrance could be found except, of course, the wire mesh. However, it seems almost impossible that a snake of this size could have squeezed through such a small opening as canary-proof netting." (Snake in Canary Cage, 15 Mar 1923, p.4)

As Cobb & Co. expanded into Queensland, the Darling Downs and Warwick regions, including Rosenthal and Canning Downs, emerged as a vital hub of economic growth. Queensland's proclamation as a separate colony in 1859, followed by territorial adjustments, underscored the increasing demand for settlement and development during this transformative period.

George Francis Train
(By One Who Knew Him.)

On January 19, 1904, a Reuter's Telegram from New York announced the passing of George Francis Train, described as "one of the most remarkable men in America." He died at the age of seventy-five. Train often recounted that he "began his business career at the age of ten." Tragically, he was "left a penniless orphan in a strange city when only four years old." Yet, by twenty, he had risen to lead George Francis Train and Co., earning "a yearly income of two thousand pounds" through commission trading between Australia and the United States. His contributions to infrastructure were immense—he built railways connecting Lake Erie with the Mississippi and Ohio Rivers, and planned and constructed the first Pacific Railway. In 1857, he personally laid down tramway lines in what would become the modern city of Omaha, where he owned "five thousand town lots." By the time he was forty, he had amassed "a fortune of ten million pounds sterling." Train displayed "such inventive genius or such manifold enterprise" across numerous fields—he was a farmer, merchant, railway constructor, builder, and author. He journeyed four times around the world. Beyond his achievements, he was renowned for his "handsome and distinguished" appearance and even considered a candidate for President of the United States. He never drank spirits throughout his life, remaining "an honest man, a truthful man." His intellectual prowess was astonishing—he "knew the whole of the Psalms, and the Gospels, and most of Isaiah by heart." He could also recite entire chapters of Plutarch's Lives, after just one reading. Among his philosophies, he believed that "Sunshine, children, and birds are the life of the world." Yet, he was "certainly an eccentric man." (George Francis Train, 15 March 1904, p.3)

Portrait of George Francis Train from 'One of the Few Sane Men in a Mad, Mad World', New England Historical 28 Society, 2015

1894 Canning Downs near Warwick – Courtesy State Library of Queensland

1915 Troops on parade at Rosenthal training camp, Warwick, Queensland – Courtesy State Library of Queensland

ca. 1863 Gilbert Davidson in a carriage in front of the stables on Canning Downs station, Warwick district – Courtesy State Library of Queensland

Chapter Four

Communication & Cobb and Co.
1860s

THE BUSHRANGER.
By Edward H. Morgan, Bowral

Rogue by heredity, felon by birth,
Ancestors often the scum of the earth ;
Bred on 'duffed' mutton and other folks' beef ;
Horse-stealer, brand-fakir, rowdy, and thief.

Rides like a centaur—no country too rough—
Lithe as a warrigal, wiry and tough ;
Joined by a comrade, some human reproach,
Plucks up his courage and sticks up the coach.

Then becomes 'wanted,' and warrants abound ;
Troopers are eager to run him to ground ;
Aye, to be hunted and hounded his lot ;
Finally hanged, or, if lucky, is shot.

Never the hero some writers aver,
Seldom the scoundrel his critics infer ;
Two great attractions for men of his mould—
Lots of excitement and lightly-won gold.

(The Bushranger, 8 Feb 1896, p.10)

By 1866, main roads connected key settlements across Queensland. Maps of squatting runs show key locations such as Cleveland, Brisbane, Ipswich, Alfred, Gatton, Toowoomba, Drayton, Warwick, Maryland, and Tenterfield, marking significant areas of pastoral activity and future growth. See *Appendix A*. Extreme weather was often recorded at these locations.

A terrific storm on October 27, 1866,

"buildings unroofed and town flooded, and loss of life through the upsetting of Cobb's coach at South Brisbane." (Queensland's ... notable events, 8 Dec 1909, p.26) Back in 1841, Ipswich and Brisbane had already experienced severe flooding, as recorded in the chronicles of Queensland's history: "Jan. 17.—Great Flood Ipswich and Brisbane." (Queensland's ... notable events, 8 Dec 1909, p.24)

While the 1860s were a time of expansion and settlement in the Tenterfield district, where squatters established pastoral holdings across the landscape. From Reminiscences of the Late Issac Whereat, we learn that early squatters managed vast stations, shaping the development of the area: "The squatters in the Tenterfield district in the early 'sixties' were: Messers. Riley and Cowper, managers of Tenterfield and Clifton Stations for Sir S. A. Donaldson; Bolivia, owned by Edward Irby; The Mole, by Dr. Fraser; Mingoola by J. Logan; Barney Downs, by James G. Dickson; Boonoo Boonoo, by Cullen; Maryland, by M. H. Marsh, managed by Greenup; Bookookoorara, by James Irvine McKenzie; Millera, by Alex Stewart; Cheviot Hills, by Smith Bros.; Wellington Vale, by R. R. C. Robertson; Deepwater by Arch Windeyer and Co., and managed by Collins." (Tenterfield, 1949, p.26)

By April 7, 1861, official stock returns documented substantial numbers of animals across the state: "Horses, 23,086; cattle, 425,896; sheep, 3,285,734; pigs, 7,115; area under cultivation, 4000 acres." (Queensland's ... notable events, 8 Dec 1909, p.25)

Cobb and Co. business

Opening up Queensland

In 1862, "James Rutherford was appointed Manager of New South Wales. Cobb and Co." (Advertising, 20 Aug 1862, p.1) Early in 1863, he "went over to Queensland, where most of the mails were carried on pack horses. People did not think that coaches could be run through the bush and laughed when they heard of Cobb and Co.'s intentions. Mr. Rutherford put coaches on all the roads in the north while buying up the best of the traps, and when mail tendering time came around, he put in a price for the whole lot, which he knew would be accepted. *I did not go over there for nothing*, he told the interviewer, adding, *I intended to fight the game afterwards*. As he anticipated, he secured the mail contract. It was the policy of the company never to pull the plant off a road that had been paying, no matter who got the mails, and Mr. Rutherford carried out this policy in its entirety.

When mail tendering came around the next year, he put in for all the mails he wanted under a new system. He submitted the tender in the ordinary way and then lumped the whole lot together, fixing a new period of duration, saying: *We will carry the whole lot for three years at so much*. Along with the tender, he sent a strong letter stating that, as the government well knew, the company had lost money during the last year and had done much for the benefit of Queensland in opening up the country and paving the way for the railway. It was also pointed out that the tender was submitted with the objective of making a fair profit.

The business people of Brisbane and other places were so pleased with the regular delivery of mails that they would not hear of anyone else getting the contract, and so Cobb and Co. were again successful. Bulk tenders were submitted ever afterward." (Late James Rutherford, 11 Nov 1911, p.2)

Dissolution and reformation

In 1864, the firm underwent restructuring. On January 27, 1864, the existing partnership was dissolved by mutual consent, and the business was continued by Alexander William Robertson, John Wagner, and James Rutherford: "Notice is hereby given, that the Partnership heretofore existing between us, the under-signed, Charles Russell, William Warren, Alexander William Robertson, John Wagner, and James Rutherford, trading in the colony of New South Wales as coach proprietors under the style of Cobb and Co.'s Telegraph Line, New South Wales branch, has this day been dissolved, by mutual consent.

The business will be continued as heretofore by Alexander William Robertson, John Wagner, and James Rutherford, who will receive all monies due to and pay all monies due by the late firm. Dated this 27th day of January, 1864. C. Russell. W. Warren. A. W. Robertson. John Wagner. James Rutherford. Witness—Alfred Malleson, solicitor, Melbourne." (Advertising, 30 Jan 1864, p.7)

Expansion beyond coaching

The success of Cobb and Co. was not limited to coach transport: "The firm of Cobb and Co ... did not confine their energies and enterprise to coaching alone. They were the first to export jarrah timber for railway purposes to Bombay and Madras—in India—in 1865, and for that purpose erected large sawmills in Western Australia. They were also (in conjunction with the late Colonel Robins) large exporters of horses to India for military purposes. In a large way they were pastoralists, too, being at one time the owners of a number of sheep and cattle stations. Amongst those were Perricoota ... Midkin ... Momalong ... Claverton and Burrenbilla in Queensland, and others in the three States. They also operated largely in mining.

In connection with the coaching business, the firm established five coach-building factories at Goulburn, Bathurst, their chief centre, Castlemaine, Hay, Bourke, and later Charleville. There were also railway contractors, and were the constructors of the northern line from Glen Innes to Tenterfield, one of the most costly pieces of railway work in New South Wales. This contract, which was entered into in Mr. Rutherford's absence, and against his strong advice, resulted in a loss of £80,000." (Coaching in Australia, 1917, p.19)

The Bathurst coach factory

The first coaches used in Queensland came from the Bathurst factory. The Bathurst Times on May 2, 1866, described the vast scale of the operation: "Proof of the immense establishment ... perhaps very few residents in the country, aware of the extensive workshop ... Being struck with the number of vehicles of all sizes and descriptions, in various stages towards completion ... The large contracts for mail services held by Messrs. Cobb and Co., requiring the employment of so many coaches, naturally led the company to the establishment of workshops in which they could more economically effect such repairs as were needed to their vehicles, and accordingly on the three principal routes, north, south, and west, shops have been opened ... Mr. Rutherford ... seeing the importance of its position, as the key to the interior of the colony, selected it as the most suitable district in which to place the headquarters of the company ...

From all parts of the colony (even from Sydney) and from Queensland, work pours in to the Bathurst factory ... blacksmiths ... carriage makers ... The company find it cheaper, however, to import American wheels, as well as nearly all their materials ... At the rear of the smith's shop ... painters ... trimmers ... sinking platform, a simple contrivance invented by Mr. Brown for fixing tires to wheels ... a portable eight horse power engine is situated, which works extensive chaff-cutting machinery overhead, and supplies motion to a lathe and circular saw ... perhaps unequalled by any other firm in the colony ...

Cobb have cut out an entirely new trade, and established a factory which, without their energy and skill, might never have been called into existence ; and in doing this they have, whilst increasing the importance of the district, opened, quietly and perseveringly, an avenue to labor, and set an example which might well be copied by those who rave so loudly upon the necessity of protection to native industry." (The Sketcher, 19 May 1866, p.12) Note: Coach Factories see 'Along the tracks of Cobb and Co. - The New South Wales Headquarters'.

Post offices, mail & coach services

Tenterfield, 1860 "The ever-memorable 1st of April was not allowed to pass quietly by. Our Postmaster, Mr. O'Connell (who, by the bye, is not very popular just now), played a hoax upon some of our worthy townsmen on Sunday evening. The mail bag has usually been delivered as soon as sorted, but on Sunday last between 20 and 30 people were quietly discussing the affairs of the nation until past 9 o'clock, when they were stayed in their chit-chat by observing that the light in the post-office had been extinguished. *No letters*, said one ; *Nonsense*, added another ; *surely, after waiting* (which many had done upwards of an hour and a half), *the mail will be delivered*. But alas, no ! (Country News, 7 Apr 1860, p.2)

In 1860, the Brisbane General Post Office was already a hub of communication, handling a significant volume of correspondence. "The post office passed 280,000 letters, 250,365 papers, and 4,456 packets." (Geographic History of Queensland, 1895, pp.12–15).

By 1862, attention turned to integrating bank services with postal operations in Ipswich. "Mr. O'Sullivan, pursuant to notice, asked the hon. the Colonial Secretary 'if it was the intention of the Government to provide a room in the new Post-office, Ipswich, for a Savings' Bank and if there was any objection to allowing the Postmaster there to act as manager under proper restrictions, and at a small salary.' The Colonial Secretary said that the Government considered that the Savings' Bank should be in a central situation, and a room either in the Post-office or the Telegraph-office should be devoted to the purpose. The appointment of an accountant would, he presumed, rest with the trustees of the bank." (Legislative Assembly, 29 May 1862, p.2).

Despite these developments, mail delivery remained inconsistent in some regions. In 1863, concerns were raised about the Maryland mail service. "There is only one mail a week from Queensland to the borders of New South Wales (Maryland), and if the postman were to start from Warwick on Tuesday mornings instead of Saturday, we would have the benefit of Queensland news four days earlier than by the present arrangement, while the mails which reach Maryland twice a week from Tenterfield … could be conveyed to Warwick without any loss of time. It seems altogether a mal-arrangement that more than a week should elapse in the receipt of news from Warwick to Tenterfield—a distance of only 80 miles." (Notes and News, 15 Aug 1863, p.3). 1865 saw the frustrations with the Maryland mail service persist. "What we want is … a mail twice a week from Toowoomba to Maryland … we call the Postmaster-General's attention to the necessity of at once amending the present unsatisfactory postal arrangements … that it required eighteen days to obtain an answer to a letter sent to Tenterfield … the present contractor … would be willing to convey the mail twice a week between these places for £125 annually, over that paid for conveying a weekly mail." (The Queensland Telegraph Lines, 25 Jan 1865, p.4).

That same year, "Cobb and Co. expanded into Queensland, starting with 16 coaches, first line from Brisbane to Ipswich.

The tenders of the well known mail contractors, Messrs. Cobb and Co., having been accepted for services between Ipswich and Brisbane, and Grandchester and Toowoomba, very commodious coaches have been placed on these lines, I fear, however, that the coaches used between Brisbane and Ipswich may prove too heavy in bad weather." (1865 Report of the P.M. General, T.M.L. Murray-Prior). Note: "Grandchester (as Bigge's Camp is now absurdly and grandiloquently called)." (The Line from Helidon to Bigge's Camp, 7 Apr 1866, p.11)

By 1866, Cobb and Co. coaches were becoming a familiar sight. "One of Cobb and Co.'s coaches arrived here (Warwick) from Toowoomba on Monday morning, and started again yesterday. We are not aware whether the company intend to make regular trips on this line. Mr. Cook has again commenced to run regularly, and we hope, for the sake of public convenience, he will carry out a thorough system of regularity, as far as the weather will permit." (Warwick Coaching, 7 Jul 1866, p.8). Advertisements also promoted the coach service from Warwick to Toowoomba.

In 1867, mail contracts were expanded. "Mail Contractor Cobb and Co. Brisbane and Ipswich, five-horse coach, twice a day, one year contract, £691; Cobb and Co., Toowoomba and Warwick, three times a week, £683; James Fox, Warwick and Maryland, by horse, twice a week, two year contract, £85 per annum." (Tenders accepted for Carrying Mails, 12 Dec 1866, p.3) "In 1865 … Brisbane to Ipswich being the first route exploited, and by 1867 coaches were running from the capital to Ipswich, Toowoomba, Warwick, Dalby, Condamine, Roma, and Gympie." (Cobb & Co., 14 Jan 1931, p.9) The schedule being "Mail Coaches. Cobb and Co.'s. Run from Brisbane to Ipswich daily, 6 a.m., 11.46 a.m., and 4 p.m.; Ipswich to Brisbane, Helidon to Toowoomba, Toowoomba to Helidon, Toowoomba to Dalby, Toowoomba to Warwick, Dalby to Condamine, Condamine to Roma." (Pugh's Queensland Almanac, Directory and Law Calendar, 1867).

Bushrangers & mail robberies

1867—THE GERMAN BUSHRANGER

"On Tuesday night last, says last Saturday's Burnett Argus, Christian Beiermeister, the Burnett mail-robber, very nearly effected his escape from the lock-up in this town. At about half-past 10 o'clock the lock-up keeper heard a dull, heavy noise, and on opening the slide in the door discovered prisoner

clinging to the iron bars of the ventilation-window, his handcuffs slipped, and he naked, with the handle of an iron bucket in his hand, picking away the bricks and dropping them onto his clothes inside.

As soon as the lock-up keeper saw what was up he obtained a revolver and walked into the cell with it in his hand and ordered the prisoner to come down. Prisoner saw the revolver and immediately did so." (The German Bushranger, 8 Mar 1867, p.2)

1868—MAIL ROBBERY NEAR TENTERFIELD

"The Northern Mail hence on Thursday last was stuck up, by highway robbers, at the Bluff, about ten miles from Tenterfield on the Armidale road. The robbers ordered the mailman (A. Pillar) to go off the road into the bush, when they rifled the mailbags of their contents, and opened all the letters.

The only available booty the gang possessed themselves of was a solitary one pound note—although there were cheques, drafts, &c., to a considerable amount, which the robbers flung back again into the bags in most admired confusion. The mail man returned to Tenterfield with the opened bags, and delivered them at the post office." (Tenterfield, 27 Jun 1868, p.3)

1868–Robbing the mail coach

"William Jenkins, alias John King, was brought up on remand at the Brisbane Police Court on Friday, charged with robbing the mail coach between Ipswich and Brisbane in January 1867. The prisoner was asked if he would like to hear the depositions already taken read over, to which he replied, *No, it will only be a waste of time.*" (Jenkins the Bushranger, 4 Jul 1868, p.4)

1869–Bushrangers and capture of Rutherford

"Jan. 6.—Gympie coach (to Brisbane) stuck up by two bushrangers. W. E. King (Bank of New South Wales) and Rev. G. King behaved gallantly, wounded bushrangers, who escaped, however, with £25. W. Bond arrested, and on Oct. 26 sentenced to 20 years … Sept. 7.—Capture of Rutherford (in Sydney), Thunderbolt's mate." (Queensland's … notable events, 8 Dec 1909, p.26)

1871–Decrease of crime in the colony

"At the Goulburn assizes yesterday, his Honor the Chief Justice in discharging the jury said he was glad to be able to say that crime was on the decrease throughout the colony, and the offences committed were of a less serious character than formerly.

> *It was always the case here that when there was plenty of wealth and high wages crimes were more numerous than when the contrary was the case;*

but in England just the reverse occurred, crime arising there from poverty. Here when man had little money there was less resort to public-houses. The very heavy punishments inflicted upon bushrangers had had a great deal to do with putting down crime.

The last bushranger, Thunderbolt, had been shot; and the leader in bushranging, Gardiner, was not likely ever to be at large again. Some part of the credit for the present decrease in crime was due to the great activity of the police in finding out offenders; and cases were now got up far better than they were previously. All these things combined had led to the decrease of crime. The extension of temperance societies throughout the colony spread habits of peace and good will. Those grand institutions were doing much for society; and the thanks of the community were due to those gentleman who were endeavouring to extend them. It gave him great pleasure in bearing testimony to the very great moral improvement noticeable in the places he had visited." (Goulburn Police Court—Decrease of Crime in the Colony, 14 Oct 1871, p.3)

Bushranger—Thunderbolt

Fred Ward, known as Thunderbolt, became one of the most infamous bushrangers in New England during the late 1860s and 1870s. "Many are the legends, handed down by early residents, referring to this 'Gentleman Outlaw.' It was said in 1864 that the highwayman gave himself this distinguished name whilst committing very mean thefts on the Northern Road. Next to Morgan, perhaps no individual bushranger earned greater notoriety than did Thunderbolt. He was an old 'Cockatoo' bird, and one of the few prisoners who escaped from that gruesome island in 1863." (Tenterfield, 1949, p.28)

A splendid horseman, fearless and daring, Thunderbolt roamed the New England District, striking fear into mailmen. If Mr. Pillar was here today, he could attest to that, as could Bob Bates, who was driving a Cobb and Co. coach on the main northern road when it was "stuck up by Thunderbolt, who looted the coach and passengers of all he could find. From the driver the outlaw took a watch and chain and a half sovereign. Some months later, however, these were returned through the post office at Tamworth to Mr. Bates. There was nothing with them to indicate where they came from, but it was evident that Thunderbolt had desired that the driver should not be a loser at his hands." (Thunderbolt Scene, 9 Jan 1931, p.7)

By 1866, more details about Thunderbolt emerged, thanks to a female informant who attended to Mrs. Thunderbolt during one of her confinements.

She revealed that

> Thunderbolt's wife "always accompanied him (dressed in men's attire) out to plunder …

She has a large butcher's knife fastened on the end of a stick, rides up alongside the cattle, and with this instrument, she hamstrings the beast, then kills it, as they principally lived on beef, wild yams, and wattle gum … She asserts that there is no one else with Thunderbolt except his wife and three children." (Capt. Thunderbolt, The Maitland Mercury, 29 Mar 1866, p.2)

"The Colonial Secretary's Office issued a £200 reward for Thunderbolt's capture and £50 for each of his accomplices, further cementing his reputation as a feared outlaw." (The Armidale Chronicle, 27 Aug 1904, p.8)

By 1868, "News reached Roma from Currawillinghi of an affray with Thunderbolt (the notorious bushranger) and his companion, Rutherford, Constable M'Cabe shot dead." (Queensland's Half Century, 8 Dec 1909, p.26)

Despite his crimes, some remembered Thunderbolt fondly. John Telford Morecroft, ex-driver of Cobb and Co., recalled "the days when Frank Gardiner and Frederick Ward—'Captain Thunderbolt' to most people—held the roads. *I've spoken to Thunderbolt hundreds of times*, he said *A real good fellow. The whole district was sorry when he was shot by the police.*

John's acquaintance with the bushranging fraternity wasn't always so happy. It was at dawn one morning, a mile outside Gympie. As the mail coach, with its golden load, approached a clump of trees, a masked figure leapt out. 'Bail up!' he ordered sharply. A loaded revolver is a strong argument; and John bailed up. But later John's identification led to the robber's capture and sentence to fifteen year's imprisonment. John still chuckles when he thinks of that. It was all in the day's work; and there was £10 at the end of each month, with everything found except the whip." (Knew Thunderbolt, 15 Dec 1932, p.7)

While "the Warwick (Queensland) Times mentioned a few days ago that the bushranger Thunderbolt had stuck up several parties on the Maryland road. It is now in possession of further particulars. When the bushranger had obtained possession of the money from a band a little parleying took place, the bandmaster stating that it was very hard to take money from poor men, and that the sum the bushranger had got was the result of several days' playing. Thunderbolt replied he did not care—if it was his own brother he would take it ; but coolly said if the party would give him their names and addresses he would return the money to them if he succeeded in sticking up some person who had a good sum. When parleying with Hart, whom he had stuck up and robbed of £105 the day previous, he said he wanted money, and he had a good mind to take the horse as well as the money. Hart expostulated upon the hardness of taking all the money, stating he was a poor man, and his horse 'Minstrel' had won him the money. The bushranger said as he was a poor man he would return him £5, which he did. A report was circulated on Monday morning last that Thunderbolt had been in the town on Sunday evening, and that he had been at various publics, shouting for all hands. There is, however, not the slightest truth in the report." ('Monday, April 13, 1868', 13 Apr 1868, p.4)

The legend of Thunderbolt came to an end in 1870 when "Thunderbolt was shot dead by Constable Walker." (Chronicle of Occurrences, 31 Dec 1870, p.4)

False reports and mistaken identities continued. It was reported in 1882 that "this notorious housebreaker and burglar made a desperate attempt to escape from custody yesterday afternoon, whilst being conveyed into the gaol after receiving a sentence of 20 years' hard labour from Mr. Justice Windeyer. He was found guilty of having shot at Constable Chapman in order to resist lawful apprehension. For this offence, he was sentenced to 10 years on the roads, and a further period of 10 years for breaking into the ironmongery store of Mr. Henry Evans in Oxford Street. Whilst being removed from the court by Sergeants Pirie and Keating, he made a sudden plunge and a rush towards the door, but the officers were prepared and immediately seized him, conveying him safely within the walls of the gaol. His attempt to escape caused much excitement." (Thunderbolt, 15 Nov 1882, p.5)

Then in 1890 "one day a half-drunken bushman made into the township and proclaimed himself to be the outlaw … Information had, meanwhile, been given to the police, and a party soon put in an appearance. The pretended bushranger became alarmed, rushed to his horse, jumped on him, and rode away with one of the constables in pursuit. He was overtaken and shot, and the news quickly spread, but the genuine Thunderbolt took the opportunity of dropping out of the bushranging industry and returned to a farmers life … Truth." (Thunderbolt, 26 Sep 1890, p.6)

Even years after his death, Thunderbolt remained a familiar figure in Australian history. "Mrs. Emma Youmans, 82, wife of Mr. John Youmans of Arding. As a young girl, when resident of Scone and later in the Uralla district ... saw 'Thunderbolt', the bushranger who was afterwards shot at Uralla. She used to tell of an occasion when Morgan, the bushranger, called at her parents' place. Mrs. Youmans was a native of Derbyshire, England." (Remembered Thunderbolt, 16 May 1934, p.14)

From his daring raids to his infamous escape from Cockatoo Island, Thunderbolt's legacy endured, leaving behind stories of adventure, lawlessness, and mystery in the Australian bush. Interestingly "between Bookookoorara and Wilson's Downfall, on the eastern side of the road, there is a building. Until a few years ago this was occupied by Mr. Jack Dillion, well-known drover. The people ... had often showed kindness to him [Thunderbolt] ... somewhere he had found a young fruit tree and brought it to them ...

The large pear tree ... is known as Thunderbolt's Tree."
(Tenterfield, 1949, p.28)

As bushrangers vanished from the landscape, their stories remained deeply embedded in Australia's history, serving as a reminder of both the hardships and resilience of the pioneering era. With mail coaches, expanding settlements, and courageous individuals shaping the nation's growth, the legacy of Cobb & Co., early settlers, and infamous outlaws like Thunderbolt continues to echo in Australian folklore.

Constable Alexander Binning Walker, who killed the bushranger Thunderbolt, ca. May-June 1870, photographer A. Cunningham, Armidale – Courtesy State Library of New South Wales

Post-mortem photograph of Fred Ward Captain Thunderbolt) – Courtesy Powerhouse collection, Gift of Royal Australian Historical Society, 1981 (Presented by Harry Burrell 24-7-44)

ca. 1890-1898 Cobb & Co Factory, Lower William Street, Bathurst (David Brown in Charge)
– Courtesy Bathurst Historical Society Museum

1870-1875 Bathurst, part of panorama looking north east and taken from the tower of the
Catholic Cathedral – Courtesy State Library of New South Wales

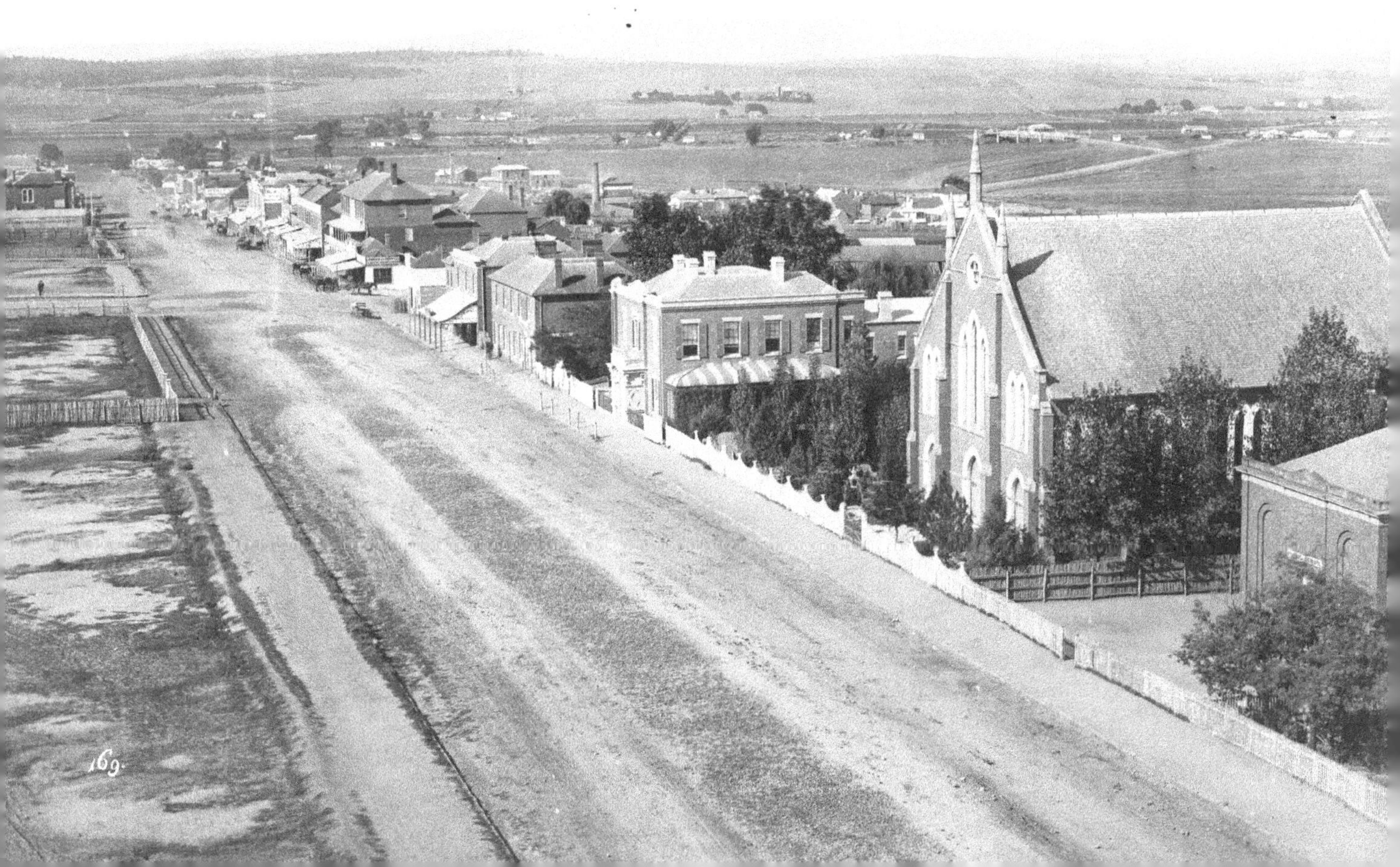

Chapter Five

Cobb and Co.'s mail conveyancing 1870s

JAMES RUTHERFORD.
By Cecil Poole

Till, circling to our journey's end;
Where Queensland rivers sometimes flow;
We greeted, like an ancient friend,
The furtherest coach of Cobb and Co.

Of Cobb and Co.! The name is one
That's blazoned wide across our years;
Recalling all the labors done
By hosts of doughty pioneers.

Who tamed a raw and hostile land;
Who scaled the pass and found the ford;
And foremost, in that giant band,
Was mighty-hearted Rutherford!

Not his the meagre soul that goes
Where phantom stars of self may lead;
But, selfless, to his happy close,
He spent his pow'rs for others' need.

The old colonial school may die,
But still, the merits shall be sung
Of those, like him, of nature high,
And open hand and guileless tongue …

(James Rutherford, 16 Oct 1911, p.2)

Cobb and Co. business

By the 1870s, Cobb and Co. had solidified its dominance in transportation across the eastern colonies, expanding its mail services and acquiring rival businesses. The structure of Cobb and Co. in 1871 was as follows: "Robertson and Wagner took over the Victorian plant, whilst Rutherford, Hall, Whitney, and Bradley assumed control of the New South Wales and Queensland lines. Bradley sold out about 1875, Walter Hall retired in 1880, and Whitney died in 1893. This left Rutherford, at the time of his death in 1911, the sole representative of the original Cobb and Co., Robertson and Wagner having died before him." (Cobb & Co.—The Roaring Days, 14 Jan 1931, p.9)

While Cobb and Co. expanded across New South Wales and Queensland, the firm had no connection to the Sydney omnibus service but maintained ties with Beresford's vans."James Rutherford, Walter R. Hall, William B. Bradley, William F. Whitney and Colin Robertson trading under the firm 'Cobb and Co.' in New South Wales and Queensland, were not connected to Cobb and Co. omnibuses running in Sydney." (Advertising, 30 Dec 1871, p.8)

By the end of 1872, Cobb and Co. successfully eliminated competition in Stanthorpe. "The Stanthorpe correspondent writes on November 30:—The opposition to Cobb and Co. has at last 'caved in,' and a rich harvest, no doubt, will be reaped by Cobb and Co. during the approaching holidays. Mr. J. T. Lethbridge, who must have been running at considerable loss for some time, has sold his horses and plant to the above enterprising firm, the sum, I believe, to be between £300 and £400. The fares are already announced to be raised to 10/ ... A public meeting of the promoters of a company to form a people's line of coaches is to take place next Monday evening (December 2)." (Links with the Long Ago, 8 Dec 1932, p.9)

At the same time, Cobb and Co. expanded beyond coaching and entered livestock trading, selling cattle, for example:

- "It seems, says the 'Dubbo Despatch,' as if Cobb and Co. will be as great a name in the stock market as in the coaching world. On Monday last, in a full market (1100 being penned), 300 head of fat cattle from Messrs. Cobb and Co.'s Buckinguy stations, sold by Messrs. Powers, Rutherford, and Co., made £10 9s per head—the highest average for the day." (Sixty Years Ago—Gleanings from The Queensland Files, 25 Jan 1934, p.14)
- "Mr. James Rutherford passed to-day with 380 fat cattle from Davenport Downs for Cobb and Co., Cunnamulla." (Queensland News, 23 Feb 1888, p.5)
- "800 bullocks, from Davenport Downs to Ambuthalla, Mr. James Rutherford (owner) in charge; 1000 cows, from Vanrook to Davenport Downs, Messrs. Cobb and Co. owners, Mr. H. Medhurst in charge." (Longreach, 25 Sep 1906, p.3)

It was written that "Mr. James Rutherford is, in some respects, one of the most remarkable men in Australia ... He was one of the Cobb and Co. syndicate and is now Cobb and Co. altogether. He is a squatter, a sheep breeder, a miner, a newspaper proprietor, a churchman, a hospital guardian, a mail carrier, a contractor, and a railway authority—all boxed up in one.

In fact, in addition to running the chief of the country's coaching routes, he laid down or built one of the biggest of our railway sections ... An extraordinary man ... in all things, and with extraordinary virility and hopefulness. He was not a young man fifteen years ago but could drive day and night over rough and smooth against the best whips known, and he is much the same today, fifteen years older ... He is a figure right through western New South Wales and is known from one end of Queensland to the other; also, perhaps, from one end of Victoria to the other." (Our Sydney Letter, 30 May 1907, p.5)

In 1875 James Rutherford, was honored at a farewell dinner before his departure for America. "At Bathurst a complimentary dinner was given on the 3rd inst to Mr James Rutherford, previous to his departure for America. The Mayor presided; and the dinner was largely attended. Mr Rutherford and Mr Colin Robertson, both of the firm of Cobb and Co." (Latest European Intelligence, 12 Jun 1875, p.3)

While "on this day in 1911, James Rutherford, whose name will always be associated with Australia's coaching days, passed away ... After passing through several hands, Cobb and Co. (as it was always called) was eventually purchased by a syndicate, with J. Rutherford ... In 1865, Rutherford went to Queensland, and within 10 years, Cobb and Co.'s service covered 4,000 miles of road. By 1870, Cobb and Co. were harnessing 6,000 horses a day across the three eastern colonies. Their coaches covered 28,000 miles of road weekly, earning £95,000 a year from mail contracts alone, and their annual payroll exceeded £100,000." (It happened Today, 13 Sep 1934, p.10)

While it was stated in 1894 "As coaching contractors, they harnessed 6,600 horses a day alone, employed, directly and indirectly, some thousands of hands, and paid in wages the startling sum of over £200,000 a year, while their contracts for the mails were of such an extensive character that they ran into £100,000 a year at least." (Local and General News, 15 Nov 1894, p.4)

Written in 1879, "we find from the estimates that the entire cost of inland mail conveyance for the last year was about £50,000. Of this amount, it seems, more than two-fifths was paid to Messrs. Cobb and Co. It seems also that the new tenders for the horse mails show a general reduction; yet the great coaching firm, having established a practical monopoly, refuses to abate one jot from rates demanded in time of drought and direful scarcity." ('Wednesday, October 15, 1879', 15 Oct 1879, p.2)

Post offices, mail & coach services

- 1870 – Cobb and Co. secured a MAIL CONTRACT "No. 44 Cobb and Co., Warwick Maryland (N.S.W.) and Tenterfield (N.S.W.) twice a week, coach, two years." (Conveyance of Mails for 1870, 11 Dec 1869, p.2)

- 1871 – The railway between Toowoomba and Warwick was completed, replacing Cobb and Co.'s mail service along that route: "The event which has occasioned most interest in Brisbane, since last mail left, has been the opening of the Warwick railway. This, although not strictly an item of Brisbane news, is still, from its intimate connection with our future, possessed of an importance to all Brisbanites. This important event, which successfully completes the Southern and Western railway scheme, took place last Tuesday." (Brisbane, 21 Jan 1871, p.2) That same year, Cobb and Co.'s services included six mail routes: "Cobb and Co., six mail services, for two years, at £5775 per annum including a mail from Warwick, via Maryland, to Tenterfield, by coach, twice a week." (Tenterfield, 21 Nov 1871, p.2)

- March 1872 – Quart Pot Creek "Proposed by Mr. Kelly and seconded by Mr. Ross,— 'That a local Post Office be urgently required; the numerous population already settled here having to go to Maryland, in New South Wales, a distance of 10 miles, for the purpose of posting and procuring correspondence'." (Tin Mining at Quart Pot Creek 30 Mar 1872, p2)

- 1872 – Cobb and Co. MAIL CONTRACTOR "Coaching firm of Cobb and Co. have secured the mail contracts for next year between Murrurundi and Maryland ... There is little doubt that they will have the contract between Warwick and Maryland also." (Warwick, 1 Nov 1872, p.3)

- August 1872 – It was questioned "What has become of the much talked-of daily mail to Tenterfield, which was to commence on the 1st instant?" (Tenterfield, 24 Aug 1872, p.6)

- September 1872 – "A Post office was opened at Mr. Lee's store on Ruby Creek, last Monday, the mails being conveyed from Maryland by horses twice a week. Mr. T. Shepherd has been appointed Postmaster." (Tenterfield, 28 Sep 1872, p.6)

- November 1872 – "We arrive at the Border Custom-house and the Post-office of the old township of Maryland, which is chiefly remarkable from the absence of houses and stores." (At the Tin Mines—Warwick to Stanthorpe, 11 Nov 1872, p.3) While the Stanthorpe post office was "a miserable shed attached to a store, but is quite in proportion to the miserable salary of the postmaster, only £12 a year. This is simply disgraceful to a Government, every member of which must be aware that a large amount of correspondence passes through the Stanthorpe office ... another instance of official blundering, that the mail from Warwick arrives here at noon, and the coach returns at 1 o'clock, passing by the Post-office without calling for a mail. There is no earthly reason why the coach should not be delayed until half-past 1, and on hour left for business men to receive and reply to their letters. By this arrangement there would be in some cases a day's gain in the period of communication between Stanthorpe and Brisbane." (At the Tin Mines—Warwick to Stanthorpe, 11 Nov 1872, p.3)

- 1873 – E. M. Mcleod MAIL CONTRACTOR "Conveyance of mails No. 119 Maryland to Ruby Creek, 7 miles, two per week, horseback £52 until 31 Dec 1873. E. M. McLeod (Address Ruby Creek)." (Advertising, 19 Oct 1872, p.1)

- 1873 – Cobb & Co.'s Telegraph Line of Mail. Queensland Branch "The Coaches of the above Line run as under:—
Between Brisbane & Ipswich.—Twice daily, meeting trains to and from Toowoomba, Warwick, and Dalby.
Brisbane and Gympie.—Twice a week.

Gympie and Maryborough.—Three times a week.
Brisbane and Nerang Creek.—Three times a week.
Warwick and Murrurundi, N.S.W., via Tenterfield And Armidale.—Three times a week.
Warwick and Stanthorpe.—Twice a day.
Dalby, Condamine, and Roma.—Twice a week.
Passengers booked through from Brisbane to any of the above-named places, Railway fares excepting. For full particulars see daily papers. Fred. Shaw, Manager." (Pugh's almanacs 1862-1866, Issue 1873)

- 1874-1875 – Cobb and Co. MAIL CONTRACTOR "Cobb and Co., Glen Innes, Dundee, Deepwater, Tenterfield, Bookookoorara and Maryland … 119 miles, three times a week, 2/4 horse coach £1333 (with other runs) until December 1875." (Government Gazette Tenders and Contracts, 19 Jan 1874, p.174)

- While in Stanthorpe, in 1874, "considerable annoyance has been caused by a lot of loafers who have prowled about from claim to claim, and either in the absence of the owner or because his claim was not formally granted, have taken the tin on the ground and sold it for 4lu. per lb., that being the price which can be obtained for it here. The presence of the police, however, has been of great service, and many disturbances might have occurred had they not been here. All is quiet now, and when we get a telegraph and other offices, Stanthorpe will be no mean place. Every coach that comes either from Warwick or Tenterfield is loaded with passengers, to say nothing of the numerous drays and horsemen that are pouring in all day long. We shall shortly have 40 hotels open, which will offer some accommodation to the weary traveler. At present, let all who come here with the intention of staying a night or two

    bring plenty of warm clothes and a good supply of blankets ; for it is fearfully cold and we have had a white frost."

- 1874 – The mail route was from "Warwick to Maryland (N.S.W.) … 28 miles thence to Stanthorpe … 9 miles. Total 37 miles. Mails conveyed by Cobb and Co.'s coach. Canning Downs is 2 miles from Warwick ; Rosenthal, 2 miles; South Toolburra, 14 miles ; North Toolburra, 7 miles ; Gladfield, part of Maryvale, Bank of Australasia, 12 miles ; Killarney, 17 miles ; Talgai, 25 miles ; Pikedale, 50 miles ; Pike's Creek, 55 miles ; Ballandean, 55 miles ; Nundubbermere, 45 miles ; Mangoola, 65 miles ; Maidenhead, 90 miles ; and Undercliffe, 50 miles. Goomburra is 15 miles from Warwick ; Acacia Creek, 22 miles; and Koreelah, 30 miles." (Pugh's almanacs, 1862-1866, Issue 1874)

- During that same period "the railway terminus is at Warwick. Fare thither, is 7s. by Cobb's coach to Ipswich, thence per rail, 143 miles, 24s., second class ; 36s., first class. Coaches start from Warwick to Stanthorpe, 40 miles, at 5.30 and 9 a.m. Fare: 15s.; box seat, one shilling extra. Very good refreshment on road, with substantial dinner at Gap Inn. Coach returns from Stanthorpe to Warwick at 9 and 12.30. Warwick to Tenterfield, by coach, passing through Maryland, Monday, Wednesday, and Saturday, at 5.30 a.m. Coaches also run from Stanthorpe to Tenterfield, about 40 miles, twice a week. Stanthorpe to Thirteen Mile Creek, every Tuesday and Friday at 12.30. Also to Bookookoorarah, every Wednesday and Saturday, at 12.30." (Pugh's almanacs, 1862-1881)

- 1874 – T. W. Simms MAIL CONTRACTOR "Conveyance of mails No. 127. Maryland to Ruby Creek, 7 miles, two per week, horseback £75 until 31 December 1874, T. W. Simes (address Maryland)." (Government Gazette Tenders and Contracts, 19 Jan 1874, p.176)

- 1875 – F. Mossman MAIL CONTRACTOR "Conveyance of mails No. 132. Maryland to Ruby Creek, 7 miles, two per week, horseback £50 until 31 December 1875, F. Mossman (address Ruby Creek)." (Conveyance of Mails, 13 Jan 1875, p.97)

- 1877 "Royal Mail Coaches. The Coaches … will run as follows until further notice—From Warwick to Tenterfield—Mondays, Wednesdays, and Saturdays, at 5.30 am; From Tenterfield to Maryland—Sundays, and to Warwick Tuesdays and Thursdays, at 5 am; From Warwick to Stanthorpe—Daily (Sundays excepted), at 5.30 am." (Classified Advertising, 7 Jul 1877, p.8)

- 1877-1879 – Cobb and Co. MAIL CONTRACTOR "Mail conveyance No. 151 "Cobb and Co., Glen Innes, Dundee, Deepwater, Tenterfield, Willson's Downfall, and Maryland, distance 119 miles, three times a week, 3 years, 2 or 4 horse coach, £1700 per annum, date of termination 31 Dec, 1879." (Government Gazette Tenders and Contracts, 20 Jan 1877, p.315)

- 1878 – "Warwick Post Office. Arrivals From Brisbane, Ipswich, and Toowoomba; Cambooya, Clifton, Hendon, Allora, and 'Travelling Post Office'; Tenterfield, Maryland, and New South Wales generally (overland);

Leyburn to Talgai via Cambooya ; Darky Flat and Pratten ; Stanthorpe; Swan Creek ; Killarney; Northern Ports and Southern Colonies via Brisbane by every opportunity ... Receiving Offices Letter bags are made up for Sandy Creek and Talgai ; Freestone and Swan Creeks, Farm Creek ... Letters may be posted at 'T.P.O.' Railway Station daily (Sundays excepted) ... All correspondence from or to the above Receiving Offices must bear country postage rates: 1s. 2d. per half ounce for letters ... Pillar Post Boxes—Located at corners of Percy Street, Dragon Street, Guy Street, and Wood Street. Emptied daily ... Undelivered Letters—Letters not claimed within three months, and British letters not claimed within six months, are advertised in the Government Gazette before being returned to the sender ... Mail is usually dispatched in the morning and delivery made between 6 a.m. and 8 a.m. ... Sale of postage stamps from 5 p.m. to 6 p.m. S. Marshall, Postmaster." (Warwick Post Office, 20 Jul 1878, p.6)

- 1879 – Cobb and Co. MAIL CONTRACTOR "Western, Southern, and Northern Roads. Messers. Cobb and Co's tender, by two or four horse coaches, at £17,500 per annum for three years for the following services, viz.:- ... 77. Tenterfield and Maryland. Should it be determined to afford a six, instead of a three, times a week communication between Tenterfield and Maryland, a further sum of £281 per annum to be allowed, and Contractors to make a reduction of £250 per annum if a certain time-table is fixed between Armidale and Maryland ... 77. Tenterfield, Willson's Downfall, Amosfield, and Maryland, three or six times a week—Cobb & Co. See combined tender." (Government Gazette Notices, 31 Oct 1879, p.4877) See *Appendix H* for more mail contractors & routes.

Coach accidents

1872 – Cobb and Co. coach incident at Bookookoorara

On Sunday, as Cobb and Co.'s coach was crossing the creek at Bookookoorara en route to Tenterfield, (says the Tenterfield Star), "the horses plunged when they got into the bog ... one of the swingle-bars having become unhooked, they bolted, throwing the driver, Michael Hart, out upon his back, and galloping up the hill in the direction of Tenterfield. There was only one passenger at the time, a little girl, and further on the road she was thrown out, fortunately sustaining no greater injury than a few bruises. The horses continued bolting along the road until the coach came into collision with a tree, when its progress was arrested, and one of the horses broke away and galloped to the company's stables. Hart having picked himself up, and although very much shaken, followed after the runaway coach, and found it about half a mile further on against the tree referred to, with one horse attached to it. The coach was too much damaged to proceed even with fresh horses, and the mailman at once determined to carry the mail on horse-back ... Every credit is due to the mailman for the promptitude with which he acted to deliver the mail." (New England, 11 Apr 1872, p.4)

1872 – Buggy accident on the Maryland Road

While "Mr. Jas. Partridge was driving his buggy along the Maryland road on Thursday last, when about two miles from Bookookoorara station, from some unaccountable cause the vehicle came in contact with the thick end of a fallen stump, the concussion throwing a young lady who was in the buggy violently to the ground." (Tenterfield, 24 Aug 1872, p.6)

1873 – Queensland Coach Breakdown

On Saturday, last "the Queensland coach, filled with passengers for Tenterfield, broke down between here and Boonoo Boonoo, which delayed it about two hours. We believe one of the swingle-bars was broken and had to be replaced by a small sapling from the bush. None of the passengers received any injury." (New England, 24 Apr 1873, p.3)

1874 – Serious coach accidents near Warwick

"During the past week, two significant accidents occurred involving Cobb and Co.'s mail coaches. Our Stanthorpe contemporary complains of neglect in the management of Cobb's Coaches on that line—very unusual complaint, by the way—and seems disposed to attribute the following might-have-been serious accidents to want of better men on the box ... either of which might have been attended by serious and even fatal consequences.

In the first instance, the afternoon coach proceeding to Warwick on Friday last (fortunately without any passengers), on arriving at the Gap Hotel, a horse belonging to Mr. W. Gillum was substituted for one taken away by the up-coach. The driver, Mr. Crow, then started to cross the Gap, accompanied by Mr. Gillam, and on arriving at the top of the Range, Mr. Gillam returned, the horse appearing perfectly quiet.

However, on descending the other side, the fresh animal became obstinate, and after a short struggle caused the buckle of one of the reins to go through the hames-ring, the driver thus losing all power over the horses.

> He then tried to capsize the coach to prevent the horses from getting away but could not succeed, and the horses bolted away down the precipitous ridge, running the coach over a log, which threw the driver out, and after that against a tree with great force.

We are sorry to say the driver was very seriously hurt. The second accident occurred on Wednesday last. When the mid-day coach ... driven by Mr. J. Highfields, was nearing Fagg's selection, one of the reins broke, and the horses immediately started off, running the coach against a tree. We believe the passengers were not injured and succeeded in getting as far as the Gap Hotel." (The Courier, 24 Feb 1874, p.2)

1875 – Great Northern Road coach breakdowns

Several breakdowns occurred along the Great Northern road between Tenterfield and Glen Innes. "The Great Northern line of road, between Tenterfield and Glen Innes is getting as almost as bad as the streets in this Municipality ... Cobb and Co. must assuredly be justified in forming such an opinion when the expense of a series of breakdowns on Sunday and Monday, the 15th and 16th instant, is presented for liquidation. On the Monday after the mail had crossed the Bluff ... the coach capsized, but fortunately without accident to the passengers. Some few miles further on, the thorough-brace broke ... no person was injured, owing to the exertions of J. Dilworth, the coachman, and R. Bowers, of the coaching staff, who was present.

Again ... on the return trip ... breaking of the axle, some of the passengers being much shaken and slightly bruised. Those who travelled by the coach that day speak in terms of praise of the coachman and his assistant and justly attribute the accident to the right cause—the dangerous state of the road. Trial railway surveys are progressing in the district." (Tenterfield, 25 Aug 1875, pp.2-3)

1875 – Cobb and Co. coach breakdown Near Wilson's Downfall

"News arrived here on Friday that Cobb and Co.'s mail coach that left Tenterfield for Warwick on Thursday morning had a spring broken when about four miles from Wilson's Downfall, on the Great Northern Road, but owing to the cool activity of Tom Rumley, the coachman, the restive horses were restrained, and no further casualty occurred." (Tenterfield, 30 Jun 1875, p.2)

1877 – Severe injuries sustained in coach accident

Two serious accidents occurred within a week. The first happened to Mr. T. Rumley, a Cobb & Co. driver travelling from Stanthorpe to Tenterfield. "It is with much regret that we are obliged to make mention of two very serious accidents which happened in our locality within the past week. The first occurred on Sunday evening last, to Mr. T. Rumley, the driver of Cobb & Co.'s coach from Stanthorpe to Tenterfield ... he left Tenterfield at the usual hour on Sunday morning, but when about two or three miles from Boonoo Boonoo the coach broke down ... owing to the horses swerving off the road, and running it against a tree, which necessitated the driver to return to town for the spare coach ... same day he resumed his journey, and when crossing the stony creek on the plain, his horses bolted, and he was thrown heavily to the ground. A report of the occurrence being brought to town, several gentlemen proceeded to the spot, and found Mr. Rumley lying on the roadside, in a state of insensibility. He was conveyed to Brown's Hotel, when it was found that he had sustained a compound fracture of his right leg, in addition to other serious injuries ... He is now happily improving in health, and it is to be hoped that he will soon recover from the shock to his system." (Tenterfield, 5 Jan 1877, p.6)

News along the tracks

Tenterfield

"HOW TENTERFIELD GOT ITS NAME. Towards the end of last year, the Millions Club (Sydney) launched a scheme to send cases of Australian jam to Britain, mainly to advertise Australian fruit in the homeland and as a gesture of goodwill. The Tenterfield Municipal Council received a letter setting forth the scheme and decided to join in. It was suggested that the gift should be sent to the town in Great Britain from which this town gained its name. The question then arose—how did Tenterfield get its name? The Town Clerk (Mr. E. A. Wallace) communicated with the Mitchell Librarian, Sydney, who replied that this town was named after the home of two sisters of Sir Alexander Donaldson, which was situated in the Tenterfield at Haddington, Scotland. Therefore, the case of jam was forwarded to the Mayor and aldermen of Haddington.

The Tenterfield Town Clerk has received a reply from William Davidson, Provost of the Ancient and Royal Burgh, Haddington, Scotland, in which it is stated: *Our Tenterfield still stands and is in daily use as an orphanage school for homeless girls. I read your letter to my Town Council, and they decided unanimously and with acclamation to return your warm greetings and wish you and all your Council hearty greetings and the hope that the foster-child in Australia of our Ancient and Royal Burgh would extend and prosper."* (How Tenterfield Got its Name, 8 Mar 1934, p.1)

During the year 1872:

- "We learn from a reliable source that the tender of Messrs. Cobb and Co., for the conveyance of mails from Armidale to Tenterfield, and vice versa, has been accepted by Government and that we are to have three mails every week. This is a decided improvement on the old system. We understand that this arrangement is to take effect at the beginning of the ensuing year ...

- A horse belonging to Mr. James Logan, junr., of Mongola, while running in Murray's paddock, about three miles from Tenterfield, was bitten by a snake last week, and died a short time afterwards. This will be a heavy loss to the owner as the animal was valued at £70. About six weeks ago Mr. Logan, senr., sustained a similar loss, while going to Lawrence with two horses. One of these, for which £70 had been refused, died it is supposed from over-driving, while the second, worth about £25, was crippled and rendered useless.

- To facilitate the apprehension of criminals and others, at the tin mines on the border, and other parts of Queensland, the whole of the police force of Tenterfield are now made constables of that colony also. Messrs. Brassington, Bickley, and Beck, the only three not previously members of the Queensland police, were sworn in last Thursday by the Police Magistrate, who, by virtue of his position as a Justice of the Peace for Queensland, had full authority to do so.

- Concerning the Stanthorpe diamond, Mr. John Ruxton has written to the 'Telegraph' stating that its value is not more than £22. It contains some flaws otherwise it would he says be worth £80 ...

- The Tenterfield Steam Flour Mill, which opened in February last, closed about the 20th instant. The quantity of wheat ground during the interval amounted to 10,283 bushels." (Tenterfield, 9 Nov 1872, p.6)

Boonoo Boonoo

Meanwhile ANSWERS TO CORRESPONDENTS:

- "'Bull's Eye.' – The steamer City of Sydney was wrecked on November 6th, 1862. The following is a list of the male passengers by her, including the riflemen who were returning from Melbourne, where they had won the intercolonial rifle match: Messrs. Jackson, Russell, Rowland, Byrnes, Brush, Ashmore, Mitchell, Walker, E. Walker, Windeyer, Sharp, Shannon, Rayner, Lynch, Webb, Malcolm, Strong, Hellyer, Windham, Dickson, Fosberry, CWT, Roilston, Heath, Phelps, Lees, Captain Garrard.

- 'G.' asks: *I am 180 miles due west of Sydney; will you kindly inform me what is the difference of time for that distance; also, whether the sun sets here before or after Sydney setting?*—The further west a place is, the later the sun rises and sets. At 180 miles west of Sydney, the true time is about sixteen minutes behind that at Sydney.

- Prospector asks: *Was Boonoo Boonoo, near Tenterfield, ever a declared gold-field?*—Yes; but was usually included in the Timbarra Gold-field.

- 'J. C. C'.—New South Wales, with an area of 478,801 square miles and a population of 503,981, has 2,014,888 head of cattle and 16,278,097 sheep. Victoria, with 88,198 square miles and a population of 731,528, has 799,509 head of cattle and 10,002,381 sheep.

- Nurse asks: *Can you inform me how to prepare night-lights for a nursery?*—Make fine cotton wicks and wax them with white wax. Melt the grease and pour it into pill boxes, either fixing a cotton wick in the center beforehand or dropping it in just before the grease sets. If a little white wax is melted with the grease, all the better. When set to burn, place in a saucer with sufficient water to rise to the extent of the sixteenth of an inch around the base of the night-light.

- 'J. W.' asks: *Should a postmaster deny having any letters lying at his office when asked for by the owner, what is the best way of proceeding?*—Write to the Postmaster-General if you have reason to believe there are letters for you which the postmaster refuses to deliver." (Answers to Correspondents, 28 Dec 1872, p.8)

The following year "On Thursday morning, as the coach was proceeding from Tenterfield to Maryland en route to Warwick, it

capsized near Boonoo Boonoo due to the roughness of the road caused by recent heavy rains.

There were about nine passengers on board, including a constable and a prisoner. While they escaped serious injury, the driver was severely shaken and bruised.

BORDER PARCEL REGULATIONS. Authorities advise all individuals sending parcels by coach across the border—whether to Queensland or New South Wales—to ensure they contain goods exempt from duty. If parcels include dutiable goods, proper payment of duty must be ensured, or they risk being seized. Due to past instances of smuggling across the border, Custom House officials now find it necessary to examine coaches upon arrival." (Tenterfield, 1 Feb 1873, p.3)

Bookookoorara

During 1872 "Early on the morning of the 31st ult., the premises of Mr. E. Jenner, of the Half-way house, Bookookooara, were discovered to be on fire. The fire, which had evidently been burning for some time, was speedily extinguished before much damage had been done." (Tenterfield, 24 Aug 1872, p.6)

Wilson's Downfall, Wilson's Downfall & Sugarloaf

"In the early seventies Mrs. Palmer, with her husband, opened a hotel at Wilson's Downfall, known as the Coach and Horses Hotel. Although not on the main road to Tenterfield at first, Cobb and Co.'s coaches adopted that route, and it was for a time one of the changing stations for that firm." (Obituary—Mrs. Palmer, 10 Jun 1924, p.4)

During that same period, "We have been informed that a lad at Willson's Downfall was recently bitten by a snake in the region of the stomach. It appears the snake was enclosed in a hollow log, which the lad was carrying in his arms, and in a most dastardly manner, the reptile put its head out and bit him in the belly." (Country News, 24 May 1873, p.6)

By 1874, "We had a capital evening out at the Sugarloaf on Wednesday night, 27th May, with about 200 persons attending the new school, now nearly finished, for a social gathering to commemorate the building of the school and also in connection with the Church of England. A capital tea was provided, and there were a good few of us from Stanthorpe. After the tea and a few words from the parson, Mr. Richmond, singing became the order of the evening. Some good songs were sung; the manager of the Joint Stock Bank particularly pleased us, as he always does at every entertainment, with his capital songs. We were really astonished at the number of people present; Sugarloaf is becoming a very important part of the tin mines. Our tin getting does not decrease, and as the market seems steadier, we may look forward to better times than ever." (Stanthorpe, 4 Jun 1874, p.3)

Herding Yard, Amosfield & Liston

In 1876, Ashton's Circus was delayed at Herding Yard near Stanthorpe. "As may be seen by an advertisement in another column, Ashton's Circus will not perform in Warwick till Tuesday evening next, the night before the races. This delay has been caused by the company being detained at Herding Yard, near Stanthorpe. We learn by telegram that the company performed at the latter place on Monday night to a crowded house. The Japanese are said to be wonderfully clever, and the feats of horsemanship unsurpassed." (Local and General Items, 20 Apr 1876, p.2)

By 1877, "New Post, Telegraph, and Money Order Offices. – The Gazette of March 2 says that the post office known hitherto as Herding-Yard Creek will after April 1 be known as Amosfield. The Post Office Money Order system has been extended to Frogmoor, Gerogery, and Haymarket. Telegraph offices have been opened at Stroud and Lithgow." (Local News, 6 Mar 1877, p.5)

While further along the road in 1878 "Crown lands set apart for the Village of Liston." (Site for a Village at Liston, 8 Jul 1878, p.2654)

Quart Pot, Stannum & Stanthorpe

Firstly, "A word about the name by which this place is to be designated. It has for years been known as Quart Pot ; it has since been changed to Stannum (by somebody, I suppose, who wishes to show his proficiency in Latin), and now the Government are going to call it Stanthorpe. But why this changing of names? Surely the unassuming name of Quart Pot is as applicable to a tin country and, when seen in print, will arouse as many 'tinny ideas' as the far-fetched Latin name. And what has Latin to do with Queensland? Surely we have plenty of good old English names—and if not, some Australian names that would suit—instead of going back to the days of the Romans to find a name." (The Tin Mines, 28 May 1872, p.3)

"Stannum, as the people call it (though Stanthorpe, as the Government persists in designating it, is built on the base of a huge granite hill, named Mount Marlay). All the buildings in the main street are at present made of wood with iron and calico coverings ... The stores are numerous and are well supplied with all the necessaries. With the option of meat and potatoes, provisions are almost as cheap as in Toowoomba. There are many shanties (miscalled hotels) all doing a good trade. The accommodation for visitors is as well provided as it is possible to conceive." (Stanthorpe, 10 Aug 1872, p.3)

Later that year, "things are not as brisk here as they were a week or two ago, not through any scarcity of tin, but many squatters having interests in claims here have caused some of the works to be stopped, and the men discharged, in order, it is said, that they may be supplied with hands for the shearing." (Stanthorpe, 7 Sep 1872, p.2)

But a month later, "I started from Warwick by Cobb's coach ... It was crowded inside and out, the seats on the outside evidently being most in favor, and the passengers perching themselves anywhere on the roof where sitting room could be found." (At the Tin Mines—Warwick to Stanthorpe, 11 Nov 1872, p.3) "The new settlement at Quart Pot—Stanthorpe ... The population may be estimated at about 1600 to 2000 inhabitants, and there is considerable trade done with the tin mines ... the influx of people is said to have been so great that scarcely standing room could be obtained at the daily ordinaries, and a private room could not be had till after a long residence in the town or until some of the present occupants had left. The most we could obtain was a 'shake down,' and at the well-ordered inn kept by Mr. Groom, a member of the Queensland Legislature, we were as comfortable under the circumstances as it was possible to be. The house was full to overflowing, with doctors, captains, and others ...

After so much sojourning among the mines and miners, we were delighted with the attention we received at Mr. Groom's, where a well-ordered table greets every guest, the attendance being of the very best kind. A real live butler attended to our wants—a bill of fare bespoke the luxuries that we could regale ourselves with—while the wines and sparkling beverages were of the choicest kinds. We preferred a good kind of champagne termed Creuze. In short, every luxury seemed at our call. Besides Mr. Groom's good inn, there are several others—Mr. Scowen's, almost the next door—while over the way are Mr. Tevlin's and Mr. Farley's, both occupying corner sites, and Mr. Kelly's, close by ; still, there is not accommodation enough for the many visitors that frequent the place en route to the mines.

Stores are numerous—Mr. H. George's, Mr. Scowen's, Messrs. Davis, Harris, & Co.'s; Mr. Howitz's, and Mr. Merry's being among the principal ones. Mr. George has the post office.

There are three banks—the Commercial, Joint Stock, and National. A spacious auction mart is owned by Mr. Ransome, and there are some fine livery stables, kept by Messrs. Stewart & Home, where horses and vehicles of all descriptions can be hired, and if needs be, be driven by one of the proprietors, who, possessing intimate knowledge of the mines, find their services frequently called upon ...

There is a local weekly paper—the 'Border Post, and Stannum Miner'—but it is as well known as the 'Border Peg.' Thirteen policemen sport the uniform of that useful body of men ... Mr. Pollett Carden fills the office of chief magistrate.

Cobb & Co. have reduced the fare by their coaches between Stanthorpe and Warwick, a distance of 40 miles, to five shillings. This seems to be for the purpose of running the people's line of coaches off the road. It is to be hoped such monopoly will not be successful, but it is feared it will.

The fare may then soon rise to fifteen shillings. There are four coaches daily each way—two by Cobb & Co., and two of the people's line of coaches—and they are generally well filled. The driver of Cobb's coach assured us he would run the next week for half a crown and give his passengers a feed on the road. The booking office of Cobb & Co. is at Groom's, and that of the people's coaches at Farley's ...

Among its other places of amusement, Stanthorpe has a theatre. I think it is called after the Prince of Wales. The opening night was celebrated with a dance; the invitations were general, and sixteen ladies were guaranteed. The building is situated near Scowen's hotel and is at present but a rude building, there being a deal of that material called bark in the structure." (A Trip to the Mines, 23 Nov 1872, p.3)

The next year, "relics of old times at Quart Pot Creek—seventeen bottles of brandy—were found buried in the bank of the creek, not far from where once stood the public house of 'Darkly Ross,' on the Queensland Company's claim, the other day, supposed to have been placed there 10 or 17 years ago.

The premises of Mr. Scowen, the Melbourne Hotel, were broken into on Saturday night or early on Sunday morning, and a box taken from the bedroom where Mr. Scowen was sleeping, containing property to the amount of £200.

The box has been recovered, and also the property. Some of the thieves were taken with part of the property on them.

On Sunday night last, three ruffians were walking down Maryland Street. Two young men were standing talking in front of a saddler's shop, when those fellows knocked one of these young men down. A barber living opposite, hearing the cries of this man, turned out to save him; the ruffians immediately turned on him, giving him an unmerciful kicking. His wife, hearing his cries, ran out to his assistance ... She lies under the doctor's care and is in a very precarious state." (Stanthorpe, 29 Mar 1873, p.3)

STANTHORPE–THE ROLL UP TREE

Also of interest in Stanthorpe is the famous 'Roll Up Tree.' "Many lively (yet orderly) scenes occurred in the early days of the field, and probably the most notable was that which occurred at the Roll Up Tree (a tree which stood in the roadway of Maryland street and the scene of the principal meetings of the miners), where the miners decided to drive away all the Chinese miners who had been introduced by Mr. H. C. Ransome, and

this gentleman was to be ducked in the Quart Pot.

Ransome, who feared violence, communicated with Brisbane, and a strong force of police arrived, but they only had to report 'that all was quiet,' and the Chinamen 'sought fresh fields and pastures new.'

Other notable scenes at this famous tree, were when members of Parliament were burned in effigy and probably the one who came in for most derision when the ceremony was taking place was Hon. R. Pring, who had accepted Cabinet rank against the wishes of his constituents. "This Day. Great indignation is felt here in consequence of Mr. Pring's desertion of the constituency. At a large meeting held last night under the Roll-up-Tree, the honorable gentleman was hung in effigy, and burnt amidst loud groans." (Stanthorpe, 3 Jan 1874, p.2)

Following this "On Saturday morning the bellman announced a caucus meeting at the Roll-up Tree, and such was the indignation of our citizens that in a few moments a subscription was made to erect a substantial hustings, and a well-appointed list of speakers was duly nominated. The object, to take into consideration a lying telegram published in the Courier in the issue of 26th ultimo, to the effect 'that this town was deserted; that tin ore was worth but 4d per lb.,' and other statements equally untrue.

A large number of storekeepers, miners, and others met at the time appointed, and the result was as follows:—*Public meeting to counteract the wired lies of the Stanthorpe correspondent of the Courier*. Mr. Tyrrell proposed to the chair, Mr. Austin moved the first resolution, to the effect that the telegram which appeared in the issue of the 26th ultimo, from their Stanthorpe correspondent, was untrue, and calculated to do great injury to the mines by the withdrawal of capital, thereby throwing large numbers of men out of employ. Mr. Austin spoke with great warmth. After being duly seconded, the motion was carried.

Mr. Scowen proposed the second resolution, to the effect *that the Courier be requested to contradict the telegram*, and in doing so said that although the Northern Eldorado appeared to offer great attractions, he firmly believed that the district would for many years hold a large settled population, and that although his interest was not now so largely identified with Stanthorpe as it had been, he should always be a well-wisher of the district.

If the presumed correspondent of the Courier was now retiring from the trade of the town, he should not forget that he owed his present ease to the tin mines. Seconded and carried.

The third resolution, proposed by Mr. Bathurst and seconded by Mr. Austin, *That the Courier correspondent's conduct is deserving of the severest censure*, was met by cries of 'Who is he?' An amendment was moved by a Mr. Arbouin, amidst great confusion, and ultimately lapsed, the mover of the amendment being accused of a weakness for the celestial labor. The resolution being put and carried with considerable cheering, and concluding with a vote of thanks to the chair, the meeting broke up. Mr. Arbouin, on leaving the platform, was somewhat roughly handled, and but for timely police protection, which enabled him to take refuge in Groom's Hotel, would most likely have come to grief.—Corr. D. D. Gazette." (Affairs at Stanthorpe, 7 Mar 1874, p.2)

Shortly after,

"a great calamity has befallen Stanthorpe, and at present, it is difficult to say what dreadful consequences may arise from it.

Ever since the 'roll up' on Saturday, the last day of February, the unfortunate tree that upheld 'the stump' on which the stump orators aired their eloquence has sickened, and now it is in the last stages of existence, blighted and dying.

In vain, efforts have been made to save it. The indignation that evoked the 'roll up' has died out, and the 'roll-up tree' is dying with it. Our orators will mount crape and conceal onions for the loss of the poor old tree, which must now yield to the axe. Future 'roll ups' must provide for their own roll-up tree. Many at the Palmer will think kindly of the red gum tree under which, in earlier days, many a good grievance was ventilated and many a yarn spun about the days of 'auld lang syne'." (Stanthorpe, 14 Mar 1874, p.3)

By 1885, "Stanthorpe is busier just now than it has been at almost any period of its existence since the days when the roll-up tree flourished in front of Groom's Hotel." (The Stanthorpe-Border Extension 28 May 1885, p.2)

Maryland

1878 MARYLAND SELECTION "Many of your readers are perhaps not aware of the fine opening there is in this locality for a number of industrious free selectors with families … You are doubtless aware that at the separation of Queensland from this colony this station was divided in two, the Queensland portion being designated Folkstone … every acre between Warwick and the New South Wales border is now occupied … such rich alluvial soil here … situated as this place is on the top of the New England Range. The whole country is thickly timbered, with the exception of small flats erroneously called swamps, but the facilities for transit of produce to Warwick and Brisbane by the railway, now in course of construction, will more than counterbalance the extra cost of clearing. Another advantage not to be over looked …

The Queensland Government are destroying the marsupials in this district by thousands … so that by the time the navvies reach this place, a kangaroo or wallaby will be a curiosity … As a fruit-growing district it would be impossible to find a better. We have apples (without blight), in great variety; pears, plums, quinces, cherries, gooseberries, grapes, &c., in fact any kind of English fruit will thrive here. In agricultural produce, wheat, oats, barley, lucerne, &c. is grown with great success, and there will be an unlimited demand for these productions for years to come. In vegetables the finest cabbages, carrots, onions, cauliflowers, potatoes, and pumpkins have been grown. But the best of all is that Maryland is one of the most healthy places in Australia. In proof I need only mention that when

measles and scarlet fever were raging in the township of Stanthorpe, only nine miles distant, not a single case was to be found in Maryland …

Suitable reserves for camping, water supply, and recreation have been made. At present there are two hotels, a store and post-office, blacksmith's shop, a nice little English Church, and a Public school capable of accommodating sixty children, besides private residences. As we are on the border of the colony, of course, the Government know little of our requirements—a member of Parliament has not visited us for the last four years." (Maryland, 1 Jun 1878, p.780)

Warwick

"Mailmen and coach drivers did a lot towards the development of Australia, and it was no occupation for a waster—only brave men, full of resource, could hold the position. Just here it might be as well to mention that the originator of Cobb and Co. was a Yankee, who came from California when our gold diggings broke out. He and Ashton, of circus fame, came to Australia about the same time …

COBB & CO.'S COACHES. Cobb introduced coaches like they had in California, but after a time he dropped out of the firm, and, of course, he has been dead now for many years. It is a pity that some pen better than mine would not write the history of Cobb and Co.; all I can do is to recount a few instances that came under my own observation.

When I was a boy my father used to take me by horse buggy from Pikedale to Warwick, where I would get into a coach driven by 'John the Coachman,' who used to take me from Warwick to the railhead, about Clifton. The worst part of the journey was crossing Glengallan swamp. I used to think I was somebody on this coach, because the driver was an old servant of Mr. John Deuchar, and was well known to us before he took up coach driving. After taking the train one was astonished at the flash first-class carriage, which, to a bush boy, was a luxury hitherto unheard of. The train stopped at Ipswich, and my father and I used to stop at the hotel for the night, leaving next morning for Brisbane by coach or steamer, whichever one preferred.

Of course, a seat on the box seat of the coach was the ambition of all boys, and extra money was charged for this seat. After a rough but short trip, the coach would land us at the ferry situated not far downstream from where Victoria Bridge now stands. The coach was driven onto the punt, which was pulled over the river by hand power, and on reaching the eastern side, about opposite where Mr. Ryan's statue stands, the coach drove up a slanting cutting to near the end of the present Victoria Bridge. When going up this cutting the coach driver used to blow his horn.

All mailmen were compelled by law to do this, crack his whip, and land his coach in great style at the post office, which was not far from where Allan and Stark's now stands. After delivering the mails, the coach used to trot down Queen Street with many small boys running after it, but this did not last long because the coach pulled up at the Royal Hotel, which still stands where it stood then—opposite the present post office.

RUNNING TO THE TIN MINES. Then the tin mines were discovered, and Cobb and Co. ran a coach from Warwick to Stanthorpe. Billy Richardson drove one of the coaches and Harry Lumby the other; both were splendid drivers. Richardson afterwards became manager for Cobb and Co. The coach used to run from Warwick to Stanthorpe via Maryland. Later on, a coach was run from Stanthorpe to Tenterfield via Sugarloaf. The coach used to stop the night at Tenterfield, and a fresh driver would take charge.

'OINTMENT' TAYLOR. One of them was called 'Ointment' Taylor because whoever had a box seat was persuaded to buy a pot of ointment of his own making—according to him, it would cure sore backs, etc.; in fact, it would cure anything! Every time I rode in his coach, I bought a pot of ointment in place of tipping him; he seemed better pleased to sell the ointment than to get a tip. I remember my brother Bob being persuaded to buy a pot, and some months later, when he took another trip, he was asked by Taylor how he got on with it. My brother said, *First rate*, and he was then asked by Taylor if he would give a testimonial stating particulars of the cures he had effected. This cornered my brother, so he told Taylor he had only used it to grease the buggy! After this, 'Ointment' had no time for my brother!

THE WILY HOTELKEEPERS! From Tenterfield to Glen Innes was a day's stage, and we were glad when it was over. Not only on this road but on all other coach roads,

> no matter what hotel you stayed at, they gave bacon and eggs for breakfast (very salty, home-made bacon it was). This gave the passengers a raging thirst, which they got rid of at the next hotel!

From hotel to hotel, they seemed to delight in feeding one with salty things, of course, to the benefit of each other!

THE PRISONER AND HIS ESCORT. About 1890 I had occasion to travel by coach from Charleville to Cunnamulla, and on the way, we spent a night camped out. On the return trip from Cunnamulla, we had a policeman and a prisoner on board. What amused me was that the prisoner used to have his meals at the different eating places with the passengers, while the policeman sat on the doorstep eating sandwiches which he had brought with him. From the coachman, I gathered that the prisoner was fed by the Government, but the policeman had to feed himself, and as he had a family, it paid him to carry sandwiches. The night we camped out, the policeman leg-ironed the prisoner to himself and gave me the key of the irons to keep until morning.

GOONDIWINDI MAILS. About 1861 Goondiwindi got its mail from Maitland, and the stations around Goondiwindi had to send in for their mail; we had to send 60 miles for ours. Our newspaper came from Sydney—the 'Sydney Morning Herald.' By 1877, mail communication had very much improved. From about 1870, our Queensland Government deserved a lot of praise for the way they ran mails to outback places. In cases where the population warranted it, coaches carried the mails, mostly by Cobb and Co. One of the postal regulations was that the mailman or coach driver had to sound a horn on nearing a post office, and neglect in this respect meant that the mailman was subject to a fine.

Before ending, I would like to say a word in praise of the way these coaches contrived to get through in all sorts of weather. A noted driver was Billy Hood; with his scramey hand, he could drive anything with hair on—so also could Jack Dallas. Then there was the careful and efficient George Lucas.

Joe Hurshburg was also a good driver—he left to go north for Cobb and Co.—and there was a host of other drivers, to say nothing of good and bad coach boys. Being a coach boy was a hard life; the hours were too long for boys, but they seemed to be able to sleep anywhere, no matter how rough the coach was. Then another coach mail was run between Goondiwindi and Mungindi. George Lucas had the first contract, and Charlie Death drove the coach. Later on, Bill Carter got the contract, and although not a first-class driver, he was a good mailman. He got through, no matter how bad the roads were, and, best of all, he always brought the latest news. He was by far the best news medium we had. They used to consider the 'Mulga Times' and the 'Bagman's Gazette' good news givers, but they weren't a patch on Bill Carter!

I enjoyed the old coach journeys far more than the trains we now have, notwithstanding that I often had to walk in bad weather and shove through the bog-holes!" (The Coach Days, 10 Nov 1934, p.8) Note: For more information about Western Queensland runs see 'Along the tracks of Cob and Co. - The Western Run'.

Toowoomba

Worthy of note in 1870: "Aug. 2.—Execution at Toowoomba of Brown, alias Bertram, bushranger." ... 1878 "April 22.—Outbreak typhoid fever at Toowoomba, many deaths." (Queensland's ... notable events, 8 Dec 1909, p.28)

Brisbane

In 1870 "COBB & CO.'S TELEGRAPH LINE OF ROYAL MAIL COACHES. QUEENSLAND BRANCH
Head Office: Royal Hotel, Brisbane
On and after the 1st January, 1870, the coaches of the above line will run as follows:
- From Brisbane to Ipswich—Daily (Sundays excepted), at 5:30 a.m. and 12 noon.
- From Ipswich to Brisbane—Daily (Sundays excepted), at 12:30 p.m. and 5:40 p.m.
- From Brisbane to Gympie—Mondays and Thursdays, at 4 a.m.
- From Gympie to Brisbane—Mondays and Thursdays, at 6 a.m.
- From Brisbane to Pimpama—Tuesdays and Saturdays, at 9 a.m.
- From Pimpama to Brisbane—Mondays, Wednesdays, and Fridays, at 9:10 a.m.
- From Allora to Warwick—Daily (Sundays excepted), at 7 p.m.
- From Warwick to Allora—Daily (Sundays excepted), at 5:30 a.m.
- From Warwick to Maryland and Tenterfield—Sundays and Wednesdays, at 5 a.m.
- From Tenterfield to Maryland and Warwick—Mondays and Thursdays, at 5 a.m.
- From Dalby to Condamine and Roma—Sundays and Wednesdays, at 4 a.m.
- From Roma to Condamine and Dalby—Sundays and Thursdays, at 6 a.m.
Parcels booked through to the above-mentioned places at reduced rates.
A. R. Bennett, Manager, Fred. Shaw, Agent ... THE TURKISH BATH, ALBERT STREET
Open daily (Sundays excepted) from 9 a.m. till 6 p.m. On Tuesdays and Fridays, open for ladies from 9 a.m. till 1 p.m.; and for gentlemen at 2 p.m." (Classified Advertising, 31 Jan 1870, p.1)

Meanwhile in 1872 "June 15.—Victoria Bridge opened; Cobb and Co.'s coach first vehicle to cross it." ... "Feb 1 to 7—Heavy floods throughout Queensland." (Queensland's ... notable events, 8 Dec 1909, p.28)

In conclusion, the 1870s marked a significant expansion of Queensland's postal and transport networks, with Cobb & Co. at the forefront of mail delivery and coach services. However, this progress came with challenges, as the rugged terrain and harsh conditions posed considerable risks for drivers and passengers alike.

ca. 1917 Mr. James Rutherford – Coaching in Australia, p.4

QUEENSLAND "No state in the Australian Commonwealth, and few countries in the world, possess the diversity of resources and living conditions with which Queensland has been endowed. Her climate ranges from the altitudes of Stanthorpe, on her southern border ... the cold nights and fresh crisp days ... to the burning arid plains of her western interior, and the sweltering humid sunshine of her rich tropical coast ...

Her scenery is rich in many types, from glaring desert sands to tropical and forested mountains where rivers gurgle among overhanging shrubs and ferns, and the landscape blazes with the heterogeneous splendour of mile upon mile of gleaming foliage ...

Queensland is best known to people outside its borders by reason of her pastoral industry. No doubt the stock-breeding enterprise has for years been the mainstay of her prosperity ...

Queensland is rich in minerals and prolific in coal, and numbers of large high-grade deposits await but the drawing nearer of the iron road to become abundantly reproductive. Timber forms an industry which until lately was exploited in only the most unscientific and wasteful manner ...

The intending grower may select his land and cultivate apples, peaches, and other cold-climate species on the hills of Stanthorpe." (The History of Queensland, Matt J. Fox, 1919-1923)

ca. 1870s Pillar Post Box, Lower Fort Street, Dawes Point (John Paine) – Courtesy State Library of New South Wales

ca. 1870 Tenterfield, NSW, Kuskey's blacksmith shop and coach building works – Courtesy State Library of New South Wales

ca. 1874 Cosmopolitan Hotel (paddocking on the hotel grounds) – Courtesy State Library of Queensland

Horses in mud with coach - Courtesy Sovereign Hill Gold Museum

ca. 1870s Edward Jenner's (1835-1900) Halfway House Hotel, Bookookoorara – Courtesy State Library of Queensland

Thomas Merry's general drapery, men's clothing, millinery and fancy goods store,
Stanthorpe (William Boag) – Courtesy State Library of Queensland

1872 Britannia Hotel in Stanthorpe (William Boag) – Courtesy State Library of Queensland

ca. 1873 Ruthven Street, Toowoomba – Courtesy State Library of Queensland

1870 The first Brisbane General Post Office, Queen Street, Brisbane – Courtesy National Archives Australia

ca. 1873 Buildings on the north face of Edward Street between Adelaide and Queen Streets, Brisbane – Courtesy University of Technology

Chapter Six

Along the mail routes
1880s & 1890s

COBB & CO.
By G. M. Smith

One day in our big medical ward (We'd had word from the station)
A traveller passing through became ill And was ready for transportation.

He was brought up by the ambulance And placed in a corner bed.
And when his history was being taken, "My name is Cobb," he said.

I told him the only Cobbs I knew Were those of Australian fame,
And while I thought of romantic days, He said, "I belong to the same."

He wore a well-clipped pointed beard And his eyes were keenest blue,
And when I asked him, "What's your age?" He said clearly, "Ninety-two."

Although he chewed the plaited whip Belonging to days of yore,
He told me tales of coaching days And all his travels galore.

He told me of the fast proud horses, All of the finest breed.
And of the shoesmith always ready To shoe in time of need.

He told me too of the dogs they kept And all their whims and ways;
Remembering how they guarded the camps In the good old coaching days …

(Cobb & Co. 27 Mar 1942, p.3)

Railways

In 1881, Cobb & Co.'s mail service from Warwick to Stanthorpe ceased, marking the end of an era in coach-based mail delivery. The railway took over, offering a faster and more efficient route, replacing the traditional coach mail run with rail transport. At the same time, Maryland township, once a significant settlement, saw major changes. "In pre-railway days Maryland township was a settlement of some importance, but the completion of the railway from Warwick to Stanthorpe in 1881, and the consequent diversion of most of the road traffic along the line by way of Dalveen, had far reaching effects as far as the endurance of the place was concerned." (Echoes of the Past, 24 Jun 1933, p.7)

By 1883, railway expansion was in full force. "The railway contractors are prosecuting vigorously their Tenterfield section of the Northern railway. Large numbers of men find employment on the works. The weather is fine and bracing. The border traffic has been unusually great during the past week. No less than 30 teams loaded with merchandise or tin ore passed through the town. The traffic would be far greater were the border duties lower, and more attention paid to goods by the Queensland railway authorities." (Telegraphic Intelligence, 5 Jun 1883, p. 3)

However, progress came with tragedy. "A terrible and fatal accident happened yesterday morning at the railway works, Cluff River, 13 miles from Tenterfield. One of the navvies employed, named White, was engaged drawing a charge which had failed to go off the previous evening when it suddenly exploded. The unfortunate man received the full force of the blast in his chest. He was hurled fully 15 yards away, and when picked up was quite dead. Coroner Graham proceeded to the scene of the accident today and held an inquest. The result was a verdict of accidental death." (Telegraphic Intelligence, 5 Jun 1883, p. 3)

COACHING SERVICE 1881—Cobb & Co.'s Telegraph Line of Royal Mail Coaches
- Brisbane & Beenleigh
- Brisbane to Pimpama and Nerang Creek
- Nerang Creek, Southport, Pimpama
- Noosa & Gympie
- Gympie & Maryborough
- Cherry Gully & Stanthorpe
- Stanthorpe to Tenterfield
- Stanthorpe to Warwick
- Yeulba, Surat and St. George
- St George to Cunnamulla
- Roma to Charleville
- Charleville, Cunnamulla
- Comet to Springsure
- Emerald & Clermont & Copperfield
- Withersfield & Aramac
- Clermont & Copperfield
- Withersfield & Blackall
- Blackall & Isisford
- Riedville & Charters Towers and Ravenswood
- Maytown & Cooktown … Fredk. Shaw, Manager. (Advertising, 28 Mar 1881, p.4)

COACHING SERVICE 1891—Telegraph Line of Royal Mail Coaches
- Yeulba to Surat and St. George
- Charleville to Cunnamulla
- Cunnamulla to Thargomindah
- Cunnamulla to Barrangun
- Thargomindah to Hungerford
- Charleville to Adavale
- Charleville to Tambo
- Blackall to Tambo
- Hughenden to Richmond Downs
- Richmond Downs to Cloncurry
- Cloncurry to Normanton
- Port Douglas to Herberton to Thornborough
- Laura to Maytown
- Blackall to Jericho
- Tambo to Blackall
- Barcaldine to Isisford
- Barcaldine to Aramac
- Aramac to Muttaburra
- Muttaburra to Winton
- Croydon to Georgetown
- Winton to Hughenden
- Haydon to Croydon
- Herberton to Georgetown
- Adavale to Windorah. (Classified Advertising, 29 Aug 1891, p.387)

News along the tracks

Warwick

In 1880, travel between Warwick and Stanthorpe was available with Cobb and Co.'s Telegraph Line of Mail Coaches. "On and after May 1st, 1874, leave Warwick for Stanthorpe at 5:30 a.m., Maryland at 10 a.m., and arrive at Stanthorpe at 11:30 a.m. Will leave Stanthorpe at 1 p.m., arrive at Maryland at 2:45 p.m., and arrive at Warwick at 7 p.m.

MAIL COACH TO TENTERFIELD. The Mail Coach for Tenterfield leaves every Tuesday, Friday, and Saturday at 5:30 a.m., returning the following days. Booking Office at Warwick:—Evenden's Commercial Hotel, L. H. Shaw, Manager, S. Evenden, Agent." (Advertising, 3 Jan 1880, p.1)

By 1883, the overland route to Sydney via Warwick and Stanthorpe was used by notable individuals. "Amongst the less public people who availed themselves during the last week or so of the overland route to Sydney, *via* Warwick and Stanthorpe, there were a trio of notabilities. J. M. Macrossan, ex-Minister for Works (accompanied by his new partner M'Sharry, both bound to the scene of their railway contract); and Charles Hardie Buzacott, managing proprietor of the Courier and Queenslander. Buzzy is on a holiday tour." (Fistiana, 5 May 1883, p.7)

In 1885 "the tender of Mr. T. J. Quinn for the lease of the refreshment room at the Warwick railway station, for a period of one year, has been accepted. Amount, £35." (The Warwick Argus, 22 Dec 1885, p.2)

By 1888, Warwick faced severe water shortages, leading to increased regulation. "Water is now so scarce at Warwick that men are employed to watch persons who waste the precious fluid. They detected a man named Michael Sweeney in the act the other day. He was summoned before the Police Court and fined in all £1 9s. 3d. Speaking of this case, the Examiner says: *We hope in this crusade against water wasters there will be no favouritism shown, but that all offenders will be treated alike. It has been told us that in one case a man has a lucerne paddock, a vegetable garden, an orchard, &c., all irrigated night and day, and he says he is perfectly safe—first denying that he uses the water, and if so, that the authorities will not touch him. Strange, only a three-railed fence divides this beautiful half or three-quarters of an acre of luxuriance from the dry, arid, and desert-like land adjoining.*" (Country News, 24 Nov 1888, p.935)

Interestingly, in 1895 "I reside in Southport, Queensland, and have lived there for some 15 years on account of its being a calm place for yachting, which pastime I am extremely fond of. My wife and I decided to start our journey from Goondiwindi, as that was the furthest point we could commence from when the rivers were low, in order to have an uninterrupted trip by river through to South Australia. In order to reach this point, we had to travel by rail to Warwick, a distance of 130 miles, and then head south to Goondiwindi. The latter was a very rough journey of 140 miles, and any inclination the scenery and coach trip might have had towards monotony was dispelled by the antics of the various teams driven in the vehicle. The coach was chiefly occupied in breaking in horses, as the broken colts to a great extent comprised our horseflesh. Several poles were broken, but luck seemed to favor us from the outset, and fortunately, no serious accidents occurred. We arrived safely at Goondiwindi and stayed there for a week with Dr. Woodforde, an old friend of mine …

Our now memorial journey by river was commenced on 2nd March, when we boarded the Snipe on the McIntyre River. … The large number of trees which had fallen across the river … so impeded our progress … One or two that we could not overcome, we got under by emptying the boat, sinking her, and so getting under what we could not get over. We also met a great many waterfalls between these places, some of which were 7ft or 8ft high. Some we shot, but in a good many cases, we had to lower the boat down. This was very unpleasant and at times dangerous work, as my wife stood on the rocks on one side of the fall and on the other with ropes by which we lowered the boat from rock to rock … At the various stations we stopped, the tale was told that thousands and thousands of sheep were dying from want of food, and on one station 85,000 had died out of the 150,000 that comprised the run. That was five months ago, and as there has been no rain since, the experiences of the squatters must have been awful. Travelling along one mile, I noticed 59 dead sheep, 5 cows, and 3 horses, and that was only an average mile. We saw such sights as these day after day …

With a fair wind, made Goolwa at 5 o'clock on Monday, 4th November, and thus completed our journey through Queensland, New South Wales, and South Australia of 2,574 miles … The weather was fine all through the journey, and rain only fell on three days. It was very cold in the winter, but our sleeping arrangements prevented us from feeling that at night … We stopped the boat every night and tied her up to the bank. On only twenty-five occasions did we sleep away from the Snipe, and we then accepted the hospitality of the owners or managers of some of the stations we visited. If we had remained at all the stations we were asked to stop at, our trip instead of taking eight months would have occupied eight years." (Down the Darling in a Canoe, 7 Dec 1895, p.8)

STANTHORPE

In 1882 "Stanthorpe, which is really the beginning of the New England country, stands at an elevation of 2656 ft … Cobb's coach is in waiting at the railway station when the train arrives and conveys passengers and their luggage to Farley's hotel, which is clean and comfortable, though the building is much in the bush style of architecture. Cobb and Co. have an agent here, so that travellers who have not booked their places before leaving Brisbane can now do so.

The charge by coach from Stanthorpe to Armidale is £4 2s ... From Stanthorpe to Tenterfield is about forty miles, and the coach starts at 9 a.m. The country is chiefly of granite formation and is very hilly ... About one-third of the way is Wilson's Downfall, once a considerable tinfield. On the whole the road is passable, for large sums of money have been spent in cutting and macadamising. Amongst the ranges is Boonoo Boonoo, near which place are the silver mines; here a refreshment-room is kept by the wife of the groom (Fox) who has charge of the horses; the building and the fare are of the simplest kind." (From Brisbane to Sydney Overland, 6 May 1882, p.556)

Then in 1893 "A very sad and fatal accident happened last Friday. Mr. John Sheahan, jun., only son of Mr. Daniel Sheahan, one of our local butchers and a very old and highly esteemed resident of Stanthorpe, was bringing in the sheep that had been killed that day. The slaughter-yard is on the further side of Funkers Creek, which was flooded. Nearing the further end of the bridge, the wheel became jammed against the guard fence, and the horse, growing restive, reared up. In his plunging, he wheeled sharp round to the right, and his head at first went under water. Seeing this, Mr. Sheahan took off his coat and jumped into the water. It does not appear that he was able to hold on to the horse or cart before being carried down by the stream. There is a two-rail fence three or four yards below where he jumped. He was at this fence for about a minute, but it could not be seen whether he had hold of it. He then drifted over it and was seen to head for the bank he had left. After taking a few strokes, he suddenly sank and never rose again.

The body was recovered the following morning not far from where he had been last seen. One of Sheahan's arms had been dislocated at the shoulder joint some time previous, and when the body was found, the shoulder was out. It is conjectured that it failed him while he was swimming and that this caused him to sink so suddenly. A crowd soon collected at the spot, and a young man stripped off his clothes and extricated the horse without much difficulty. The funeral took place on the following Tuesday and was very numerously attended." (Fatal Accident at Stanthorpe, 28 Feb 1873, p.6)

Maryland

"In pre-railway days, Maryland township was a settlement of some importance, but the completion of the railway from Warwick to Stanthorpe in 1881, and the consequent diversion of most of the road traffic along the line by way of Dalveen, had far-reaching effects on the endurance of the place ... the boundary fence of old Maryland station, New South Wales, is within a mile of Dalveen." (Echoes of the Past, 24 Jun 1933, p.7)

By 1885, progress continued with the establishment of a telegraph station at Dalveen. "For the information of your subscribers between Warwick and Stanthorpe and others, I enclose you a copy of a communication just received by me from Mr. Commissioner Curnow, stating that the Railway Department has, on the application of the inhabitants around Dalveen, decided to place a telegraph office and operator at that station. This office will not be solely departmental but also for the use of the general public." (Telegraph Station at Dalveen, 15 Apr 1885, p.2)

That same year, an opportunity arose for those seeking land in the New England District, adjacent to Maryland. "For private sale ... Cattle Station.—New England District, 48 miles south of Warwick, Lightle Stocked and well watered, adjoining the following well known stations, Undercliff, Acacia Creek, Maryland, and Balandean, abundance of grass and water in all seasons has an area of 59,800 acres of Lightly Timbered, Well Grassed Country. Together with 400 Head of nicely Bred Cattle; and 20 Head of horses. The improvements consist of Substantial house, of 9 rooms in good repair, detached Kitchen, and Stockman's Cottage, A Splendid Orchard, Drafting and Branding Yards, Capable of working 2000 head of Cattle, 2 secure Heifer Paddocks." (Advertising, 8 Jun 1885, p.2)

By 1887, Maryland, a township about one mile from the Queensland border, had been "left in the shade ... About fourteen years ago it was a lively little place, having two hotels, a store, and blacksmith and butcher's shops, etc. But the discovery of the tin mines at Stanthorpe led to the advancement of that town, and Maryland was soon left in the shade, and at about the time of making this trip, it can only boast of one hotel, two dwelling houses, State school, and a church." (A Trip to Maryland, 15 Jan 1887, p.2)

Wilson's Downfall, Willson's Downfall & Boonoo Boonoo

By 1883, "the coach (a two-horse buggy) is ready to carry you to Tenterfield ... Wilson's Downfall, a change of horses, and away again for another fifteen miles to Boonoo Boonoo then on to Tenterfield where the mail is delivered ... A change of horses, and away again for another fifteen miles to Boonoo Boonoo. Too dark to see what the place was like, but on pulling up opposite the hut, a young girl (Fox) stepped gaily out, and, in the most business-like manner, unhooked and walked off with the horses to the stable, from whence she shortly returned with fresh ones, and put them in with the calm and business-like style of an experienced groom.

And such on inquiry we found she was. Her father had been groom J. B. Fox at the same place for many years, and, dying, had left a large family unprovided for. This plucky damsel, with a fondness for horses and a thorough knowledge of the duties, begged to be allowed to take up the position of breadwinner. To the honour of Cobb and Co. and her own credit be it recorded, that she is earning the full wages paid by them for the work, and with the reputation of being the best groom on the line." (Brisbane to Melbourne, 24 Mar 1883, p.453)

During 1886-1887, life along the Great Northern Road was serviced by the roadside hotels. Among them was the Coach and Horses Hotel at Wilson's Downfall, where Anastasia Palmer was the licensee. The hotel bore a grim past—"In 1882 William Palmer died from a blow to the head when trying to break up a fight." (Government Gazette Notices, 3 Sep 1886, p.6024) "The Fatal Fracas at Willson's Downfall. Our telegrams on Tuesday contained brief particulars of a fatal fracas which took place at Willson's Downfall on Friday evening last, during which a man named William Palmer, landlord of the Coach and Horses Hotel, received injuries which resulted in his death eight or nine hours subsequently. William Allison, a well-known storekeeper and tin buyer, residing at Sugarloaf, was afterwards arrested, charged with having inflicted the blows on the deceased ... Mr. Coroner Graham, of Tenterfield ... a large bruise was noted on his right cheekbone with three bruises on his right temple. On turning down the scalp, the markings were very distinct on the inner surface. Removing the skull cap, he found in that region a clot of blood—about four ounces in weight—which completely flattened the brain. This clot was caused by the rupture of one of the chief arteries that supplied the membrane of the brain. From the symptoms described and the post-mortem appearances, it was evident that compression of the brain was clearly the cause of death." (The Fatal Fracas at Willson's Downfall, 9 Sep 1882, p.3)

"This sad affair has caused a great sensation not only at Willson's Downfall and the immediate neighborhood but also in Stanthorpe and Tenterfield, where the deceased was well-known. He was a very quiet, unassuming man and was greatly respected by all who knew him for his peaceable disposition and his honorable and straightforward character. He had been the landlord of the hotel at Willson's Downfall for about eight years and was, we believe, a native of Hull in the County of York. He leaves a widow and one child to mourn his untimely passing at the early age of 43. All the circumstances surrounding the case are of a very painful nature, as the accused, William Allison, holds a respectable position as a storekeeper and is reputed to be very wealthy. The consequences of his rashness must, under any circumstances, be very serious." (Tenterfield, 15 Sep 1882, p.4) Not far away, the Boonoo Boonoo Inn at Boonoo Boonoo was managed by Samuel Brown. (Government Gazette Notices, 3 Sep 1886, p.6024)

By 1891, "Influenza is very prevalent throughout the district, and scarcely a family has escaped. Mr. F. Burne, C.P.S., is unable to attend to his duties, and the Boonoo Boonoo school is closed owing to the teacher having the complaint. The attendance at all the schools in the district is affected by it." (The Influenza Epidemic, 18 Nov 1891, p.5)

In 1895, disaster struck when a fire engulfed the hut of Mr. W. Cullen. "On Saturday morning, the hut occupied by Mr. W. Cullen, at Boonoo Boonoo, near Tenterfield, was completely destroyed by fire. The whole of the contents, including wearing apparel, powder, etc., was destroyed. It is supposed that a spark from the fire caught the bark, and the flames spread unchecked. The explosion of the powder quite alarmed those in the neighborhood, who congregated upon seeing the conflagration. The loss is a severe one to Mr. Cullen, who has lost his all." (Country Notes, 12 Jul 1895, p.3)

Amid these events, confusion persisted regarding the name of Willson's Downfall. "I ... beg to tender as evidence a letter received from Mr. Robert Willson, a son of the late Mr. George Willson, ... who, as nearly everybody from Pittsworth to Glen Innes knows, spells his name 'with two little l's.' Mr. Willson ... writes: That the place was named after George Willson is absolutely correct. The facts of the case, as they have been told to me by my own family and also by such a good authority as Mr. D. G. Smith, of Downfall fame, are that my father was traveling in a buggy from Maryland to Tenterfield in company with my mother and my two eldest sisters (one an infant in arms, the other a year or so older). When crossing a gully, the trap capsized, and they were all precipitated into the water. The place was called Willson's Downfall, and the name stuck to it. If you look up the area of the N.S. Wales Government Gazette, you will find the name given as Willson's Downfall." (No Title, 25 Oct 1904, p.3)

Tenterfield

Written in 1880 "From the Border Post of Friday last:—We learn that Mr. H. Lumley, so long and favorably known, as driver for Cobb and Co., between Warwick and Stanthorpe, has severed his connection with that firm, and purposes running an express waggon between Tenterfield and Grafton. Few drivers in the employ of the universal coaching company have merited and secured more public esteem than 'Harry' ...

Whose obliging demeanor and accomplished manipulation of the ribbons has gained for him the respect and confidence of all who have travelled either on the box or inside under his pilotage, and the well-wishes of the general public are fully accorded him.

Mr. Lumley's engagement with Cobb and Co. has extended, we believe, over six years, during which period he has acted faithfully and well to his employers, and he leaves the company's service simply with the view of bettering his position. We heartily wish him success in his new undertaking. A testimonial to 'Harry' is on the tapis, and will no doubt assume a substantial form. We also can bear testimony to 'Harry's' skill as a whip. One who has driven the difficult road between Warwick and Stanthorpe for a period approaching five years without a single accident is deserving of something more than the thanks of his employers and the travelling public. 'Harry's' many box-companions in this district will be glad to hear of his success in his new venture." (The Warwick Argus, 1 Jun 1880, p.2)

By 1886, the opening of the Great Northern Railway Extension occurred. "The opening of the Great Northern Railway Extension Line from Glen Innes to Tenterfield took place today. Great preparations had been made for the occasion, and a large number of guests, including His Excellency Lord Carrington, the Ministers of New South Wales and Queensland, and members of the Legislative Houses of both colonies, had been invited … The railway track from Stanthorpe to Wallangarra, the Queensland terminus, was sufficiently completed for the train to continue straight to the last-named station. Upon arrival, Cobb's coaches awaited passengers for the twelve-mile journey between the border and Tenterfield." (Opening of the Great Northern (N.S.W.) Railway to Tenterfield, 21 Oct 1886, p.5)

In 1892, there was a remarkable act of bravery in the Tenterfield district. "There would have been a vacant place in the family of Mr. B. Woolnough, at Tenterfield Station, on Monday last, but for the plucky conduct of his son, a youngster of nine summers. It appears that several children were playing on the bank of the creek on Monday morning, which was very high and running rapidly in consequence of the previous night's storm, when a little fellow, four years old, son of Mr. Woolnough, overbalanced himself as he was throwing stones in the whirling stream, and fell into the water, which carried him rapidly down. His plucky brother had to run a distance of fifty yards to cross a hand-bridge along the creek, and plunged into the water up to his arm-pits only just in time to seize his little brother by the foot as he was passing down the rapid current and pull him out. The child was conveyed home in an insensible condition, but under parental attention, he revived and is no worse for his untimely immersion." (New of the Day, 25 Oct 1892, p.5)

Meanwhile, local governance continued with the operations of the Tenterfield Stock and Pastures Protection Board. "A meeting of the Tenterfield Stock and Pastures Protection Board was held on Thursday last, with Sir W. H. Walker in the chair. Mr. Walker was re-elected chairman, Mr. J. Bishop treasurer, and Mr. M. J. St. Clair secretary for the ensuing year. In answer to an inquiry, the secretary was instructed to reply that the board would not be in a position to pay for marsupial skins before the rate was fixed in June next. At a meeting of the Sheep Board held last Thursday, the inspector (Mr. H. J. St. Clair) presented his annual report, showing that he had traveled 1,403 miles on duty during the year. The number of horses returned in the district was 6884, an increase of 564; cattle 71551, an increase of 4072; and sheep 125689, an increase of 8930. There were no diseases to any extent among horses and cattle, but the excessive wet weather had caused footrot, fluke, and worms among the sheep, which had been successfully treated by various remedies. The returns by stock owners having less than 500 sheep were 13,195. The average weight of the clip was 5 lb 7½ oz, a decrease of ½ oz per sheep compared with 1890. The stock traveling in the district by road, as reported to the inspector, were: horses 732, cattle 5482, sheep 94096." (Tenterfield, Australian Town and Country Journal, 19 Mar 1892, p.16)

COACH FACTORY—CHARLEVILLE

- 1886, factory moved to Queensland. "Cobb & Company Limited, coachbuilders, factory relocated to Charleville As our coach routes extended out west we commenced to notice that our vehicles built with the coastal seasoned timbers would not stand the dry inland climate, they would crack and gape at all joints. This became so serious at last that we decided to move our Factory to a suitable inland locality, and after considerable thought Charleville, nearly 500 miles inland, was chosen, and our whole plant and equipment moved to there in 1886 … We had another Factory in Bathurst, N.S.W., and the machinery and plant from there were also removed to Charleville at the same time." (Cobb & Co.'s Catalogue of High Class Vehicles, 1897, p.3)

- 1893 Bathurst Cobb and Co. "Vehicular.—Messrs Maddy, Fleming, and Mollison, coachbuilders, of Keppel street, are turning out some really first class vehicles at their establishment … although the factory of Cobb and Co. has been closed." (Bathurst Free Press, 17 Jul 1893, p.2)

Post offices, mail & coach services

- 1880 – "Conveyance of mails No.77. Tenterfield, Willson's Downfall, Amosfield, and Maryland, three or six times a week—Cobb & Co. See combined tender." (Government Gazette Notices, 31 Oct 1879, p. 4877)

- 1891-1893 Mail contracts – "No 96. Tenterfield, via Clifton, Mole, and Mingoola Stations, and the south side of the Severn River, twice a week—James Gallagher, horseback, 3 years, £90 per annum, conditionally; 97. Railway Station and Post Office, Tenterfield, twice or oftener daily—John H. Collins, spring van or cart, 1 horse, 3 years, £40 per annum; 98. Tenterfield, Steinbrook, Timbarra, and Lionsville, twice a week—James M'Lean, horseback, 3 years, £200 per annum; 100. Tenterfield and Bryan's Gap, twice a week—John Finn, 3 years, £17 18s per annum. 101. Willson's Downfall and Acacia Creek, via the surveyed road and Cullendore, once a week—David G. Smith, horseback, 3 years, £52 per annum." (Conveyance of Mails, 6 Nov 1891, p.8861)

- 1880 – "Tenders.—The Works Department invites tenders until July 23, for fitting clock, new post office, Toowoomba." (Official Notification, 10 Jul 1880, p.6)

- 1897 – "Queensland Brisbane, Thursday. Warwick Post Office. The Cabinet has accepted a tender for the construction of Warwick Post Office for £5,437." (Queensland, 4 Jun 1897, p.5)

1898 Postal stations, mail roads and telegraph offices – Mail routes Tenterfield (Receiving Office), Bryan's Gap (Post Office), Boonoo Boonoo (Receiving Office), Wilson's Downfall (Post Office and Money order Office) to Rivertree (Receiving Office) or to White Swamp. (Postal Stations, Mail Roads & Telegraph Map, 1898) Mail route no longer directly shown between Liston and Maryland. See *Appendix A*. 1897 – Corduroy roads are laid down in boggy country to prevent horses and carts from sinking in the mud. "The endeavour to get over the difficulty … construction of corduroy roads … roads made of logs of wood laid side by side … cost £800 a mile." (Tour of the Minister for Works, 25 Sep 1897, p.5) "Lengths of timber, sometimes split, sometimes young saplings, were laid close together across bush tracks, forming a rough but fairly firm surface. The name was suggested by the ridges, which are parallel to each other, much like the texture of corduroy cloth. That was originally termed 'Cord de Roy', meaning 'King's Cord'. This type of road either originated from that kind of load used in tin mining or was given the name based on early road construction techniques. They were described by an eminent writer eight years ago." (Corduroy Road, 31 May 1910, p.9)

Bushrangers & robberies

In 1880, the town of Yeulba had a post-office robbery. "Post-Office Robbery Tuesday.—The post office at Yeulba was broken into last night, and three mail bags were stolen. Two of the mail bags were for Brisbane and one for Dalby. The police are investigating the matter." (Post-office Robbery, 19 May 1880, p.2)

Nineteen years later, in 1899, another example of a post office burglary which caused a stir. "The Post Office Burglary Brisbane. Wednesday. In connection with the burglary at the post office … F. T. Spencer, the officer in charge … was yesterday found lying on the office floor." (The Post Office Burglary, 14 Sep 1899, p.6) The case took an unexpected turn when Spencer was discharged from the hospital and arrested. "Fred Spencer, the post office official, who was found apparently unconscious yesterday at the George-street post office after the robbery, was discharged from the hospital today. Subsequently, he was arrested on a charge of stealing £140." (Queensland, 14 Sep 1899, p.6)

Notorious bushranger Thunderbolt continued making headlines

By 1890, rumors swirled about Thunderbolts disappearance. "The notorious bushranger Ward, better known as 'Thunderbolt,' kept the Clarence country in a state of terror … and reaped a fairly good harvest until he suddenly disappeared. The general impression is that he was shot, but this is incorrect. He was known to be in the district … dropping out of the bushranging industry and returned to a farmers life. He belonged to a respectable family, and is now, it is said, a prosperous and worthy member of community. — Truth." (Thunderbolt, 26 Sep 1890, p.6)

Later that year, a sensational discovery was reported near the Goulburn River. "We have pleasure in reporting the most sensational find of its nature which has taken place for some time. The district in which the find took place has been known as the rendezvous of the celebrated bushranger, Thunderbolt, whose exploits are well known to old hands in this part.

On Saturday last a little boy, the son of Mrs. Munns, the housekeeper for Mr. D. Campbell, was enticed to a spot on the mountain near the house by reason of a hen cackling. The mother and son went to look for the nest … the boy at once seized an old olive oil bottle and took it to his mother in a childlike manner.

She noticed it was filled with something of a bluish tinge ... Close examination proved the writing to be that of bank notes, tightly packed in the bottle, and closed with a stick. ... It is impossible to state the value, as they are not opened, owing to the finder being anxious to deliver the parcel into the hands of the police. It most certainly is a valuable curiosity, and from the nature of the place in which it was found it would seem to have been placed there for Thunderbolt's so-called wife, who eventually died there." (Goulburn River, 11 Dec 1890, p.6)

In 1882, Thunderbolt, along with Owens and Gordon, faced trial. "This notorious criminal, togethers with two others named Owens and Gordon, were tried at the Central Criminal Court this morning for the burglary at Mr. Graham's shop, George-street, on August 12 last. The jury, after listening to powerful Appeals from the prisoners, who asserted their innocence, found them all not guilty." (Thunderbolt, 10 Nov 1882, p.2)

1898 "Ward alias Thunderbolt, The 'Winghain Chronicle' says : A man named Ward, supposed to be Thunderbolt's brother, stole a horse near Tamworth, rode it to a place close to Walcha, where he left it, and took another. The police have been in pursuit, but so far have not yet caught him. He was seen near Yarras a few days after he left Walcha. A number of persons, believe he is the real Thunderbolt, as they say Thunderbolt was in a different part of the colony, when the supposed Thunderbolt was shot, and persons who knew him well have repeatedly seen him since. The local police have, we believe, been on the lookout for a man who 'sweated' a horse, from Swamp Oak and made for Armidale. If it was Ward he has warded off the efforts of the police to capture him, but as a cast of Thunderbolt's skull was taken some time after death, it cannot be that individual.

Still, there may be more Thunderbolt's about."
(Ward alias Thunderbolt, 1 Jan 1898, p.2)

Cobb & Co. adapted as towns evolved, finding new opportunities even as railways replaced coach routes. Meanwhile, outlaws like Thunderbolt remained shrouded in mystery, keeping their legends alive.

James Benjamin Fox (1833-1882)

Information courtesy of Michele Claire de Courcy (granddaughter of James Fox). Some information previously came from Veronica Whitmore in 1988: "The Fox home at Boonoo Boonoo was one of Cobb and Co.'s change stations. James Benjamin Fox, also known as JB, was a groom for Cobb and Co. The Fox sisters were in charge of the change station after their father JB died—'no station had better groomed steeds.'

A story goes that JB hid the bushranger Thunderbolt once in a large salt bin so the police couldn't capture him and also hid his horse up in the hills until the police left. The Thunderbolt story continues: when Thomas Fox (JB's son) was only 19 years old, the regular mailman got sick at Boonoo Boonoo, so Thomas took the mail coach through to Maryland. Just before Maryland, he was held up by Thunderbolt, who asked Thomas his name and then his father's name. Thunderbolt told Thomas he wouldn't touch a thing of J.B. Fox's. Thomas was very relieved and continued on his way.

In 1850, JB was in the employ of Patrick Leslie as a groom and jockey while JB had the publican's license for the 'Golden Fleece Hotel' at Quart Pot Creek in 1858-1859. Thomas Fox, son of James Benjamin Fox and Mary Wall (married 12 June 1855), was born 12 June 1856 at Head Station, Goomburra, Queensland.

Thomas married Annie Peachey at Farm Creek on 23 December 1882. He lived at Murdoch's with his family until 1895 when 'Undercliffe Station' was broken up. He applied for 'Hillcrest' but then cancelled his application. Thomas then applied for 'Overcliffe' and 'Monte Cristo'. He had a house moved up from Rivertree and put on 'Overcliffe'. He and his family moved there and lived there until 1898.

In 1898, Thomas started a butcher's shop at Tannymorel and moved there with his family—the main reason being to school his children. Sometime in 1901, Thomas and his family moved to Yangan for a short time; they then moved and went to live with Bob Patterson Snr. Thomas owned land at Captain's Flat (near Canberra—site of late 1800s gold mining) but sold it to Bob Patterson Snr. Thomas Fox and his family finally moved back to 'Overcliffe' in 1903. Extract from a dairy of Thomas Fox from 1903: — June 3rd *Went to Murdoch's and started to build a house ('Overcliffe'). J. Crisp commenced work at 8/ - [8 shillings] per day.*

Mrs Irma Rickard said the original 'Undercliff Station' homestead was across the road from the present 'Undercliff' home. The second house (Cullens) was built where the present Rickard home is. It is said Thomas Fox ploughed the ground where the old pear trees are, and he was the head stockman on 'Undercliff'. Mr. Cullen sold to Gunn, and Gunn sold to Charlie Burton Senior. Syd Bonner pulled the old home down and built the present one 72 years ago. Irma lived there from when she was two years old until she passed away.

Thomas Fox (1856-1925) married Annie Peachey (1860-1909) – Courtesy Michele Claire de Courcy 'portraits of my great grandparents'

Fox Family Tree excerpt
Benjamin and Mary FOX (England)>James
James FOX m Mary Ann WINCH>James Benjamin
James Benjamin FOX m Mary WALL>Thomas
Thomas FOX m Annie PEACHEY>Thomas Charles
Ben Thomas Charles Ben FOX m Ivy Hannah Muriel EINAM

1880s Fox family at their horse change at Boonoo Boonoo, from second on left daughters Caroline and Emma, lady passenger, son James Fox Jnr with his hands in his pockets, Mrs. Mary Fox, daughters Martha and Margaret – Queensland Museum Network

Boonoo Boonoo Inn and Post Office – Liston Hall Committee, courtesy of local residents

A. J. Smith's Saddlery, Tenterfield – Courtesy Tenterfield Visitor Information Centre

The Coach and Horses Hotel, Wilson's Downfall, A. Palmer – Liston Hall Committee, courtesy of local residents
ca. 1890 Australian Hotel at Boonoo Boonoo, H. Lea licensee, Tenterfield – Courtesy State Library of New South Wales

ca. 1885 Group outside hotel, Boonoo Boonoo Inn, (A. B. Butler)
Samuel Hawkins licensee – Courtesy State Library of New South Wales

ca. 1897 Stanthorpe Commercial Hotel – Courtesy State Library of Queensland

ca. 1872 Farley's Mining Exchange Hotel Stanthorpe – Courtesy State Library of Queensland

Chapter Seven

The changing landscape 1900–1920s

THE DAYS OF COBB AND CO.
By Jack Moses

Rocking, along, singing a song, As happy as happy can be.
Jogging along, singing a song. That's the life for me.

Over the range we come to the change. And drink our billy tea;
Oh, the 'roo, and the cockatoo, An the kookas laugh aglee.

So, on we go with Cobb and Co. But, oh, how things have changed.
Alas and alack, they won't come back, They've crossed the final range.

(The Days of Cobb and Co., 4 May 1938, p.2)

Along the tracks

TENTERFIELD

By 1905, Tenterfield presented itself as a picturesque yet quiet town, reminiscent of Nelson, New Zealand. "To be perfectly candid, Tenterfield strikes the city resident as somewhat of a 'sleepy hollow,' being strongly reminiscent of the beautiful little town of Nelson, New Zealand. It is admirably looked after by the local municipal council, is well lighted by means of Kitson lamps (vaporised kerosene), and is in advance of much more important towns as regards its sanitary arrangements." (In and Around Tenterfield, 8 Nov 1905, p.32)

Two years later, in 1907, an unusual event startled travelers near Tenterfield. "On Friday last, Mr. Ben Carlill of Wooroowoolgen had a most peculiar experience. He was quietly jogging along the Tenterfield road in his sulky when he was suddenly overtaken by a storm. But it was no ordinary storm. Instead of the usual raindrops, Mr. Carlill was pelted with thousands of young green frogs, about an inch long, a good number of which fell into the trap.

For about half a mile, the little 'croakers' came down, the sight being extremely funny and novel. The frogs, Mr. Carlill states, were very thin and starved-looking but hopped about as lively as could be.

The following day, we received confirmatory reports from several travellers on the Tenterfield road, and there appears not to be the slightest shadow of doubt as to the authenticity of this strange event. We have heard of a storm of young fishes, but a storm of young frogs certainly takes the palm. The storm occurred about four miles from Casino, and we believe thousands of frogs are still visible on the side of the roadway." (A Novel Storm, 16 Feb 1907, p.6)

By 1914, "Tenterfield Shire Council ... Re Main Roads Grant for year ending 30th June, 1915 ...The requirements of the main roads were thoroughly gone into, with the following result: Deepwater to Tenterfield, £250; Tenterfield to Drake, £500, and on to Tabulam, £500; Woodenbong to Queensland border (near Amosfield between Legume and Oakey Creek), £500; between Clifton and Severn Shire boundary on to Tenterfield-Bonshaw road, £250. Total promised £2000. The Chief Engineer stated that this £200 was all that he could promise for the year, and that such a high grant was principally due to the high valuations and the increase in the rating. I was also given permission to inform the Council that the Minister had decided to reduce the grant considerably to shires that have a low rate struck and whose valuations are low." (Tenterfield Shire Council, 19 Sep 1914, p.1)

In 1926, the town's 'quiet night' made its way into the local newspaper. "Constable Completes His Day. In the early hours of Wednesday night, there was some animation in Tenterfield's main streets, with two picture shows and a dance attracting a good number of patrons. Constable Milan, after taking an affectionate farewell of his wife and children, passed through the police station yard and proceeded up Molesworth Street, along Rouse Street, meeting various citizens along the way. In some cases, he greeted them with a cheery remark, while in others, he engaged in conversation. He was in his usual good spirits, and his witty remarks created many a laugh as he completed his patrol up and down the street. Passing a dance in progress,

he exchanged words with two or three young citizens enjoying a smoke outside the hall.

When the clock struck 11, signaling the end of his shift, he was at the post office corner. At that moment, Mr. Joe Kelly, a Tenterfield saddler, crossed the street from the School of Arts. As both he and the constable lived in the northern section of the town, they joined company and walked to the corner of Rouse and Molesworth Streets. After a few minutes of conversation, they parted, with the constable making his way home. As he left, he remarked to Mr. Kelly that 'it was quiet in the street'." (Quiet in the Street, 27 Nov 1926, p.4)

Just a year later, in 1927, nature took a destructive turn as heavy rains caused widespread flooding. "Since January 23 more or less rain has fallen every day, with last night's fall making a total of 621 points registered at the post office. While much heavier rain has been recorded in the river districts from Tenterfield, 262 points fell in the town in a very short time last night, and considerably over three inches fell outside the town ... brought the river up to the highest flood mark in many years. Considerable damage was done to bridges on high roads leading to Tenterfield, and an enormous amount of harm done to the main roads. The whole of the flood gates for miles up and down the river have been washed away. The Tenterfield Agricultural Society was one of the biggest losers. The damage done to the society's grounds is very regrettable, as their jubilee show event is only three weeks distant.

It will cost several hundred pounds to repair the damage done by flood waters. Portion of the rural public school fence has been swept away, and the whole of the large rural school vegetable plot was many feet under water. This morning, then, shows every appearance of more heavy rain. Later—The floods at Tenterfield are the worst for 27 years. Families were forced to seek safety during the night. The approaches to bridges on the main roads have been destroyed, and traffic blocked. The bridge on the service route to Casino is damaged. The Showground fences have been washed away, and widespread damage done." (Floods in the North, 28 Jan 1927, p.9)

TENTERFIELD—SADDLERS

"In well-settled districts, one rarely comes upon a shop in which saddles are actually made. The trade in these places is often confined to harness-making, repairing, and selling saddles made in city factories to set patterns. In far inland towns, however, the saddler is a tradesman of much importance, as most people find the horse practically indispensable, and saddles are made on the spot to suit each customer's needs. In towns such as Bourke, Forbes, Warren, and Tenterfield, saddle-making is an important trade. Saddles unique to the far-back regions are the stock and break styles. These feature deep, hollow seats and high knee and thigh pads, ensuring the rider can grip securely while pursuing stock over rough terrain or staying seated on a bucking horse. These saddles have evolved from English designs to suit Australian conditions, although English saddles are gaining popularity in flatter areas and near towns.

In the far west, the travelling saddler is quite an institution. Sometimes he is employed by a business house in a larger town, but often he works independently. With a wagon loaded with saddlery and harness, he travels from station to station, staying long enough to perform necessary repairs, visiting 30 or 40 homesteads on his rounds, which span hundreds of miles. Back in the city, locally manufactured harnesses differ only slightly from their English counterparts. In New South Wales, harnesses are generally lighter than those used in England. Most harnesses, except small saddles, are made locally due to cost considerations, with lower-grade products dominating the market. Only a few first-class sets are produced, priced similarly to their English equivalents—though colonial leather is cheaper, higher local wages offset the savings. Another branch of the trade includes bridle-making and strapping, such as coat and luggage straps, usually crafted by youths.

Regarding the industry's condition, a well-known manufacturer comments: *The saddle and harness industry is currently in a depressed state. Several factors contribute to this, primarily the recent prolonged drought, which has significantly weakened consumer spending. Another factor is the rise in mechanical transportation—railways, tramways, and bicycles are reducing the demand for saddlery. The Arbitration Court's rulings have also affected the industry, as its awards granted workers nearly all their requests despite the market downturn. This has led to the dismissal of inexperienced, older, and slower workers, with the minimum wage and imposed conditions negatively impacting business. Whereas we previously employed 100 men, we now have only about 25. A few good seasons will likely reverse this trend, but it remains challenging that, in the industry's weakest moment, we must endure such severe restrictions.*

Additionally, leather production plays a role in manufacturing bags and portmanteaux, with imports now minimal. Though this industry does not employ a large workforce, it is steadily growing alongside the population." (Our Industries, 11 Feb 1905, p.12)

- 1905 – A. J. Smith's Saddlery and Harness Maker. "It is more than 20 years since the proprietor started this business—the oldest established saddlery in the town. A large and flourishing trade is done in teamsters' and buggy harness, whilst the saddles, of which Mr. Smith makes a specialty, are well and favourably known throughout the northern districts and Southern Queensland … The coach which runs to Lismore is owned by Messrs. Morrissey and O'Keefe, who are the mail contractors between Tenterfield and Lismore, a run of 100 miles, the trip to Lismore taking 17 hours, the return journey—an ascent of about 3000ft—lasting 20 hours. Drake, Tabulam, and Casino are passed en route." (In and Around Tenterfield, 8 Nov 1905, p.33)
- 1908 – "F. Kneipp, Saddler, Tenterfield. Stock Saddles – £5/10/-, Park Saddles – £5/5/-. The Champion Saddles of N.S.W. Delivered free to any railway station in the state for cash with order. Mention 'The Freeman'." (Advertising, 21 May 1908, p.5)
- 1910 – "TO THE MAN WHO RIDES A HORSE. Perfect-fitting saddles are essential for the comfort of both horse and rider. Nothing makes a good horse look poorer than an ill-fitting, badly finished saddle. My staff of high-class saddlers work tirelessly to craft saddles that are unmatched in shape, fit, and comfort—built to withstand hard wear without showing it. Bridles, bits, stirrups, rings—everything is in abundance. Every description of harness is made—everything a horse owner needs is in stock. For over 20 years, I've been the leading prize winner at Tenterfield and other shows. A. J. Smith, Leading Saddler Tenterfield." (Advertising, 30 Dec 1910, p.3)

- 1910 – "Fred Kneipp, For saddles, harness, collar, saddlery in all its branches. The combination of high-grade materials, skilled workmanship, and reasonable prices has brought Kneipp's business to the forefront. Give Him a Trial. Address: Saddle & Harness Emporium, Rouse-Street, Tenterfield, Phone No. 33." (Advertising, 30 Dec 1910, p.3)

'TENTERFIELD SADDLER' SONG ... Written in The Australian Women's Weekly on October 1, 1975, Peter Allen reflected on his inspiration for a truly Australian song, stating, *"I wanted to write an Australian song with a true Australian flavour—not a comical song ... I was born in Tenterfield in Northern NSW, and my grandfather* [George Woolnough as stated by the N.S.W. Government, 2025] *was a saddler-maker there—so what could be more natural than this song?"* (Guess who popped up among the paintings?, 1 Oct 1975, p.29)

In 1914, Woolnough's trade faced regulatory challenges. "George Woolnough, Saddler, was charged with employing an apprentice in excess of the number he was entitled to, based on the proportion of journeymen employed. Mr. Huntley stated that during his visit, he found the defendant had an apprentice under indentures dated January 1914. At that date, and at the time of the visit, the defendant employed no journeyman, which was a requirement before having an apprentice. It was unfortunate that the apprentice was unable to properly learn his trade under such circumstances, but this constituted a breach of the award. The defendant explained that he was unable to find a journeyman,

as they refused to leave the city.

Mr. Huntley acknowledged that he did not doubt this. George Woolnough was fined 10 shillings, with 7 shillings court costs and 10 shillings complainant's costs." (Industrial Court, 4 Jun 1914, p.5)

Beyond his work as a saddler, Woolnough was actively involved in local events, including the popular Swastika Club dances, where he played a role in organizing and managing the floor. "The Swastika Club held one of its very enjoyable dances in the Gymnasium last evening, and the attendance, numbering about 100—on an evening that was cold, bleak, and wet—was ample evidence of the popularity of these social gatherings. Dancing continued until a little after midnight, with all attendees having a most pleasant time. Mr. Archie Fletcher, with the assistance of Mr. George Woolnough, had charge of the floor, while music was voluntarily supplied by Misses Eileen Krahe and Eileen Fletcher, along with Mr. Ernest Tooley. These two ladies also serve as the secretaries of the Club and are largely responsible for its success. During the evening, a very nice supper was served." (Personal, 18 Jun 1914, p.2)

By 1946, his reputation extended well beyond saddlery, earning recognition for his expertise in horticulture and breeding poultry. "MEET THE SHOW JUDGES Noted for his punctuality, Mr. George Woolnough of Tenterfield was a worried man yesterday morning when the car in which he was traveling to Glen Innes to judge the horticulture broke down a mile or two this side of Dundee. Fortunately, a south-bound motorist happened along, and Mr. Woolnough got a lift, arriving at the showground late but apologetic. Knowing their man, the stewards had realized that the delay was no fault of his, and everything was in readiness for an immediate start with the judging when he arrived. Mr. Woolnough almost rivals our own Mark Marshall for versatility. He is a remarkably fine gymnast and still finds the time—and energy—to run a boys' club in Tenterfield. He has a fine garden and is a noted authority on horticulture. Additionally, he breeds and judges poultry and caged birds. A member of a very old Tenterfield family, Mr. Woolnough is one of the best-known and popular identities of the northern town, and no old Tenterfieldian returns to the town without calling in on him for a chat." (Meet The Show Judges, 21 Feb 1946, p.2)

Boonoo Boonoo

In 1900, "the pupils attending the Boonoo Boonoo Public School will be treated to a picnic by their teacher (Miss List) at one of the pretty resorts in that district. The parents and friends of the children attending the school are sparing no pains to make the day an eventful one for the juveniles. Invitations have been issued to a number of people in town, and it is likely many of them will take advantage of the outing.

FIREWORKS CELEBRATIONS. The juveniles are busily engaged collecting bushes for a bonfire display, which for a brief space will illuminate the town at night in sundry directions. Stores of fireworks of every conceivable description are also being stored up for the eventful occasion." (Queen's Birthday 22 May 1900, p.2)

By 1906, "the annual Boonoo Boonoo School picnic took place amidst the picturesque surroundings of the once promising mining village on Friday. The weather conditions were not of the brightest description, but Jupiter Pluvius was most kind in withholding his moistening drops, and as a result of this circumstance, together with excellent management, the function was immensely successful. Sports of all kinds, for both young and old, were run off during the day, the principal event being the Boonoo Boonoo Champion Sprint, the honors in which fell to T. Funnell, with J. Forbes second, and T. Cleary third.

The children were liberally regaled with dainty refreshments, which had been generously donated and subscribed to by Tenterfield and Boonoo Boonoo residents, and in this connection, Mesdames Williamson, Weir, Sweedman, Miss Hurtz, and others are deserving of great praise for their indefatigable and effective attention to the children.

After the midday meal, Mr. Brawn (teacher) explained that in order to encourage the children, he had offered prizes for good work, good attendance, and good conduct, and he had much pleasure in asking Mr. Thomas Funnell to present the prizes to the children. Mr. Funnell said it gave him much pleasure in complying with the request, and he had no doubt the children had earned their prizes or they would not have got them. Prize Winners:

Good Work – George Youngberry, Stanley Sweedman, Hilda Weir, May Hurtz, Aden Glasgow ; Attendance – Lionel Sweedman, George Youngberry, Christina Youngberry, May Hurtz, Edie Weir, Rose Youngberry, Albert Hurtz, Eva Glasgow ; Good Conduct – Mavis Glasgow ; Messrs. Brawn, Glasgow, Hurtz, and Youngberry managed the sporting events, and every child was given a prize or a toy of some kind.

At night, a most enjoyable dance eventuated at Williamson's hotel, where about 20 couples enjoyed themselves till daylight. Mr. T. McAllister as M.C., and Messrs. D. Hooten and P. Hurtz as musicians, gave every satisfaction, while songs were excellently rendered by Misses B. White, M. Hurtz, Eva Glasgow ; Messrs. J. A. Brawn, W. J. Clarke, and D. Hooten. Refreshments were served at midnight and 4:30 a.m., and proceedings terminated at daylight.

LIST OF DRESSES WORN BY THE LADIES
Mrs. Williamson – Black Silk, Cream Trimmings
Mrs. Alderman – Black Lustre
Mrs. Glasgow – Book Muslin
Mrs. Weir – Pink Silk Blouse, Black Skirt
Mrs. Sweedman – Delaine Blouse, Black Skirt
Mrs. Jenner – White Muslin
Miss B. White – Pink Silk Blouse, Light Skirt
Miss A. Weir – Red Silk Blouse, Dark Skirt
Misses J. and E. Weir – White Delaine
Miss Glasgow – Brown Cashmere
Miss K. Fox – White Silk
Miss M. Youngberry – Green Cashmere, Silk Trimmings
Miss J. Youngberry – White Muslin
Miss Hurtz – Cream Voile
Miss Dwyer – Blue Silk Blouse, Dark Skirt

The committee wish to thank all the people who kindly assisted at the picnic and dance, also Mr. E. H. Juergens, C. L. Garr, and others for donations etc." (Boonoo Boonoo, 2 Oct 1906, p.3)

In 1908, "Coach and Horse Hotel, Wilson's Downfall. A. Hoskings licensee, Mrs Palmer owner; Boonoo Boonoo Hotel, H. Williamson licensee and owner … All in good order, well conducted, sanitary conveniences ample and clean ; licensees comply with law." (Special Licensing Court, 23 Jun 1908, p.2)

Following that in 1912, "at the Tenterfield Licensing Court last week, Hugh Williamson, licensee of the Boonoo Boonoo Hotel, applied for the approval of the Bench for the removal of his license from Boonoo Boonoo to premises at Acacia Creek." (Tenterfield Licensing Court, 23 Jan 1912, p.4)

That same year, "While coming in from Boonoo Boonoo with a load of wood, Mr. Sam Dickson, who had stopped to tighten up his load, was startled by hearing groans coming from a creek in the paddock of Mr. A. Sommerlad. On investigating, he came across Mr. A. Sommerlad's two boys, aged 5 and 6. The elder brother was lying on the bank, holding his brother, who had slipped into the water. The boy was unable to pull his brother out, so he had to scream out to attract the attention of passers-by. Mr. Dickson pulled the lad out of the water, but as the boy had been immersed for nearly an hour, he collapsed. Mr. Dickson at once began to try to revive him, but his efforts did not seem to be doing any good, so he immediately took him to his home, where he was revived and is now doing well. It was fortunate that Mr. Dickson happened to hear the screams; otherwise, a double drowning accident might have occurred. The stamina of the elder brother is to be commended, and that he must have suffered is shown by the fact that his arms had become completely black from the strain of holding his brother." (Brave Young Australian, 28 May 1912, p.5)

Later in 1925, Boonoo Boonoo Falls gained attention as a tourist attraction. "The Tenterfield Council has decided to advertise Boonoo Boonoo Falls as a tourist resort. The Mayor (Alderman F. Kneipp), at the last meeting, stated it was 'a sight second to none in the State', and as it was only a few miles off the main Northern Road, many tourists would be glad to visit the place.

It is suggested that advertisements, with pictures of the locality, should be placed in public vehicles, railway carriages, etc. Additionally, the Government will be asked to construct a permanent road to the falls, as the current route consists only of a bush track. Although motors can reach the top of the falls without difficulty, the Council aims for a more accessible road for travelers. The falls are located 21 miles from Tenterfield." (Boonoo Boonoo Falls, 15 Jul 1925, p.16)

Wilson's Downfall & Wilson's Downfall

- 1900 – "SOCIAL … at the Coach and Horses Hotel … Mr. Piper … Dear Sir: On your retirement from the Police Service, we the undersigned residents of Wilson's Downfall and district do hereby tender you our compliments together with a watch-chain as a mark of our esteem for your long and valuable services among us … to Mr. Hosking's Hall, where dancing and songs occupied the time till daylight." (Wilson's Downfall, 10 Jul 1900, p.2)
- 1901 – COACH AND HORSES HOTEL "A meeting of the Wilson's Downfall Jockey Club was held on Saturday evening last at Mrs. Palmer's Coach and Horses Hotel for the purpose of receiving the balance sheet of the past year's transactions, and arranging a date and programme for the annual meeting. There was a fair attendance of members, Mr. D. Cullen, J. P., occupying the chair … that £4 be spent in repairing the Racecourse fence; also that £8 be spent in repairing the track and course. The date of the annual races was fixed for Monday, 11th November, King's Birthday … the meeting terminated with the usual compliment to the chair." (Wilson's Downfall—Annual Races, 16 Aug 1901, p.2)
- 1902 – COACH LICENCE "Before Mr. G. Martin, P. M. Charles Shoblom, hotel keeper, Boonoo Boonoo, made an application for a coach license to run from Wilson's Downfall to Tenterfield. Granted." (Wilson's Downfall, 11 Feb 1902, p.2)
- 1903 – HORSE AND JOCKEY HOTEL "Anastasia Palmer, licensee of the Horse and Jockey Hotel, Wilson's Downfall, applied for a liquor license for a booth at the Wilson's Downfall Races to be held on November 9th. Mr. Readett appeared for the applicant, and on his representations the Bench decided to extend the hour of closing from 6 to 6.30 p.m., the license being granted for the date applied for, the hours being fixed from 6 a.m. to 6.30 p.m." (Licensing Court, 23 Oct 1903, p.2)
- 1905 – WILSON'S DOWNFALL "A Charitable Act.— Mr. W. Moron, of Tenterfield, very generously gave a phonograph entertainment in the local hall recently in aid of the fund for clearing the local cemetery … A horse sale was held here on Wednesday last, but was poorly attended, probably on account of the dry season we are experiencing … A Social is to be held here on Saturday night next in aid of the local Cricket Club. On the following Saturday a picnic will be held, and judging by the energy being displayed by the ladies in the district it should be a big success." (Wilson's Downfall, 3 Oct 1905, p.2)
- 1920 – COACH AND HORSES FIRE "The Coach and Horses Hotel at Wilson's Downfall, (one of the old landmarks of northern New South Wales), was completely destroyed by fire. The well-known Coach and Horses Hotel at Wilson's Downfall, which has been conducted for many years by Mr. A. Hosking, was burned to the ground the other day (says a Tenterfield message). The flames were noticed about 3 a.m., and had a firm hold of the building, which was quickly enveloped. Nothing could be done to save the building or furniture. Mrs. Hosking only saved what she stood up in, and the men folk were somewhat similarly placed. The building, which belonged to Mrs. Palmer, of Wilson's Downfall, was insured." (Hotel Burnt Down, 4 Feb 1922, p.5)
- 1924 – MRS. PALMER'S PASSING "The memories of the old coaching days are recalled by the death of Mrs. A. Palmer, who, at the age of 85, passed away… In the early (eighteen) seventies Mrs. Palmer, with her husband, opened a hotel at Wilson's Downfall, known as Coach and Horses Hotel." (Obituary—Mrs. A Palmer, 10 Jun 1924, p.4)

Naming of Wilson's Downfall

1904 "The 'Argus' story is, that Wilson's Downfall received the appellation through the late George 'Willson' (who was in business in Tenterfield in the early sixties [1860s]) coming to grief at the particular spot. This is pure fiction. In the first place the gentleman referred to did not spell his name with 'two little l's,' and in the second, Wilson's Downfall was so named from the fact of a mishap occurring to a bullock driver in 1840, and the circumstances have been detailed to the examined by a very old hand who obtained the facts nearly 50 years ago. Some teams were engaged taking wool to the Clarence, and in the party was one William Wilson, nicknamed Bill the Sluggard, from his weakness to turn in early and rise late. The teamsters camped not far from Maryland the first night, and on the morrow had decided to make an early start … Bill, as usual, overslept … his mates had struck camp and were well on the road … he lost no time in yoking up and was soon following in the wake of the other teams … he did not overtake them, and in trying to negotiate a declivity in the track he capsized the load, and by some means got pinned underneath … four mounted men put in appearance … even outlawed as they were and steeped in crime, they yet had a soft spot in their hearts for a fellow creature in distress...

They quickly removed Bill from his awkward position, and having assisted him to unload and right the dray … Next morning Bill and his mates returned to the gully, which from that time has been known as Wilson's Downfall. Thus it came about that a luckless teamster's misadventure has given some historical significance to the locality." (Wilson's Downfall, 14 Oct 1904, p.2)

While written in 1927 "The King of Armidale and Willson's Downfall … Mr. John Willis, St. Aubyn's, Mosman, says: —In your interesting first leading article, Saturday, August 21, occurs the passage: *What, for example, was the nature of Willson's downfall, near the northern border? Was it financial or physical? etc.* I asked the same question nearly 55 years ago, and, writing from memory, the answer I received was to this effect: *Mr. Willson (note the double 'l') was at the time known as the 'King of Tenterfield.'* In other words, he was the leading citizen of that town in the initial seventies and a few years before, and of which I became a temporary resident, remaining there from October 1872 till March 1874. Mr. Willson had the leading general store in Tenterfield, and that store became the property of Mr. Charles Alfred Lee, afterwards member for Tenterfield, and a prominent figure in the political world, as also a Minister of the Crown for many years." But to get back to the 'downfall.' Mr. Willson was driving through this dangerous depression in the road and his buggy was capsized, and he himself was thrown out. What personal injury he suffered I did not hear. It was but natural to name a place where such a prominent man in the northern area had temporarily 'come to grief' as his 'downfall,' and the name seems to have been accentuated by the fact that not a very long time after, his business passed into other hands, and he ceased to be 'King of Tenterfield,' a title which I think I am right in saying thereafter lapsed." (The King of Armidale, 3 Sep 1927, p.6)

And in 1938 "Willson's Downfall. SIR,— Mr. Clem Lack's interesting article on the disputed origin of the name 'Willson's Downfall' aroused my interest, since the little post office at that place, seven miles from Undercliffe (my home), was very well known to me. The police magistrate at Tenterfield in the 80's, Mr. J. B. Graham, presided at sessions there. I once gave him a letter to post, spelling the name 'Wilson.' He corrected me— 'always two 'll's,' and it is spelt that way in official records. The Willson who had a buggy smash there was a well-known storekeeper at Maryland, and afterwards at Tenterfield. There was also a Wilson, a bushranger, who was captured near Maryland. In a letter I had from the late Mr. Arthur Chauvel, who was interested in this question, he suggested that the confusion might have arisen from the fact that these two names are similar in sound. The Willson after whom the downfall is named was well known to my father, the late A. K. Cullen, and the story of Willson's accident during the exciting time when tin was found on Maryland was a current topic— Yours, &c., Klllarney. (Mrs.). A. H. WATKINS." (Willson's Downfall, 6 Jun 1938, p.6)

Amosfield

- 1905 – "ROAD TENDERS The following are the lowest tenders for road work in this district, which were opened yesterday: Contract 8/05-6: Tenterfield to Bonshaw – M. Hammersley, £28 9s; Contract 9/05-6: Amosfield to Acacia Creek – C. Battaglini, £30 10s; Contract 10/05-6: Great Northern Road towards Stanthorpe – E. Battaglini, £61 17s 6d; Contract 11/05-6: Great Northern Road – James Bugg, £71 15s 6d." (The Interfield Intercolonial Courier, 1 Aug 1905, p.2)

- 1912 – "BONNER-CLARK April 27, 1811, at St. Silas' Church, Waterloo, by the Rev. F. J. Dillon, uncle of the bride, Sydney James, fourth son of the late Daniel Bonnor, of Amosfield, N.S.W., to Jane, eldest daughter of the late Frederick Clark, of Watford, Hunter's Hill." (Family Notices, 11 May 1912, p.16)

- 1914 – Amosfield picnic "It is pleasing to report the thorough success of the annual outing and social function of the above district. The picnic was held on Saturday in Mr. T. Bottrell's paddock, and moreover in good picnic weather. The lady collectors, Mrs. Alcorn and Misses Bottrell, Burton and Glasby had been very successful in collecting funds for purchase of toys, eatables and what not, for amongst them they raised the creditable total of £35." (Amosfield. Annual Public Picnic., 4 Dec 1914, p.7)

- 1914 – Tennis "Tenterfield v. Amosfield. A match was played on Saturday at the Gymnasium courts between the Tenterfield and Amosfield teams, the home team winning by 20 sets 159 games to 12 sets 123 games." (Sporting Notes. Tennis, 26 Oct 1914, p.2)

- 1917 "Mrs. Bottrell and family, who are among the most respected families at Amosfield, received a cablegram from their son, Private Arthur Bottrell, advising that he had arrived safely in England and was well. However, yesterday they were officially notified that he had succumbed to an attack of pneumonia." (Personal Notes, 3 Mar 1917, p.13)

- 1919 – "SPECIAL AMOSFIELD SALE Tuesday, January 6, At Bottrell's Yards, Amosfield, 800 mixed cattle." (Advertising, 18 Dec 1919, p.1)

Liston

- 1901 – "Sale at Wilson's Downfall, Land District of Tenterfield. TOWN LOTS. Terms Deposit, 23 per cent. ; balance in twelve months, with interest at 3 per cent. In the village of Liston, fronting Stanthorpe North, Clarence, and Acacia Streets ... fronting Tenterfield, Clarence and Maryland Streets." (Land Sales, 20 Feb 1901, p.1342)
- 1908 – "In the evening, a farewell party was held at Cressbrook, with around 70 guests in attendance. The event was in honor of Mr. Harold Dickson, who is leaving town to take charge of the Liston cheese factory for Messrs. Wilson and Purkis." (Orange Blossoms, 2 Oct 1908, p.2)
- 1909 – "The new St. Joseph's School building is under way, and will prove a fine addition to those already erected in the R.C. grounds. The Liston cheese factory is in full swing, and is despatching large quantities weekly." (Stanthorpe News, 10 Apr 1909, p.5)
- 1910 – Tenterfield "The present Cooperative Butter Factory was established approximately four and a half years ago, emerging from the closure of a former proprietary firm. Since its founding, its operations have steadily expanded, with notable growth every half-year. The factory now works with 140 suppliers within a 15-mile radius, producing around five tons of butter each week ... In addition to two butter factories, the district has a well-managed cheese factory operated by Messrs. S. Wilson and A. Perkins, both from Hawkesbury College. Their operations have been so successful that two branch establishments have been opened just across the border—one at Wylie Creek and the other at Liston—bringing the total daily output of the three factories to half a ton per day ... The only cheese produced is Cheddar, known for its excellent quality. Each cheese is cured for three months and paraffined to retain moisture and enhance flavor. Additionally, the factory maintains 100 pigs, which are fed on whey, contributing to its overall efficiency. Given its steady growth, the future of the business looks incredibly promising." (Tenterfield Developments, 23 Feb 1910, p.14)
- 1910 – "A team of tennis players from the School of Arts Club met a team of Liston players at the latter village on Saturday last and defeated them by 12 sets, 88 games to 4 sets, 54 games. In the evening, the visitors were entertained at a sumptuous dinner at the Wilson's Downfall Hotel, and altogether, a most enjoyable time was spent." (Tennis, 12 Jul 1910, p.3)
- 1912 – Liston "Boundaries of village lands at Liston ... In lieu of village boundaries, proclaimed 20th March, 1885, which are hereby cancelled." (Village and Suburban Lands at Liston, 24 Jan 1912, p.458)
- 1915 – Liston "Proposed alterations of design of the village of Liston." (Proposed Alteration of Design of the Village of Liston, 10 Nov 1915, p.6656)
- 1916 – Liston village redesign "The design of the village of Liston has been altered by curtailing the village and suburban areas and closing streets." (Alteration of Design of the Village of Liston, 7 Apr 1916, p.2082)
- John Burton recalled that Henry William Burton and Charles Joshua Crome were guarantors for the building of the Liston Hall, ensuring a lasting community space.

Maryland

- 1901 – "Maryland Hotel, Maryland." (Advertising, 26 Feb 1901, p.3)
- 1905 – Maryland residents "Bott Conrad, selector; Dalley Fred, T., stkpr. & p.m.; Donnelly Jno., selector; Einam Wm., selector; Greenup Alfd, 8., stn. mgr.; Hopgood Geo., bdg house; Hunt Thomas W., orchardist; Kemp Chas., selector; Moss George, teacher; Muir, Gilbert, selector" (The NSW Post Office Directory, Issue 1905)
- 1924 – "Today the owner of Maryland is Mr. R. B. Lawson, one of the oldest and best-known pastoralists of the Stanthorpe district." (Maryland, 1 Mar 1924, p.15)

Stanthorpe

- "FINNEY'S DRAPERY STORE, on the corner of Maryland and Railway Streets, Stanthorpe, is on one of the oldest commercial sites in the town and, through the years, has lived up to its name of 'The Shopping Centre.' The old-fashioned street light right outside the store is reputed to be on the original site where the Cobb and Co. coach service to Stanthorpe terminated. Recent demolitions at the rear of Finney's buildings included the removal of the stone-flagged floors from the stables, which formerly housed Cobb and Co.'s coach horses. Over many years trading in this centre has been carried on successfully by the Barton's and McLeod's, and since 1946 by Finney's Drapery Store." (Finney's Drapery Store, 4 Feb 1954, p.3)
- 1917 – "TAXI SERVICE John C. Burton recalls that "Jack Marharg and Henry Burton owned early motor vehicles, in Stanthorpe and Liston respectively, and provided a taxi service. They would regularly ferry people from the Stanthorpe Showgrounds while Henry would take people out of town for Two-up Games."

- 1924 – "FIRE DESTROYS HOTEL AT STANTHORPE TO-DAY. Post Office Message The Deputy Postmaster-General has received advice that Ogden's Union Hotel at Stanthorpe was totally destroyed by fire early this morning ... A fire occurred in the Union Hotel, Maryland Street, this morning and completely destroyed it. The building, which was one of the oldest of its kind in the town, was the property of Mr. J. C. McKenna, and the licensee was Mr. David Ogden. It was situated on the same side of the street as the post office and immediately opposite Miss Seaman's buildings, which were destroyed by fire last year. It is understood that the hotel was insured for £800." (Fire Destroys Hotel, 27 Feb 1924, p.2)

Cobb & Co. coach factory

Cobb & Co. ceased operations in Queensland, symbolising the end of an era in coaching: "In the Days of Cobb & Co. The Old Stage Coach has been pushed off the roads by the motor, but the ghosts of the romantic past will ever linger. A few weeks ago, Cobb and Co. closed up, in Queensland, the last of its coaching lines, and the historic name, so redolent of Ballarat, bushrangers, and adventure by flood and field, vanishes into the mists of the past. The motor has taken the place of the old lumbering coach with its creaking leather springs, slouch-hatted driver, and spanking team of horses. There may be as much incident connected with the motors when the writers of three-quarters of a century hence are looking for material of these days, but the ghosts of the old coaches will ever be on the roads.

Poets are moved to burst into song at the name of Cobb and Co. Lawson and Ogilvie wrote poems about it, for it breathed the backblocks and the bush township. For years it had been outside the ken of the bulk of the population of this country, which never gets out beyond the sound of the railway engine's screech. Every schoolboy links bushrangers and Cobb and Co. together. As he grows and reads, he learns of the roaring days of the '50s, and the coaches of Cobb and Co., with cracking whips, go creaking through his dreams." (In the Days of Cobb & Co., 20 Apr 1921, p.8)

By 1920 Cobb and Co. factory closure "The Charleville Cobb and Co. factory closed, which is a distinct loss to the town and district ... Cobb and Co. will probably not carry on coaching after the present contracts are completed." (Cobb and Co.'s Factory, 20 Dec 1920, p.2)

The Queensland coaching era officially ended in 1924, when the last Cobb and Co. coach completed Mail Service No. 177: "The old thorobrace coach has been an institution in Australia for a hundred years but has gradually been superseded by train and motors." (Last Cobb and Co. Coach, 4 Oct 1924, p.27)

Post offices, mail & coach services

During the early 1900s, Wilson's Downfall and surrounding areas saw ongoing discussions regarding mail routes. "It seems to me it would have been much better if they applied for a daily mail via Stanthorpe and Sugarloaf. It is not four miles across the Border from Wilson's Downfall to the Post Office, Sugarloaf Q.— ... Tenterfield mail going through to Acacia as at present." (Wilson's Downfall, 10 Jul 1900, p.2)

In 1901, postal services saw an expansion with new infrastructure projects. "Public Works Tender. New Post Office, Stanthorpe. At the Executive Council meeting yesterday approval was given to the acceptance by the Works Department of J. Stewart and Co.'s tender of £2,848 for the erection of a new post and telegraph office at Stanthorpe. The time allowed is nine months." (Public Works Tender, 28 Feb 1901, p.4)

However, in 1902, Cobb and Co., a pioneering mail coach company, faced significant challenges as drought gripped Queensland. "Cobb and Company, according to Mr. Story, have exhausted their resources." (Stoppage of the Mail Coaches, 14 May 1902, p.4) With the ongoing drought, mail coaches ceased operations due to rising costs of fodder. "Advices from Brisbane state that one result of the drought ... mail coaches stopped running ... high price of fodder." (An Evidence of the Drought, 27 Sept 1902, p.2)

Cobb and Co.'s struggles were felt across the region. "The most dramatic, probably, of the calamities which have attended the present terrible Queensland drought is the fact that Cobb and Co. have suspended the running of their coaches ... Cobb and Co.'s coaches were, in the pioneering period, as great a factor in the making of Australia as the railways have since been. Even to-day they serve as the most rapid and trustworthy means of communication between the cities of the Commonwealth and a thousand far-away towns and townships that lie beyond the railway systems ... They have been 'stuck up' by bushrangers again and again, stopped in their course by great fires and floods, bogged on lonely plains, and saved from destruction by the skill and pluck of their drivers at the very edges of unfenced precipices. The history of Cobb and Co. is a part, often a very thrilling part, of the history of Australia." (Cobb and Co., 15 May 1902, p.4)

During the 1890s and into the 1900s drought was one of the challenges faced by Cobb and Co. The cost of feed for the firm's thousands of horses sky-rocketed—in the period 1898-1902 the bill came to £70,000 (about $10.7 million), nearly half of Cobb and Co.'s earnings during that time. (An Evidence of the Drought, 27 Sep 1902, p.2)

By 1906, Wilson's Downfall had its own appointed postmaster, ensuring continued communication despite previous challenges. "The Wilson's Downfall Postmaster was Mr. D. G. Smith." (Wilson's Downfall—Banquet to Mr. T. Olver and Mr. T. A. Campion, 14 Dec 1906, p.3)

In 1904, Brisbane's Post Office underwent renovations. "BRISBANE POST OFFICE Alterations are at present in progress in the offices of the accounts branch. Post and Telegraph Department, which are calculated to provide additional accommodation for officers and public. A brick and plaster wall is being removed and portion of a large room devoted to the use of the chief accountant is being taken in, thus allowing for more counter accommodation and a separate counter for the payout and receiving clerks. Additional accommodation will at the same time be provided for the stamps distributing officer. In the correspondence branch, a quantity of matter, books, etc., have been removed and stored in another part of the building, and the room thus previously occupied has been taken into the main office by the removal of a dividing wall. The operations of the workmen will cause some inconvenience for a time, but when finished a material advantage is looked for." (Brisbane Post Office, 19 Apr 1904, p.4)

By 1909 mail conveyance included "No 321 Willson's Downfall, Amosfield, Wylie Creek … William Goodyear (address Liston, Willson's Downfall) Horseback; No 322 Willson's Downfall, Rivertree, South Rivertree, Henry Joseph Dillion (address Willson's Downfall), Trap, horse; No 323 Sugarloaf, Kyoomba, and Stanthorpe (Q.), William Goodyear (address Willson's Downfall), Sulky, horse." (Conveyance of Mail in New South Wales, 8 May 1909, p.1094)

Mail routes across Queensland in 1907, 1908, and 1909 continued, many with the service of Cobb and Co.:
- Cunnamulla & Thargomindah … Cobb and Co. Limited Service No. 45
- Charleville and Blackall
- St. George and Hebel … Cobb and Co. Limited Service No. 49
- Mitchell and St. George … Cobb and Co. Limited Service No. 52a
- Jericho & Blackall … Cobb and Co. Limited Service No. 54
- Tambo & Blackall … Cobb and Co. Limited Service No. 62b
- Alpha & Tambo … Cobb and Co. Limited Service No. 65
- Winton & Cloncurry … Cobb and Co. Limited Service No. 107
- Yuelba & St. George … Cobb and Co. Limited Service No. 177
- Winton & Boulia … Cobb and Co. Limited Service No. 216
- Richmond & Cloncurry … Cobb and Co. Limited Service No. 248
- Longreach & Winton … Cobb and Co. Limited Service No. 250
- Charleville & Adavale … Cobb and Co. Limited Service No. 252
- Longreach & Muttaburra … Cobb and Co. Limited Service No. 350
- Barcaldine & Blackall … Cobb and Co. Limited Service No. 534

(Conveyance of Mails in Queensland, 8 Dec 1906, p.1518)

1914 saw the building commence for a new Toowoomba post office. "The new Post Office for Toowoomba will be commenced forth-with. The building will be erected on tho vacant land at the corner of Ruthven and Russell streets. It is almost time a new building was erected, for upon the arrival of the English mail on Monday night, the front portion of the present fragile structure was pushed in by the expectant crowd of mail seekers. This caused considerable inconvenience and risk of loss." (No Title, 27 Jun 1914, p.9)

Eventually, the question became, Will the mail delivery be by vehicle or horse back? "Postmaster-General Department, 13th June, 1916. CONVEYANCE OF MAILS IN NEW SOUTH WALES. CONVEYANCE being required for the Post Office Mails, either by Vehicle or on Horseback … Tuesday, the 1st August, 1916. Tenderers for motor-car service—the period of which may be for one, two, three, four, or five years, at option of tenderer—should furnish full particulars of type of cars to be used; such cars should be suitable to convey letter, packet, newspaper, and parcel mails, and adequate provision must be made for the carriage of the mails by other suitable means of conveyance, at a speed of not less than six miles an hour, stoppages included, when, for the time being, the motor-car service becomes, in the opinion of the Postmaster-General, temporarily impracticable … No. 169. Tenterfield, Leech's Gully, Boonoo Boonoo and Willson's Downfall, via Bookookoorara, twice a week. William Webster, Postmaster-General." (Conveyance of Mails, 23 Jun 1916, pp.1413-1420)

Coaches to motor buggies then aeroplanes

In 1909, Australia welcomed its first motor buggy, described as "the first motor buggy ever landed in Australia and in running order, too." It completed 300 miles on rough terrain, crossing creeks 2ft. deep and stumps 2ft. high, all without issue. "There is nothing in the machine that a blacksmith could not mend or the pastoralist himself with stringybark or greenhide … The buggy will average from 15 to 20 miles an hour." (Holsman Motor Buggy, 23 Mar 1909, p.5)

By 1920, aerial mail took flight. "A special mail was conveyed by aeroplane from Lismore to Tenterfield to connect with the train for Sydney. This was with the object of demonstrating the practicability of a permanent aerial service. The aeroplane returns on Monday with the mail from Sydney. Mails are now carried by motor car." (Aerial Mail, 28 Jun 1920, p.6)

That same year, plans were made for a long-distance mail flight. "Arrangements were completed in Sydney on Sunday for bringing the English mail for H.M.S. Renown by aeroplane from Port Augusta. Mr. C. J. de Garis, of Mildura, and his pilot, Lieut. Briggs, who have undertaken the trip, are experienced in cross-country flying in Australia. The Defence Department is lending a large plane to accompany them in case of mishap. The mail will reach Port Augusta on Thursday. The route will be via Mildura, Hay, and Cootamundra. The aviators should pass over Goulburn. Should adverse winds cause delay, the journey may not be completed until early on Friday." (Mail by Plane, 17 Aug 1920, p.4)

Meanwhile, aviation progressed with the "founding of Qantas (Queensland and Northern Territory Aerial Services Ltd) by World War I veterans Paul McGinness and Hudson Fysh, inspired by the spirit of ANZAC." (Our History Qantas AU, 2019) Aviation continued its rise, with scheduled mail flights beginning "from Charleville to Cloncurry in November 1922." (Our History Qantas AU, 2019)

By 1924, the last Cobb and Co. coach trip took place. "The last of the coaches has been taken off the road." On August 7, 1924, Mail Service No. 177 completed its journey from Surat to Yeulba, marking the end of an era. "The old thorobrace coach has been an institution in Australia for a hundred years but has gradually been superseded by train and motors." (Last Cobb and Co. Coach, 4 Oct 1924, p.27)

In 1925, a traveler recalled a journey aboard Cobb and Co.: "Never can I forget the joy I felt when my father announced … he would take me overland per Cobb and Co.'s coach to Melbourne … reached Stanthorpe in time for a splendid dinner at 'Old Scotty's' Farley's Hotel … started for Tenterfield … after heavy and continuous rain … Oh! The bumping in and out of ruts … eventually we reached Wilson's Downfall … a change of horses … then 25 miles to Boonoo Boonoo." The traveler met "a girl of about 19 or 20 who stepped gaily out … walked off with the horses … is the best groom on the line." She was James Fox's daughter, who had become the family's breadwinner. (Overland by Cobb and Co., 18 Apr 1925, p.8)

While written in 1911, "The average traveller of today, snugly ensconced in his luxurious railway carriage, has no conception of the hardships and discomforts of long coach journeys. As a rule, the journey occupied at least a day and night, if not several,

and in the depths of winter nothing but the warmest of fur rugs and the thickest of clothing would prevent the icy air from stealing in and penetrating one's very marrow.

Not infrequently an inside fare would arrive at his journey's end with a lump on his forehead as big as a pigeon's egg. It was impossible to keep awake all night, and a jolt of the coach would tilt the drowsy passenger forward until his forehead met the framework, and he awoke with a start. Then he felt his head, and swore softly.

Sometimes there were incidents in which the elements of comedy and narrowly escaped tragedy intermingled. The experience of a lecturer bound for a township on the other side of a steep mountain range will serve as an example. About 6 p.m. in winter and nearly dark, he prepared to mount the box, but to his surprise—though the coach was empty—the driver informed him in a thick voice there was no room, and that he could not go. Expostulations only elicited the stolid reply, *No room*. The lecturer climbed up and took his seat, but the coach had not gone many miles before he saw to his horror that the driver was hopelessly drunk, and he knew that the road wound about the verge of precipices. But keep his engagement he would, and on they went. Before the coach entered the great ravines of the mountain, the driver had gone fast asleep more than once, and swayed on his seat. The coach was practically in charge of the four horses. Fortunately, the traveller had with him a bag containing a dozen large apples. If the driver could be got to eat some of these, he might be kept awake. So the role of Eve and the Serpent was played for the rest of the journey. *Try another apple,* said the tempter wherever the driver's jaws ceased munching, and he showed signs of somnolence.

Down the steep inclines the coach swept, loose pebbles flying off the road into the abyss below, and at times, in the glare of the lamps, the wheels showed, travelling a bare foot from the edge of the precipice.

Lights shone out ahead eventually, and in a few minutes the horses stopped of their own accord at a small wayside inn, where they and the driver were changed. As the lecturer and his driver stood at the bar together, the latter said, *You risked your life with me tonight. I have driven that coach, drunk and sober—generally drunk—for over two years, and never had an accident. But the luck will change some day, and then they will find me at the bottom of the Devil's Gorge. Here's luck*, and he drained his glass …

The bush inns, say, twenty years ago, were of the toughest. The menu rarely rose above bacon and eggs and tough, leathery steak. Fire waters of awful potency stood on the bar shelves, and the coaches carried many a passenger the worse for liquor, but the drivers, as a rule, were moderate drinkers—fortunately, for the safety of their human freight. The proprietors of the smaller mail lines, who often drove their own coaches, bore themselves as little tin gods whose word was law. Fares were very high, and if a passenger expostulated, he was summarily informed he might walk if he chose. On the big proprietary lines, it was different. Drivers were compelled to be civil, though on the whole they were naturally a respectable and obliging class of men, always ready to assist in a difficulty. And that many of them had 'nerve,' the following incident goes to prove:

A mail coach crowded with passengers was coming down a steep incline as steadily as the retarding influence of powerful brakes and the breeching of staunch polers could hold it against the force of gravity when suddenly the brakes slipped inside the wheel on either side. It was not long then before the horses were at full gallop, with the heavy coach swaying and jolting behind them. The driver shouted to his inside fares to 'leave' if they valued their lives, and several passengers 'left' there and then, others at short intervals, and the road was soon strewn with people—mostly in recumbent positions and rubbing various portions of their anatomy. Fortunately, none of them were seriously injured. But to the driver's terse injunction to 'leave,' the two passengers on the box—a stout lady and a tall, thin man—paid no attention. They clung to the swaying vehicle like limpets on a rock swept by heavy seas. The coach, so far, by the skill and coolness of its skipper, had been kept to the road, but the bottom of the incline was not far off, and there was a sharp turn to negotiate. Once more came the solemn injunction, *You had better leave*. The thin man 'left' this time—at an unlucky moment, for a swerve of the coach threw him beyond the bushes at the side, where he intended to land, and he lit in a sweet briar a few yards ahead. Again, however, it was merely a case of scratches and slight shock. There was now only the stout lady to deal with, and the driver once more suggested the propriety of her early departure. She 'left' suddenly and succeeded in depositing herself with a dull thud, but without injury, in the middle of a plaster of soft mud at the bottom of a dried-up puddle. Finally, the coach pulled up at the foot of the incline, its bruised and scratched passengers straggled down and remounted, and the journey was continued.

But such incidents of the coaching days did not always end happily. Bones were often broken, and lives were sometimes lost—though accidents on the vast scale and with the appalling consequences of those which happen on the railways, naturally, could not occur. Occasionally, a lunatic on his way to an asylum was included with his attendant—usually a police constable—among the coach passengers. One experience fell to the lot of the writer.

The unfortunate man—an old shepherd in this instance—sang the first verse of 'Annie Laurie' over and over again for at least 20 miles of the journey and talked to an imaginary sheepdog for the remaining 30. Repetition invariably ends in creating disgust, and I think that deathless song was never before so cordially anathematised as it was on that occasion.

In the far north and west, great coaching lines still exist, but in the more settled parts of the States, the iron horse and the motor car, so far as passengers are concerned, now rule the road. Even 20 or 30 years ago, however, a long coach journey was a tame experience compared to what it was in the days of Ben Hall and Gardiner, and the bloodthirsty Morgan, when at any moment armed men might appear at the horses' heads with the stern command to 'stand and deliver.'

The modern way of travelling is no doubt preferable, but it lacks the picturesqueness of the old methods, and there are fewer cases in which, in the face of a common peril, that 'fellow feeling which makes us wondrous kind' is awakened." (In Coaching Days, 1 Nov 1911, p.46)

1873 Bridal party in front of Martin Dwyer's Rock of Cashel Hotel at the Thirteen Mile Creek, Sugerloaf, Qld (William Boag) – Courtesy State Library of Queensland

1872 Wedding at Stanthorpe's Presbyterian Church (William Boag) – Courtesy State Library of Queensland

1910 Reception setting for the celebration of the Alford & Linton wedding at Tenterfield – Courtesy State Library of Queensland

Henry William Burton and Doris A'Del Glasby
– Courtesy John C. Burton

Charles Joshua Crome and Evelyn Ellevsen Pain
– Courtesy Crome Family

Local wedding at Bottrell's home, Amosfield – Liston Hall Committee, courtesy of local residents

Marriage of G.J. Jeffrey and Lillian Stewart at back of Royal Hotel, Tenterfield L to R: Josephine Stewart, Norma Jeffrey, Lillian Stewart, G.K. Jeffrey, Bill Bishop (page boy), Daisy McLeod, Arthur Jeffrey – Courtesy State Library of New South Wales

Rivertree, Dorris A'Del Glasby (married Henry William Burton), fourth from the right – Courtesy John C. Burton

The Fox Family home at 'Overcliffe', Wylie Creek – Liston Hall Committee, courtesy of local residents

Ferris' Bark Hut – Liston Hall Committee, courtesy of local residents

Preparing a meal at Beddow's camp – Liston Hall Committee, courtesy of local residents

ca. 1870 Pikedale Station (Donald Gunn) – Courtesy State Library of Queensland

Samual and Rebecca Crome's first house – Liston Hall Committee, courtesy of local residents

ca. 1895 First home of the Elleysen family, Stanthorpe (Corner of Locke and Stannum Streets) child is Mrs Charlie Burton, aged 5 years – Courtesy State Library of Queensland

ca. 1900 Passmore family, Stanthorpe (Back row from left) Horah, Geoffrey, 'Boy' (Front row from left) Sue, John, Mrs W. H. Passmore (Mary Ann), Mr W. H. Passmore (William Henry), Mary 'Doll' – Courtesy State Library of Queensland

1872 Family on veranda of their home on the outskirts of Brisbane (William Boag) – Courtesy State Library of Queensland

ca. 1874 Lewis Perkins with his wife and sons in front of their home, Stanthorpe – Courtesy State Library of Queensland

1907 A. Gaydon, Saddler, Warwick – Courtesy State Library of Queensland

ca. 1898 Simcock's Saddlery and Harness shop, Stanthorpe – Courtesy State Library of Queensland

1910 Bonner Family in front of their home, Milford, Liston – Courtesy State Library of Queensland

ca. 1900 House at 45 Riverview Terrace, Indooroopilly, Brisbane – Courtesy State Library of Queensland

Chapter Eight

Early motoring 1900s onwards

PHAR LAP.

Although dead and gone, Australia's 'Red Terror' still touches a soft spot in the hearts of some sportsmen on the other side. The following memory tribute is taken from the New York Sun, the work of a sporting scribe who evidently admired the Australian champion:

> Where the thoroughbred immortals
> Graze in pastures ever green,
> And the steeds of song and story
> Feel the touch of hands unseen,
> There's a whinny in the distance
> And a pawing at the gate
> As the big, stout-hearted Phar Lap
> Joins the Legion of the Great ...

(Phar Lap, 27 Oct 1932, p.5)

In 1866, Maryland Races were a key event. "Easter Monday Races will take place at Maryland on Easter Monday, when Four Colonial Saddles will be run for. All hacks will be allowed to enter. A few private races will also take place, as well as other sports." (Advertising, 28 Mar 1866, p.3)

In the years that followed Maryland was a thriving settlement—"with its station buildings, church, store, hotels, and dwelling places—it was a settlement of some importance, but the completion, in 1881, of the railway from Warwick to Stanthorpe, and the consequent diversion of most of the traffic along the line by way of Dalveen, had a far-reaching effect as far as the endurance of the settlement was concerned. At the present day (1937), Maryland is quite different to what it was when the writer, then quite a small boy, first passed through it in 1874." (Echoes of the Past, 23 Sep 1937, p.3)

Eventually, discussions emerged concerning a railway expansion, with Maryland being considered in plans to link the Grafton Clarence Valley Railway to the main line at Thulimbah. "The line would run via Maryland across Woolshed Hill, through Hannon's via Duncan, Bamberry's across Wylie Creek, thence to H. Ragh's, following the Acacia Creek road, crossing the Maryland River, and then to Windaroo … This would also bring the Liston and Amosfield people nearer to railway communication. It was stated that another point in favor of the Thulimbah route was that the Queensland Government was much adverse to building further railways, and only about half a mile would need to be constructed in Queensland." (Grafton-Border Railway, 2 Jul 1925, p.4) History shows this railway connection was never established.

Back in 1870, The Great Northern Road between Tenterfield and Maryland was at that time still seen as an important road. "For a considerable time past, the attention of the farmers and public generally of New England has been drawn to the advantage of opening up traffic communication with Queensland as the best market and outlet for their produce ... The distance from Tenterfield to the boundary of the two colonies is only forty-five miles, and from there to Warwick, twenty-nine miles. Throughout this part of the route, there is a fair natural road, requiring no great expenditure to make it fit for traffic in any weather ...

On several occasions, residents of New England have expressed their desire for proper road conditions along the main road leading to the boundary of the colony ... *We, the undersigned inhabitants of Tenterfield and its district, respectfully request that £1,000 be allocated in the Estimates for the current year to repair and maintain the portion of the Great Northern Road between Tenterfield and Maryland—a distance of forty-five miles. Despite heavy and increasing traffic, little to no money has been spent on this section of the road over the past five years. Given the introduction of a mail coach service between Tenterfield and Warwick, subsidized by the Queensland Government, we urge immediate action to prevent the road from becoming impassable during wet weather. We request that the necessary repairs commence as soon as possible, ideally before the winter season begins.* ... The Tenterfield-Maryland road, situated along the Main Range summit, is uniquely positioned for improvement. With no major water sources affecting the gullies, drainage challenges are minimal, making it an ideal candidate for upgrades.

However, political hesitation surrounding projects that may benefit Queensland trade routes complicates funding approval ... Ultimately, the Queensland Government may need to step in and prioritize improvements between Warwick and Maryland. With minimal costs required to establish an effective transportation link, efforts should commence immediately to ensure that critical trade connections are not lost." (The Courier, 3 Mar 1870, p.2)

During the coming decades, infrastructure developments reflected shifting priorities, with the Maryland road diminishing in significance. A 1920 main roads map from that era recognised the routes from Liston to Stanthorpe and Liston to Acacia Creek as principal roads, while excluding the road from Liston to Maryland. See *Appendix A*.

By 1933, Maryland had faded further. "Twenty-eight miles from Warwick and nine or ten from Stanthorpe, on the old road traversed by Cobb and Co.'s coaches and the teamsters in the boom days of tin-mining at Stanthorpe, there remains just a few remnants of the ancient township of Maryland." (Echoes of the Past, 24 Jun 1933, p.7)

Along the tracks—Motor car trips

1914 Trip to Amosfield "On Easter Saturday, a gents team from the School of Arts Club [Tenterfield] made the trip to Amosfield where they met the Liston team. The journey was made in Mr. Winterton's cars. The town was left at 7.30 a.m. and at 10 o'clock Amosfield was reached. The visitors were defeated to the tune of 60 games, but were fully compensated by the way they were looked after by the home team, being entertained at luncheon and afternoon tea. The return journey was made in good time." (Sporting Notes, 26 Oct 1914, p.2)

A tourist map of the north-eastern region showcased the New England Tableland, marking key fishing streams across New South Wales. This addition reflected growing interest in leisure travel alongside essential transport developments. See *Appendix A*

1925 "In the Allora district there are a few patches of newly-made metal road. For the journey from Warwick to Tenterfield the motorist has the choice of several routes. The road via Acacia Creek takes the tourist direct to Tenterfield through Wilson's Downfall. If he desires to include Stanthorpe in his itinerary he has two roads between Warwick and Stanthorpe, one on the western side of the railway line via Braeside, and the other on the eastern side, which is known as the Gap Road. These two roads join near Dalveen. Both roads may be described as all-weather roads, but the surface is not the best. The Braeside road is the one most used, notwithstanding the six or seven gates to be opened and shut on the way. Between Stanthorpe and Tenterfield, the motorist can follow the road along the railway line through Glen Aplin, Ballandean, and Wallangarra, or take the road which crosses the border about four miles out of Stanthorpe and passes through Amosfield and Wilson's Downfall. The road surface on the latter road is better than that along the railway line, but the Wallangarra route has the advantage of keeping the motorist within easy call of a railway siding or telephone line in case of emergency." (Periodical Attention—Northern Rivers Trip, 26 Dec 1925, p.8)

By 1927, aviation was gaining popularity. "As one customer explained in the newspaper on 12 March 1927, there is no more danger in aeroplaning from Brisbane to Toowoomba, provided one has a man who understands all about the machine, than there is in motoring the distance." (Air Travel in Queensland, 2021, p.1)

And on country roads, in 1928, "motorists proceeding from Warwick on into New South Wales are advised to use the route via Killarney, Legume, Acacia Creek, Amosfield, and Wilson's Downfall to Tenterfield; this way being far better than that via Stanthorpe and Wallangarra." (Country Roads, 22 Dec 1928, p.10)

While on a trip from Lismore to Brisbane it was "327 Miles via the Great Northern Road. A great many members have inquired about this latter route, so we shall endeavour to briefly sketch the road and add as many details as possible. The first stage of the journey to Casino, Tabulam, and Tenterfield ... From this town to Stanthorpe, there are two roads, but in our opinion, the one via Wilson's Downfall is more interesting than the alternate route through Wallangarra. The first few miles are mostly upgrade, and heavy timber lines the road. At Boonoo Boonoo, the ruins of the old hotel are passed. Many creeks are encountered, but these are mostly bridged. There is a turn-off to the left about a mile past Wilson's Downfall, which leads directly to Stanthorpe, but it should be ignored as it is very rough going. At Amosfield, a big tin mining plant and dam is noticed, and 6 miles farther on the border gate is reached, and a sandy road encountered which leads directly to Stanthorpe. From Stanthorpe to Warwick, the road is often merely a bush track. Fast driving is not advisable, as there are many bad gutters." (Lismore to Brisbane, 8 Oct 1932, p.10)

Weekend motor trips in 1932 were becoming increasingly popular, with good traveling conditions reported between Brisbane and Toowoomba. "Good travelling is the order of the day between Brisbane and Toowoomba. The various routes to Warwick are all quite trafficable. On the Toowoomba-Warwick Road, traffic is advised to use the road via Deuchar from Allora, as the alternate route is still under construction. From Warwick to Stanthorpe the roads are good, and either route can be used from Stanthorpe to Tenterfield—that is, via Amosfield and Wilson's Downfall, or via Wallangarra." (Week-end Touring—R.A.C.Q. Road Bulletin, 31 Dec 1932, p.2)

By 1938, mail services had advanced to include bus delivery. "New Daily Mail Service's.—Mr. H. L. Anthony, M.P., has induced the Department to provide a daily mail service by Miller's bus service (for letters, postcards, and letter-cards) serving all centres between Lismore and Brisbane ... Tenterfield section stops will be made at Beaudesert, Rathdowney, Palen Creek, Woodenbong, Hewetson's Mill, Legume, Lower Acacia Creek, Liston, Amosfield, Willson's Downfall, and Tenterfield, with a stop at Old Koreelah both ways on Mondays, Wednesdays and Fridays only." (Local and General, 27 Sep 1938, p.2)

Cobb and Co. era comes to an end

Back in 1911 Cobb and Co. "Coaching of Today ... Queensland is the only state in which the firm still carries on coaching. The plant, including changing places, is valued at £30,000. However, coaches bearing the firm's name are running in South and West Australia. These were bought from the company, principally by old drivers, who were permitted to allow the name to remain on the vehicles." (Late James Rutherford, 11 Nov 1911, p.2)

In the early 1900s, the traditional coach began to disappear, replaced by the motor buggy. By 1907, Cobb and Co. faced financial difficulties, prompting a winding-up meeting. "A special meeting of Cobb and Co., Limited, was held yesterday afternoon for the purpose of receiving the liquidator's report on the winding up of the old company ... Mr. J. Story presided. The report stated that it had been decided to form a new company under the name of Cobb and Co., Limited, the old company being styled Cobb and Co. The liabilities of the company ... showing a debit balance of £10,856 2s. 4d.

The new company was formed with a capital of 30,000 shares. For every £200 shares held in the old company, shareholders were allotted 100 £1 shares in the new company paid up to 15s. The report was adopted." (Messrs. Cobb and Co., 18 Mar 1907, p.4)

By 1920, Cobb and Co. continued to advertise its services, but the decline of horse-drawn transport was evident. In 1924, the company ran its final horse-coach trip from Surat to Yeulba. "Slowly but surely of late years the horse coach has been disappearing from many parts of the State of Queensland, (says 'Brisbane Telegraph' of August 29) until

earlier in the week there appeared in our columns, that on August 24, the last horse-coach trip of the world-renowned firm of Cobb and Co. had been run from Surat to Yeulba.

Cobb and Co. have played a leading part in the development of outback Queensland." (The Last Coach, 6 Sep 1924, p.4)

The transition to motor transport signaled the end of an era, but the memories remained strong. "Who will forget the coach driver's cheery voice … The arrival at Surat was years ago heralded by the driver when a considerable distance away, blowing a bugle, and the same thing also applied when approaching the 'mail changes' throughout the journey. The coach, with its leather springs and six to eight horses, gave in many cases a much more comfortable ride than upon some of the branch railway lines on the Darling Downs, and the worst portion of the journey was that over the corduroy. The mail changes many times have been the scenes of miniature picnic parties, and at these, many of the prosperous selectors have made the acquaintance of their future companions for life." (The Last Coach, 6 Sep 1924, p.4)

The final Cobb and Co. coach was displayed as a historical artifact. "The last Cobb and Co.'s coach was taken off the Yeulba-Surat run in Western Queensland … is now on exhibition in the Queensland Museum, and another has been preserved in the grounds of Wentworth's old home at Vaucluse." (Memories of Cobb and Co., 13 Jul 1928, p.3)

Interestingly, "Files of November 1924 … Cobb and Co.'s coach, on the trip from Tenterfield to Glen Innes, again met with an accident on Tuesday last. On a very rough portion of the road, between Halliday's mail station and the Deepwater River, the axle gave way in the centre, necessitating leaving the coach on the road. Mr. Loveday, the driver, was obliged to convey the mail on horseback to Dundee, where Mr. Dix kindly lent him a vehicle with which to proceed on his journey." (Old Glen Innes, 18 Dec 1924, p.2)

By 1929, nostalgia surrounded Cobb and Co.'s coaching days. "Volumes could be written—tales of adventure, gold rushes, bushrangers, brave pioneers; drought and death and flood. Around them is woven a romance almost as old as Queensland itself, the romance of the famous coaching days of Australia … On one corner of the table lay some faded photographs and old prints—pictures of the coaches, and the hardy men who kept the roads open, and made habitable the uninhabited parts of Queensland. Brave men and horses that made the bush ring with the rattle, trot, trot, clicketty clack of iron-shod wheel and hoof … Last Tuesday in that same office gathered a group of people, men and women, young and old, the last shareholders of a company that has made history. They confirmed a resolution previously passed: *That the company be wound up voluntarily.*" (Cobb and Co's Coaching Days: Colourful Page of History Closed, 30 Jun 1929, p.23)

However, financial troubles persisted. "Since the last report there have been further decreases in the price of wool. This, together with the present trade depression, has made it difficult to collect outstanding debts." Property sales followed as Cobb and Co. faded into history. "The property at Surat was sold during the year for £200. Efforts have also been made to dispose of the Dirranbandi property at a satisfactory price." (Cobb and Co., 23 Oct 1931, p.10)

"Today, the excitement of the setting out of the coach lives only in memory, and the picture of the brave days fades. In 1933 … there died at the age of 89, Robert Grover, one of the first of the Cobb and Co. drivers, and a friend of the famous American drivers of their day, Levi Rich, 'Ike' Haigh, and 'Big' Sampson, and of the Tasmanian 'Cabbage Tree Ned' Devine. Mr. Grover had seen two of the Americans take their eight-horse team with loaded coaches to the Melbourne Cup and perform the figure-of-eight in front of the stand. As for Cobb, whose name we know best—because it is an easy name to remember—he eventually went to South Africa and established a line of coaches from Port Elizabeth to Kimberley. He died at Port Elizabeth on May 24, 1878, but his name seems as certain of a place in Australian legend as those of Edward Kelly [Ned] and Phar Lap." (Cobb And Co., 16 Jan 1947, p.3)

Yes, a romantic page in our history had closed, "a history that dates back to the early 1850s and the roaring days of the bushranger and the gold stampeder. Among the early Queensland drivers were H. Barnes, Jerry Murphy, Jim Hunter, Yankee Bill, Jimmy Murphy, Tom Elms, Nick Holden, Rob M'Rae, Tom Amies, and Tom Kidd.

Here's to the old days. The ramping, roaring days of Cobb and Co."

(Cobb and Co's Coaching Days: Colourful Page of History Closed, 30 Jun 1929, p.23)

Later, in 1955, Australia paid tribute to the pioneering Cobb and Co. mail coaches, which had played a significant role in the country's communication network. "Cobb and Co. Coach on new stamps. The Postmaster-General (Mr. Anthony) says that the colours of the new postage stamps, depicting a Cobb and Co. coach, to be issued at all Australian post offices on Wednesday July 6, will be sepia for the 3½d stamp and warm brown for the 2/- denomination. The stamps are being issued as a tribute to and in commemoration of the pioneers of the coaching era who over a long period of years carried the Royal Mail by coach throughout Australia." (Cobb and Co. Coach on New Stamps, 29 Jun 1955, p.5)

Today, the legacy of Cobb and Co. lives on in museums, old photographs, and stories from the coaching era.

ca. 1920 Bath Lane by Cobb & Co's stables, Ballarat – Courtesy Museums Victoria

Trackson family photo, their motor vehicle (steam Locomobile) was the first in Brisbane – Courtesy State Library of Queensland

ca. 1915 J. McDonald Motor Garage, Bath Lane, Ballarat – Courtesy Victorian Collections, City of Ballarat Libraries

ca. 1902 Early petrol-engined motor car in Brisbane, a De Dietrich – Courtesy State Library of Queensland

R L SMITH
SKIN BUYER

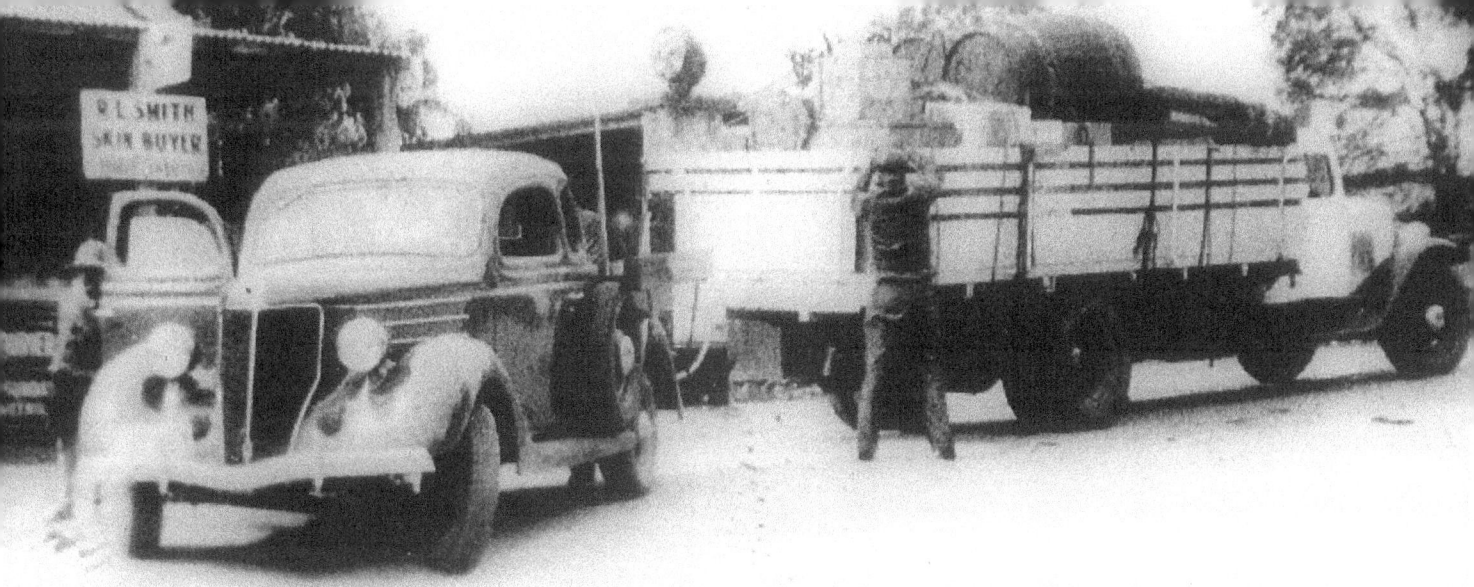

Mr. Alf Burton's taxi & Crisp's truck, Liston – Liston Hall Committee, courtesy of local residents

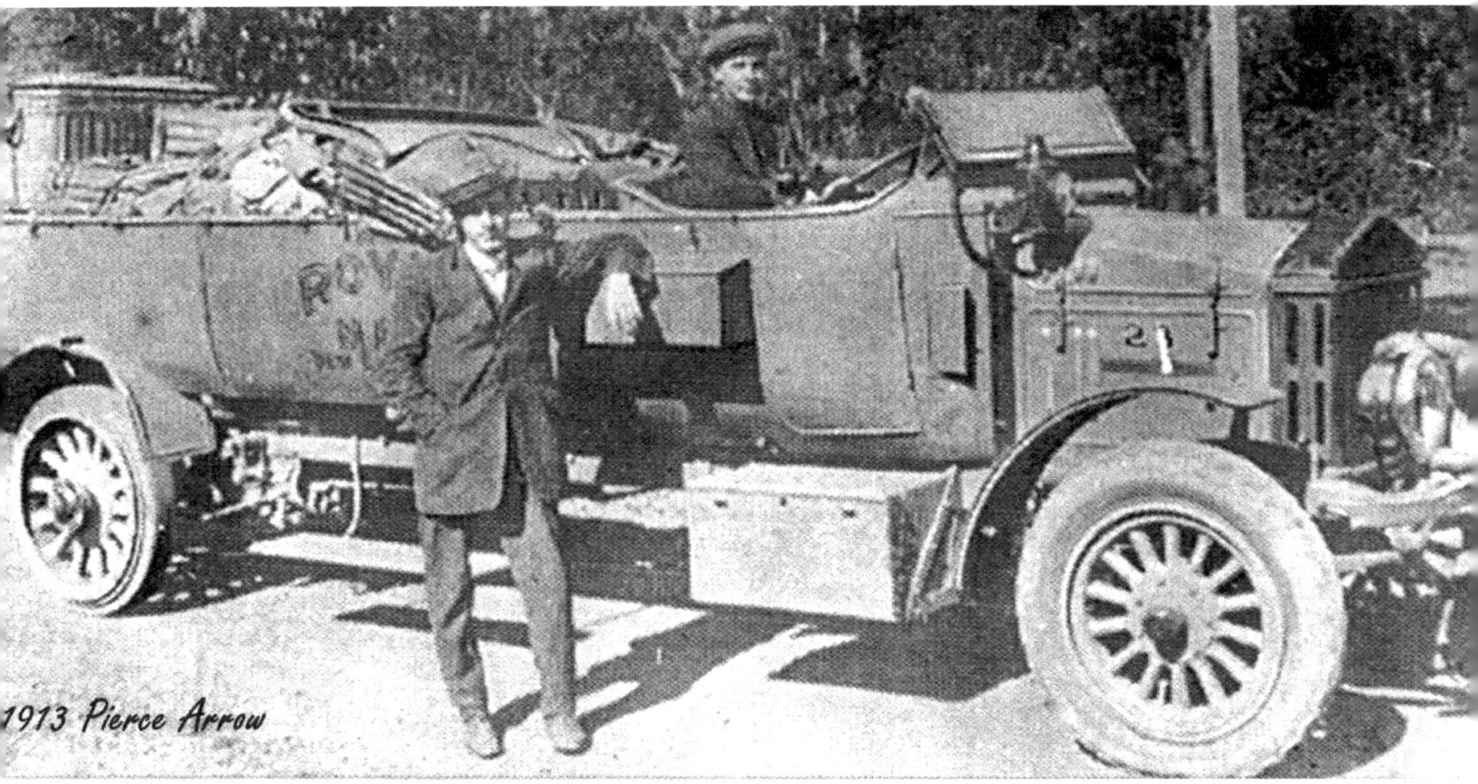
1913 Pierce Arrow

Royal Mail, New England Motor Co. – Courtesy Bruce Robinson, Tenterfield

ca. 1925 Polling booth at Mingoola Hall, Mingoola, Mole Crossing (1924 Buick on right) – Courtesy State Library of New South Wales

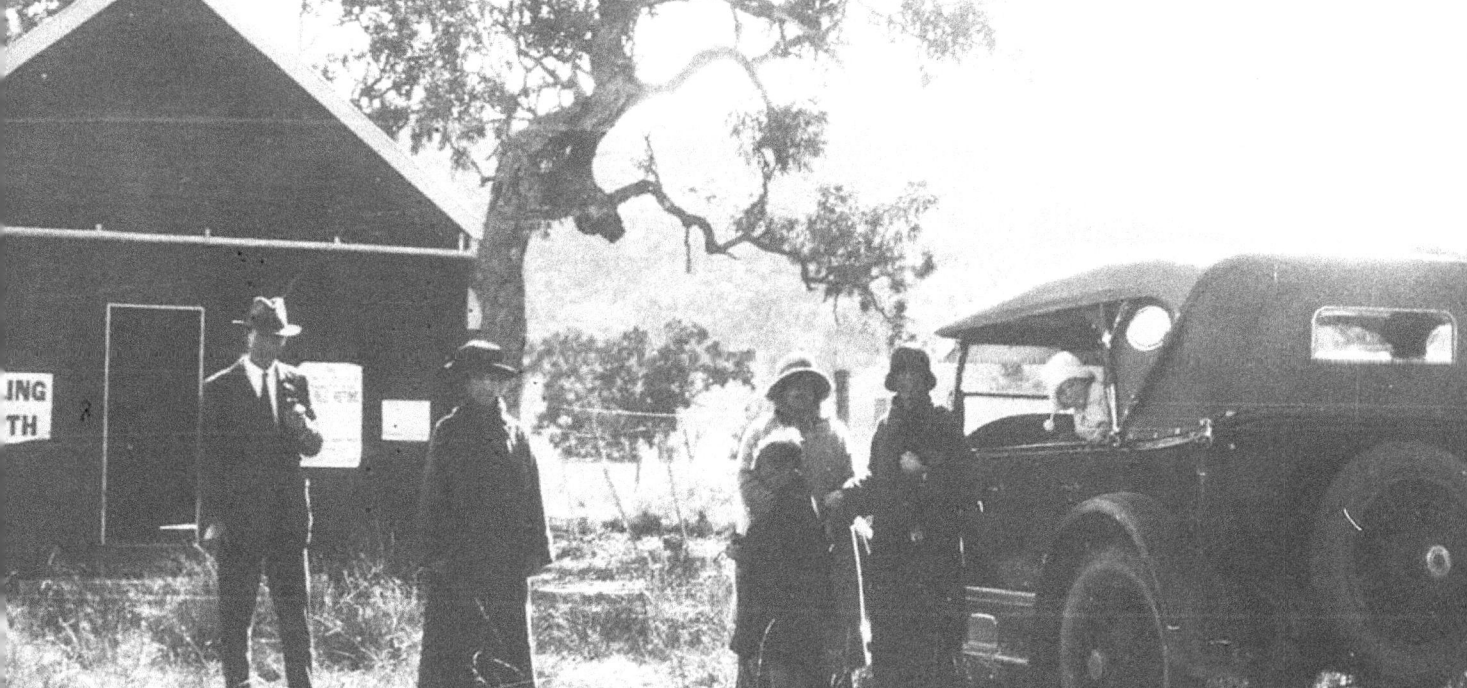

ca. 1940 New Commonwealth Bank building in Maryland Street, Stanthorpe – Courtesy State Library of Queensland

Overland car on Milford, Liston, in car left to right: W. T. Bonner, Mrs Bonner, Ethel Waltham (?), Edna Bonner, Annie Parrie, on running board left to right: Gordon & Donald Bonner – Courtesy State Library of New South Wales

1915 AUTOMOBILE CLUB'S HILL CLIMBING CONTEST

(F. W. Thiel & King Arnold) - "The Commonwealth Post Office authorities in Brisbane are gradually getting up to date. Some time ago a small automobile tricar was introduced for clearing the city and suburban pillar boxes. Now another step has been made by utilising motor lorries for transporting the mails between the General Post Office and the various railway stations and steamer wharves. The credit of this innovation, however, does not really rest with the department, for it is due to the mail contractor, Mr. W. J. Richardson, who has replaced his horse-drawn vans with the two up-to-date motor vehicles shown in the illustration, with their burdens of mail matter. One of them is painted a brilliant post office red, and the other is white." (The Queenslander Pictorial, supplement to The Queenslander, 24 Apr 1915, p.22)

ca. 1920 Winton-Longreach Mail Service in an overloaded Hudson tourer, originally by Cobb & Co. – Courtesy State Library of Queensland

Chapter Nine

Liston, N.S.W., & district on the Great Northern Road ... Just a snippet

MARSUPIAL BILL.
By J. Brunton Stephens (1878)

Where Quart Pot Creek to Severn's stream.
Its mighty tribute rolls,
There stands a town—the happiest town,
I think, betwixt the Poles ;
And all around is holy ground ;
In fact its full of Holes.

(Jubilee of Stanthorpe, 2 Feb 1922, p.3)

Let's start with a good yarn about a quart pot, but clearly not about 'Quart Pot' the town! "One very hot summer, the teller in the bank of a certain Western town used to stand behind his high counter all day in his bare legs, having all the cash and books, etc., usually required close to hand, so that he cashed cheques, etc., for even high-toned ladies at the counter, and did all other business in that light and airy fashion. I used to often go behind for a yarn and wonder what would happen if that teller's fair clients knew all that I knew. Frequently, my fingers itched to catch the bare-legged beggar by his stiff and gaudy collar and sling him into the middle of the room, just to hear the ladies shriek.

One day, however, the bank manager's wife—or rather 'lady'—and four other stylish dames came in to 'take up a collection' and do some business which necessitated the overhauling of a large book lying at the opposite wall behind where the pant-less party was standing, and he would have to walk half a dozen paces back to get it.

I went out to put my head in a quart-pot and blush when I saw the trouble coming, but I believe the ruffian got clear by pointing to the street and excitedly shouting, Look at that fashionable wedding-party going to the church! Of course, he was soon all alone in his glory. And then he got into his pants."
(Acta Populi, 21 May 1908, p.32.)

Mining in the district—1850-1920s

Mineral discoveries

In 1867, the "Qld Government offered reward of £3000 for discovery of goldfield at least distant 20 miles from existing field, providing it shall have attracted and supported for six months a population of not less than 3000 persons." (Queensland's ... notable events, 8 Dec 1909, p.28) While in 1876 "The New South Wales Government ... is a serious impediment to mining progress immediately across the Border, where thousands of acres, to all intents and purposes forfeited by the original selectors, lie dormant and entirely locked up from the miner ... As things stand at present, the individual miner in search of tin ground has no means of ascertaining what portions are or are not available for reselection ... The mining legislation of the New South Wales Government is certainly not calculated to foster the industry—indeed, it would appear from the action of that body in regard to the new industry of tin mining that their policy is rather to retard its development as much as possible than otherwise." (Tin Mining, 10 Jun 1876, p.18)

Following this, "Mr. C. D'Oyly Aplin, a Queensland geologist, after a full and careful inspection of the Quartpot Creek tin mines, made the following comments: *In my opinion the district for miles round Quartpot Creek was rich in tin, and I consider it one of the most important discoveries made in Australia, and amongst the largest finds of tin in the world.*" (Echoes of the Past—Some Border Memoirs, 23 Sep 1937, p.3)

By the 1870s, tin mining occurred at Quart Pot, Maryland, Ruby Creek, Herding Yard, Wilson's Downfall, Sugar Loaf, Ballindean and Thirteen Mile Creeks to name a few locations with "the principal tin-carrying streams of the border tin mines—Lode Creek, Sugarloaf Creek, and Brown's Gully Creek, which are the main tin feeders of Quart-pot Creek and the Severn; and Ruby, [Seven Mile or] Herding Yard, Cemetery, Two-mile, and Wylie Creeks in New South Wales." (Mines and Mining, 24 Sep 1881, p.22)

In connection with Ballindean, "A MAN MISSING ... A German named Trimbell, in the employ of Mr. H. H. Nicol, Ballindean, was lost between Tenterfield and that place ... Trimbell left Ballindean for Tenterfield ... to obtain medicine for his wife, which he received upon arrival in Tenterfield from Dr. Mason ; the same day, he made some purchases in town and cashed a cheque for £30 at the Maryland Store. Upon leaving Tenterfield, he was observed to be intoxicated and was seen galloping his horse at a furious pace along the road. Early on Monday morning, a shepherd in the employment by A. R. Riley, Esq., named George Brown, living at the Four Mile Station, found a horse with a saddle and swag—the saddle being under the horse's belly and supported by the girths over the animal's back ; both the saddle and swag were thoroughly saturated with water, which lead him to suppose that the horse had been in a creek, which was within a few hundred yards of where it was found ... The following morning several of the inhabitants of the town went out in search, and scoured the bush for miles without gaining the slightest clue of the missing man. The chief constable and his men were employed to a late hour yesterday in thoroughly examining the creek for some distance, but by the time we went to press, no further particulars had been received.—Tenterfield Chronicle." (Clever Capture of Two Swindlers, 3 Jul 1861, p.4)

The tin boom in Quart Pot/Stannum/Stanthorpe

"Captain J. Johnson, who may be aptly termed the pioneer tin prospector of Quart Pot Creek, has arrived in Brisbane, on his way to Victoria. His tin selections at Quart Pot are generally acknowledged to be amongst the very best discoveries ...

Captain Johnson will take with him the largest parcel of tin ore that has yet come to hand from the tin fields on this side of the border—over two and a half tons. The ore is in splendid condition and is of the variety known as ruby tin ore ... The tin is contained in canvas bags, each weighing approximately a hundredweight and a half ... about three and a half tons of ore have been obtained from the selections referred to—a good deal of it simply by tin dish, with the remainder by sluicing." (Australian Tin, 27 Apr 1872, p.6)

Throughout 1872, "tin discoveries in Stanthorpe district occasioned much interest ... with Brisbane practically depopulated of labour owing to rushes to various mining discoveries." (Queensland's ... notable events, 8 Dec 1909, p.28)

Before the big rush to the newly discovered Quart Pot Creek tinfield, standing "on the granite rocks, 2,656 feet above the sea level, there was in 1872 only an old bark hut of a shepherd on Folkestone Station.

> *The hut stood on Quart Pot Creek, so named from a quart pot lost at the crossing by the manager of Maryland Station."*

(Geographic History of Queensland, 1895, p.44) Additionally by November that same year, "one hundred Chinese, from the North, arrived on the Stanthorpe tin-fields." (Queensland's ... notable events, 8 Dec 1909, p.28) They "have an excellent garden here, and they are supplying the town daily with fine wholesome vegetables, and at a very reasonable figure." (Stanthorpe, 30 Nov 1872, p.3)

In response, Cobb and Co. operated a coach service during the 'stampede' to the tin mines, ensuring transportation for prospectors and fortune seekers. "Large numbers of persons are daily arriving at the tin mines from Warwick. Messrs Cobb and Co. run two coaches, one, an eighteen passenger coach, to Stanthorpe and back daily, and a second coach every alternate day, whilst Messrs. Lethbridge and Co. run a coach daily both ways. All these coaches are generally crowded with passengers. Fully twenty-five drays pass through Maryland daily with goods for the miners. In addition to this amount of traffic, there are large numbers of horsemen and tramps daily winding their way along the road." (Tin and Copper Mining, 9 Jul 1872, p.3)

While "coaches start for Warwick from Tenterfield twice a week, going through the tin country. The fare is reasonable ... On my way nothing but granite met my view, huge blocks stand high out of the ground, taking all kinds of fantastic shapes. At times one could liken them to a monster sugar-loaf, while others appear in the shape of a huge tin loaf. But granite it is, and the forty miles I travelled was studded over the surface with no other rock." (Tenterfield to Stanthorpe, 17 Jul 1872, p.9)

The production of tin ore

"The first Commissioner was F. T. Gregory. From 1872 to May, 1875, the Stanthorpe mines produced 14,000 tons of tin ore, worth £716,000. In the next five years the net result gave 16,000 tons, worth £820,000. In 1891, 1892, and 1893 the yield had fallen to 244, 246, and 240 tons." (Geographic History of Queensland, 1895, p.44)

Tin was sent "down by drays to Warwick, a distance of sixty miles. The carriage to that town, on the average, is £3 per ton. From Warwick it goes by rail to Ipswich. From Ipswich by water it is transported to Brisbane, and there transhipped for Sydney." (Tenterfield to Stanthorpe, 20 Jul 1872, p.9) By December 1872 "One hundred and fifty tons tin ore was sold in London at from £58 to £89 per ton." (Queensland's ... notable events, 8 Dec 1909, p.28)

Who claimed they first discovered tin in Stanthorpe?

"The first big impetus given to Stanthorpe was the discovery of tin there ... George Bamberry, once owner of Boonoo Boonoo station, and interested in claims on Boonoo Boonoo goldfield, near Tenterfield, relates how

> *James Fox and a man named Goldy were travelling through the district with a mob of cattle, and camped one night on the banks of Quart Pot Creek. Just below the crossing Fox went with a tin dish to try some of the wash. His prospect gave him 1/4 lb of tin*

—Goldy had worked on the Snowy River diggings and knew what it was. Nothing was done for some years, but when a big rush set in to Inverell, Tent Hill, and the tinfield southwest of Tenterfield, Goldy, who was living in Sydney, was reminded of Fox's discovery on Quart Pot Creek. He wrote to Tom Funnell and J. Andrews at Boonoo Boonoo, who got himself and a man named Tom Horton to lead them to Quart Pot Creek. They reached the spot on February 2, 1872, and pegged out on Four-mile Creek. The prospects went ¼ lb to the dish, and the creek turned out more or less a duffer. That, wrote George Bamberry, is the history of the first tin claim discovered in Queensland, and the man that first discovered it, of course, was James Fox ...

When the price of tin fell to £30 a ton, about January, 1874, the Palmer goldfield near Cooktown was discovered, and most of the old miners and able-bodied men joined in the rush there. The owners of the tin mines let their claims on tribute to the Chinese, £8 to £10 per ton being the royalty mostly charged. The Chinese came in swarms, and were all over the field for many years afterwards. It is said that between £200,000 and £500,000 worth of tin was taken out of the Stanthorpe mines by Chinese." (Tin at Stanthorpe—Some Rich Claims, 30 Jan 1922, p.11)

DEVELOPMENT OF THE TOWN STANTHORPE

"The town, 'Stannum-cum-Stanthorpe,' is advancing rapidly. In a few weeks I fully expect to see a well-laid-out town arise out of this wild, hungry-looking bush. The telegraph posts are now up, and the station is in course of erection. A meeting to establish a school and Church of England was held last night, and the very few people there stumped up the sum of £56 ... I am glad to say that I never saw a rush attended with so little 'rowdyism.' This says much for the quiet of the people and the decisive action of the police. May we all continue in this course." (Stanthorpe, 26 Jun 1872, p.3)

Stanthorpe "was situated on the bank of Quart Pot Creek in the only recess where a fine view could possibly be avoided, for generally there are some fine landscapes in the neighbourhood. The population may be estimated at about 1500 to 2000 inhabitants, and there is considerable trade done with the tin mines; and nearly every pound of sugar used over the Border in New South Wales is purchased at some store in Stanthorpe." (A Trip to the Tin Mines, 3 Dec 1872, p.3)

"Booming at a frantic pace. Land is changing hands daily at high premiums, and the demand for carpenters far exceeds the supply. In addition to the three banks, we have several well-known stores run by Messrs Greigg, George, Printong, Horwitz & Co., Kelly's Mining-Exchange Hotel and store, Farley's Hotel, and J. Brown's restaurant. Brown's sign is an amusing sight to the connoisseur—'John Bull,' fat and rotund, depicted with 'cigar in hand.' Further along, we find the pioneer bakery of D. Groom. Messrs M'Intyre, Corcoran, Merry, Sheahan, and Abrahams operate substantial stores stocked with everything—from needles to genuine Newcastle grindstones ... We now have two respectable chemist establishments, owned by Messrs Berlin and Davis, although general health is so good that they deal mostly in simple remedies—pills and plasters. Business for them is limited, and we have had no serious illness reported, except the unfortunate case yesterday of a German shepherd at a station four miles from here. The poor fellow was found in a waterhole near his hut, having cut his throat before rushing into the water. He left a note attempting to explain why he was driven to such despair. He was no doubt a monomaniac, and I am glad to say drink was in no way involved in this tragic event.

Turning to the mining interest—work is the order of the day. Several claims are hiring new workers daily, securing first-class miners at wages between 30s and 50s per week, with higher pay given to those skilled in blasting and tunneling. The Queensland Tin Mining Company is making excellent progress, yielding satisfying results. The claims of McGlew and others prove that, while tin drift sand is rich, it is not the only source of wealth—deep deposits of tin ore are expected to be found beneath the weathered granite rock. Likewise, the Ballandean Tin Mining Company is showing promising results." (Stannum-Cum-Stanthorpe, 3 Jul 1872, p.3)

In 1874 "The Stannum Miner ... says:—*He will at once advise his colleagues to bring Stanthorpe under the provisions of the Towns Police Act, which will speedily cause such nuisances as the drain in front of Merry's store to be rectified by the owner of the opposite property. The state of the main street and the crossing at Quart Pot Creek are to be brought under the notice of the Minister for Works.* The hon. gentleman has also determined upon extending the town reserve, and offering for sale suburban blocks of land varying from 10 to 200 acres, and also extending the provisions of the Homestead Areas Act to the Stanthorpe district so as to enable persons to take up homestead areas on the Broadwater and other suitable localities ... The mineral land lately held at Stanthorpe by the 'Dolcouth Company' is stated, by the local journal, to have been forfeited, and since then to have been taken up under miner's right." (Stanthorpe, 28 Feb 1874, p.10)

By 188, Stanthorpe, "at the peak year of the tin mines, 8938 tons, valued at £606,184, were won. For the 15 years—1872 to 1886 inclusive—the totals were 43,826 tons for £2,447,078, and that of 1872 to 1912 inclusive, 49,431 tons for £2,840,470." (Echoes of the Past—Some Border Memoirs, 23 Sep 1937, p.3)

1922 saw mining reach a low ebb. "Many people hold the opinion that there will still be a great revival of mining in the district, but just at present the industry is at a very low ebb." (Tin at Stanthorpe, 30 Jan 1922, p.11)

TENTERFIELD

Back to 1859 when "the Tenterfield diggings are still the prevailing topic here. The population now amounts to fourteen hundred, and daily increasing as that gold-field is extending; and every week proving more and more remunerative to the parties employed.

Stores, public-houses, and divers trades are all busy putting up buildings; and drays, with all sorts of vegetables and eatables, are continually arriving. The Tenterfield farmers are making small fortunes … The Tenterfield police district has been revised, and a large extent of country now included, which previously was in the Warwick district. The Maryland station, Boonoo Boonoo, and the new diggings, are all included." (Tenterfield, 22 Jan 1859, p.2)

By 1872 "Tenterfield is commonly reckoned to be the prettiest township in the northern districts, and the popular judgment in regard to it cannot be much at fault … The northern side of it is bounded by a pleasant stream, whose winding course is marked by the willows that grow on the banks, their drooping lower branches bathed in its glassy surface … Any tourist who visits Tenterfield … can hardly fail to be delighted with the beauty of its situation ; and however short his stay, this charming locality will likely produce impressions of pleasure … Tenterfield is about three thousand feet above sea level …

One remarkable peak, known as the 'Doctor's Nose,' always comes in for a fair share of attention, for the townsmen take great delight in pointing out a resemblance (real or imaginary) between it and the nasal organ of a gentleman who was formerly one of the principal residents in the locality. About a mile to the north-west of Tenterfield is the station owned by the late Sir Stuart Alexander Donaldson, and it is of interest as being one of the pioneer settlements in the district ; indeed, twenty years ago, this now flourishing township was part of that gentleman's run. The first Mayor of Tenterfield (Mr. Thomas Wellburn) a gentleman who appears to be held in great respect by the residents, was formerly one of Sir S. A. Donaldson's shepherds. There is an air of neatness and cleanliness about the houses which compose the town, and pretty little gardens improve the appearance of many of the dwellings … A large building is in course of erection in the town … it was 'ordained' as a flour store.

The near neighbourhood of Tenterfield to the tin mines has imparted a great deal of activity to the town … Supply of many commodities was much below the demand. At the dinner given to the Premier, beer had to be borrowed from the banker, and the wine to be telegraphed for from Queensland. The latter article, by the way, was not exactly smuggled, for the Customs officer stationed on the Border was away on official duty when the coach passed over the boundary; but it seemed to acquire a relish among the consumers from the fact that duty had not been paid upon it.

At Tenterfield, as in most of the Northern towns just now, you meet with a plentiful crop of mining 'captains.' Some are slim, overgrown young gentlemen too big for their clothes. They are commonly provided with a riding whip, more or less elegant, are profusely polite in their attentions to the barmaid, and divide much of their time between the cultivation of billiards and mustachios. If I really believed that these modest young blades were mining captains, and if, moreover, I were the fortunate possessor of tin-mining scrip, I should advise the directors of Sydney companies to order their captains into active service, for they might surely be better employed at the mines than idling away their time at public houses or pursuing dancing girls from one town to another.

The Lunatic and Boorook goldfields are situated near Tenterfield, the former being thirty-seven and the latter twenty-five miles away. Lunatic has always been regarded as a very promising field, but I believe there is not much doing there at present. About 400 men are engaged in mining. There are about 300 miners at work on Boorook, which is a field of much more recent date. Some of the reefs are highly spoken of. Boorook, I am told, was started by Mr. Donovan, and the Messrs. Amos Brothers have largely contributed to developing it and have discovered some of the best reefs there …

The road passes through many miles of mostly unproductive country. The scrubs are so dense that it is almost impossible to shepherd sheep or muster cattle, which, one would think, must inevitably become wild. This region of dense oak scrubs and granite rocks is the home of the native dingo and the kangaroo. There are, however, some fine forests of stringybark, which would be of immense value if a railway were to be constructed in these parts. As it is, it is a burning shame to see so many valuable timber trees ruthlessly destroyed in these forests merely for the sake of a sheet of bark. The runs through which the road passes are Boonoo Boonoo and Bookookoorara. The Boorook goldfields are about twelve miles to the right of the road at the Boonoo Boonoo Station, and there is an old alluvial field called after the station in the vicinity. It has, however, been long deserted. Two or three companies of swagmen were passed on the road, most of the men being Germans or Chinese. They were bound for Quart Pot, where the Celestials told us they were going to 'catchee tin.'

Twenty-four miles out from Tenterfield, we come upon the Half-way House, which has been built a little to the north of the Bookookoorara Creek ; and here mine host, a namesake of the discoverer of vaccination, is doing a roaring trade. All the way from Armidale, we had been running in the track of Bird and Taylor's Great American Circus and the 'celebrated Polygraphist Minstrels,' whose outriders had decorated the trees of the forest with cartoons and bills in red and blue; and the night before our arrival at Jenner's, the circus people appeared with immense bravado.

The Half-way House is not bigger than a working man in Sydney would require for the accommodation of a family of four or five children, and yet Mrs. Jenner contrived to breakfast one hundred persons there that morning ... There was a good deal of bustle and life at the inn; but three or four inebriates, driveling about the premises, were 'suffering a recovery' from the excitement of the previous night's entertainment. What a melancholy effect the isolation and the rough life of the bush has upon some settlers ; and how pitiful it is to see with what fond facility a lot of able-bodied men 'get on the spree' on the slightest occasion ...

The Border Consols have two hundred acres on the Two-mile Creek bend, and out of the small plot which they have commenced to work (less than a rood), they have obtained more than eleven tons of tin. Thirty-four men are employed; and half a ton of tin was the produce of two sluice boxes on the forenoon of the day ... The wash dirt runs from two to three feet deep; and the yield of a spadeful of earth washed out by one of the party was about two pounds weight of tin.

Leaving the Border Consols ... along a marked trail running to the left of the Sugar Loaf Mountain. At a point on this track, we crossed the Main Range and entered the colony of Queensland, but where that exact spot may be, I have now only a very hazy idea, for there was no slip rail to go through, no notice about trespassers stuck up, no, not even a piece of red tape to indicate the boundary between those two powerful and all-important states ... On the route, we passed the Sugarloaf Hotel and church, kept by one of that enterprising family of Scotsmen, the Lairds, known all over the Clarence ; and a little farther on, we stopped at the Bolwarra claim, under the management of Mr. Dickson. The Bolwarra Company's land consists of 200 acres; they employ twenty men and have already bagged seven tons of tin. The average production from two sluice boxes is 1,600 lbs. and 1,700 lbs. a day. A number of Chinese were at work here and had their hats tied on with their pigtails." (Visit of the Premier to the Northern Districts, 23 Oct 1872, p.5)

Boonoo Boonoo

In 1858, "within the last three weeks there has been much excitement among the inhabitants of the district of Tenterfield, by a report that a gold field had been discovered in the vicinity of the township. The report was well grounded, and it is now a known fact that a very large and paying gold field is situated in the country near Boonoo Boonoo Creek, about 12 miles north of Tenterfield." (Tenterfield, 19 Feb 1858, p.5)

"The Boonoo Boonoo diggings were discovered by Mr. G. T. Maxwell, an American, who was one of the most determined and persevering miners at Oban during the floods of last winter, after a prospecting trip of nearly three months through a great part of the Northern district. The main diggings are situated on a creek from which these gold fields take their name, or rather on a tributary of the creek, and extend about three miles from their junction. On this, for about a mile or a little more, there is a nice running stream, easily worked, and I believe all the parties (about four or five) who have succeeded in getting into their claims have earned fair wages." (Boonoo Boonoo, 27 Mar 1858, p.4)

However, "I found, on enquiry, that the exciting information that had been circulated on the Rocky was mostly false, and this, consequently, will be the means of putting many diggers and their families to vexing losses amid disappointments. I saw many packing up ... off to seek employment further north, towards Moreton Bay, showering down awful maledictions on Boonoo Boonoo and thus that were the cause of the rush ... To the Editors of the Armidale Express ... Permit me ... to make a few remarks relative to the Tenterfield or Boonoo Boonoo gold field—if it may be designated as such—as the few lines I am about to pen may be the means of preventing great losses to those desirous of visiting the miserable watery or dismal swamp of Boonoo Boonoo. Having caught the Boonoo Boonoo fever, I started on the 8th with many more ... On arriving at Tenterfield I heard a bad account of the place, and was informed that it had been raining for nearly a month ... I arrived at the Dismal Swamp, and there met my two mates leaving the place in disgust ... exciting information that had been circulated on the Rocky was mostly false ... putting many diggers and their families to vexing losses and disappointments ... the scaly gold had been found would not be workable when winter set in ... while their horses were almost starved to death, I came to the conclusion that Boonoo Boonoo would soon dwindle into its original quietness and the water wheels and pumps fall into Mr. Cullen's hands. A Returned Digger. Rocky River, 24th March, 1858." (The New England Gold Fields—The Rocky River, 3 Apr 1858, p.2)

In 1861, "From a recent visit we have paid to the above gold-fields [Boonoo Boonoo], it affords us much pleasure to be in a position to state that so far from their being worked out, as some few people imagine, there is every likelihood of a larger find of gold being struck in the immediate vicinity of the old diggings, of a more permanent character than has yet been discovered." (Boonoo Boonoo Diggings, 14 Sep 1861, p.3) Sill looking in 1867 ... "on the Boonoo Boonoo gold fields there are at present strong parties ... and as gold is found in every dish there must be a good deposit somewhere." (Tenterfield, 28 Dec 1867, p.3)

While in 1878 "The use of Wheeler's washpan at Boorook silver mine, near Tenterfield, for the treatment of tailings resulted in the company obtaining from 50 oz. to 75 oz. of silver per ton, a result considered very satisfactory." (General Intelligence, 10 Dec 1878, p.2) "The Boorook goldfield was discovered about seven or eight years ago, and a reef was opened, called the 'Nil Desperandum' reef. A ton of picked stone from this reef was sent to the Mint and yielded 105 oz. to 200 oz. of gold and 45 oz. of silver. Another ton from the 40-foot level (picked) yielded 150 oz., with about the same proportion of gold and silver. Machinery was installed on the site, and while the surface stone proved payable, the reef became poorer as it was sunk deeper, leading to its eventual abandonment. Around the same time, tin was discovered in the district, causing the entire field to be abandoned, without properly testing the stone that had been raised from many of the reefs." (The Silver Mines Near Tenterfield, 27 Jun 1878, p.6)

Tin fever—Ruby, Seven Mile or Herding Yard & Wylie Creeks

"The first Queensland gold was brought to Ipswich by J. G. Rossiter, of Glenelg Station, Darling Downs, in 1856. It consisted of 3 dwt. of scaly gold found twelve miles from Warwick, near Lord John's Swamp, on the road to Maryland. Gold had been found there even in 1852." (Geographic History of Queensland, 1895, p.39)

In 1872, found was a "stream of tin in quantity at Ruby Creek, in this colony, thirty-six miles north of Tenterfield, and six miles south of Maryland station." (Tenterfield, 17 Feb 1872, p.3) This "discovery of tin near Maryland and in the colony of Queensland just over the border (says the Tenterfield Star of the 15th February) has caused an amount of excitement in this district characterised by many, and truthfully so, as the 'tin fever.' Old and young, rich and poor, are all anxious to become the possessors of some of the tin-bearing ground and many have already secured to themselves slices of what they consider the most promising localities.

The principal portion of the mines is situated on the Maryland run, and is already occupied by a comparatively large number of men, considering the discovery of the contents of the ground to be recent, and for fully seven or eight miles blocks have been selected and marked off—averaging from twenty to eighty acres—and the usual notices to that effect posted on the boundary trees, with the applicants' names appended ... In this manner the whole, or nearly so, of Ruby Creek and its tributaries has been taken up together with Seven Mile Creek above and below the Maryland station herding yard and portions of other creeks in the neighbourhood. The area of ground not yet taken up is said to be very extensive, and fresh lots are being secured daily." (The Tin Mines, 22 Feb 1872, p.3) Later that year—"During the past few days a rush for tin land has taken place to Maryland Creek, below the junction of Ruby Creek, and East of the Warwick road. A large area has been applied for. The tin is a fine sample of ruby, and can be obtained from the surface downwards." (Tenterfield, 24 Aug 1872, p.6)

"The late rains have supplied the mines on Ruby Creek with abundance of water, and we saw considerable workings going on. Calling at Mossman's public house, which is situated near Lee's store, on Ruby Creek, for a little something after our pleasant drive over a good road from Stanthorpe ... The Great Northern Boundary Company's mine, on Herding Yard Creek, Captain Lee manager, appears at present only prospecting; I could not see any work going on. Messrs. Eldred and Spence, on the same creek, below the Tenterfield road, are sluicing with four men, and getting five buckets per diem. On Willson's Downfall Creek, near its head, Laird's claim is being profitably worked." (A Trip to the Tin Mines, 3 Dec 1872, p.3)

"The Border Post (Queensland) has reported upon the claims situated on Wylie Creek, Cemetery Creek, and the Seven Mile or Herding Yard Creek in New South Wales. This is its first report of the claims working over the Queensland border, and it appears that the prospects are really very good. The people of Stanthorpe have applied for the establishment of a bonded store." (Mining, 30 Dec 1872, p.3)

The rush—In and around Stanthorpe

"Few people in the Commonwealth have not heard of the town of Stanthorpe, and the chief reason is that prospectors flocked to the field in 1872 from all parts of the continent, serving as a great advertisement. The mining field was known as Stannum, meaning tin, while the Government township became Stanthorpe, meaning tin village.

It has been said that the population reached up to 20,000 when the tin rush was at its highest, giving some idea of the township's significance, even in the early seventies. The tin won was mostly alluvial, and in many instances, high yields were obtained with little effort from miners. The township was originally part of Maryland Station, owned by the Marsh Brothers, who, it is said, came from New South Wales to settle on Maryland in the fifties ...

DISCOVERY OF TIN. 'Twas during the latter part of February 1872 when the news began to spread that tin had been discovered at Quart Pot Creek, and early in March of that year, a sample found its way to Warwick. Many residents of Warwick refused to believe it was tin, insisting instead that 'It is only black sand'

Consequently, many who had initially considered trying their luck were discouraged. However, Thomas Nelson Rose and two of his sons were determined to see the creek and its alluvial tin for themselves. They set off by dray, carrying a good supply of provisions, and arrived at the field in early March. At that time, the population of Quart Pot Creek was well under 50 people, so it wasn't until late March that the rush truly began. When it did, prospectors arrived in droves, most of them traveling on foot.

The first hotel on the field was established by Tom Kelly, while the first refreshment booth was operated by T. N. Rose and his sons— both of which constituted the original businesses of the Quart Pot rush.

Much has been written about the number of hotels on the field, but most accounts miss the mark. As one who was there during the heyday of the rush, I can authoritatively state that the exact number of hotels was 26. By no stretch of the imagination can it be said that the rush was a poor man's venture, as the leases taken up were mostly 640 acres in area, and if memory serves, approximately 8,000 acres were claimed soon after the rush commenced. Cobb and Co.'s daily coaches from Warwick transported large numbers of Brisbane speculators, including the late Mr. George Cowlishaw. So impressed was he by the prospects that he became a major investor in several claims …

THE FIRST TIN SALE. The earliest recorded tin transaction involved approximately 28 lbs. being sold to T. N. Rose for half a pint of rum (worth about 2s.). It is remarkable that no one on the field initially knew the value of tin, and upon contacting commission agents in Warwick, they too admitted ignorance. Eventually, large quantities of tin were purchased at 4d. per lb, and in a few cases, 6d. per lb was obtained. Various other minerals were also uncovered, with some claiming that practically every known mineral had been discovered at the site.

SMELTING WORKS AND FAILED VENTURES. The field was home to two smelting works, owned respectively by Messrs. Ransome and McClay, and the Mount Marlay claim. The former was located near present-day McGregor Bridge, while the latter was built on the company's claim. Both ventures proved unsuccessful, with Mr. Andy Patterson of the Government Works Department overseeing the first facility, known as Carnarvon Castle, for a significant period." (Jubilee of Stanthorpe, 2 Feb 1922, p.3)

Written in 1937, "Records of Mr. Robertson indicate that Tom Kelly's was the first hotel built in Stanthorpe, followed by Farley's and Scowen's. Scowen's 'Melbourne' hotel was original in service.

Campfires were built nightly in the winter of 1872 in the center of Maryland Street opposite the hotel. It catered for the cold and thirsty.

Hundreds congregated here for inward and outward warmth and amusement, supplemented on Saturday nights by dancing and free suppers. Kelly's hotel bar served as a handing-out counter for mail. Soon afterward, H. George's Store (situated next to D. Sheahan's butcher shop site) became the post office, with Mrs. George as postmistress. The first Government post office was built next to the shire council office, the first postmaster being Mr. T. S. Henzell, and later the Government utilized the greater part of rooms in Groom's Hotel for a telegraph office, with Mr. Orr as postmaster." (Good Old Days, 30 Jan 1937, p.8)

Later records state "Of the first Warwick men to reach the tin mines at Quartpot Creek, on Maryland run, back to March, 1872, two 'Toms'—Kelly and Rose—pioneered business places on the field. Tom Kelly, with his bullock dray, laden with the necessary requisites for a 'pub' and store, reaching Quartpot Creek on March 21, 1872; and Thos. Nelson Rose, accompanied by two sons, in a two-horse dray, the day succeeding the arrival of Kelly. On the day after his reaching the tin mines 'Tom' Rose commenced the erection of a dwelling place and store—a one day's job. It consisted of a tent and a structure composed of bush posts and saplings, the roof being made of 12 corn sacks stitched together, while the sides were constructed on the open air system. The other 'Tom' (Kelly) was the first publican on the field, and it was his lot to act as first postmaster thereat. Standing on a cask to the bar and calling out the names, Tom Kelly delivered the mails as received from Cobb and Co.'s coaches until such time, a few months later, a post office was established to Henry George's store." (Echoes of the Past—Some Border Memoirs, 23 Sep 1937, p.3)

Back to 1872 "The Government township at Quart Pot Creek has been named Stanthorpe, and with such patronage, the private town is likely to lose its name. It is laid out on Crown lands both east and west of the purchased land of Mr. Marsh, and with Stannum in its center, it is likely to become a good-sized town as the mines are developed. It has nothing besides to recommend it, the country being productive of little else than granite boulders and stringybark trees. Two coaches ply daily between Quart Pot and the railway terminus at Warwick, which induces many Brisbane speculators to visit the mines; and being situated so near the metropolis, a great number of persons are constantly coming and going …

We visited the Blue Mountain mine and the Broadwater, where tin was being extracted by Mr. Hardaker in large quantities, and by fossickers as well; also the Thirteen-Mile and Sugar Loaf creeks, all of which we were well pleased with as rich in stream tin, but saw not a lump as large as a bean anywhere we went ... The companies that have most renown, so far as I know, are: The Maryland Ruby, the Lady Normanby, Blue Mountain, Queensland, Stanthorpe, Broadwater, and Maryland Swamp. These represent, in the aggregate, a sum of money equal to £325,000.

We arrived at Ruby Creek ... We saw every claim, beginning with Croft's, Williams', and others, and ending with Mr. Bamberry's on the top of the Sugar Loaf. The first work we saw commenced was that of the Champion Company, of which Mr. Irby, of Bolivia, is mining director. Some men were cutting a tail race through a heavy bar of rocks, and above that preparation was being made for sluicing. The ground was good and payable. The Pioneer company's ground was the next we inspected. The Ruby Creek company's land comes next. This is 400 acres in one block. I have no doubt the claim is a very rich one.

Mr. Horton of Timbarr prospected and took up this land, and for facilities of sluicing, we saw nothing like it. Adjoining the Ruby Creek Company's land, the Pioneer Company has some rich blocks. Mr. Graham, as manager for that company, was washing out a good deal of tin with four men and a Californian pump. Above the Ruby Creek Company's land, the creek narrows, and the rich dirt is shallower. It opens again, and you come on to a large swamp, taken up by Messrs. Eldred and Spence (St. Leonard's Private Company), of which Mr. Hester is manager. Mr. Hester has proved the richness of his ground with a boring rod. He proposes to work by underground tunneling ... Higher up the creek are several claims, but they were not being worked until we reached the Main Range, where Mr. Bamberry was sinking upon a quartz reef and getting good indications of a lode.

I satisfied myself that the deposit of tin that has been found eastward and westward of the Sugar Loaf has flowed from the main Dividing Range. It is a hard matter to say which deposit is richer, that to the east or west. Certainly, it is finer to the west and scattered over a larger area, but the tin found in Ruby, Wylie, and Two-Mile Creeks is very coarse compared with that of Quart Pot and its tributaries.

Herding Yard, or Seven-Mile Creek, next attracted our attention and was, in every respect, a second Ruby Creek, but as there was no water, there was no work going on, nor were there any preparations ... Herding Yard Creek has been taken up by Amos Brothers, Eldred and Spence, Trebeck, Wilson and M'Kay, Bamberry, Ward and Horton, Blake, and Merryman and party, but a few stray blocks are even now sometimes found and applied for. Wylie Creek, Two-Mile Creek, and Bookookoorara Creek, with their tributaries of Wilson's Downfall and Cemetery Creeks, have all been taken up for about the same distance downwards as Ruby and Herding Yard Creeks, the principal claimholders being Williams and Lord, Frazer, Christian, Trollope, Perbordy, Foster and Hardy, Greville and Bird, Throckmorton, and others. These creeks are quite as rich as Quart Pot and Ruby, with a better supply of water than the latter. ...

In all ordinary seasons, there is a plentiful supply of water in Ruby and Herding Yard Creeks, and the prospects of the companies on these waters are very promising, as the ore lies in such quantities that it can be taken out at comparatively little cost and without any large amount of expensive machinery ... The companies that have been floated on the mines on the border of this colony are named the Ruby Creek, St. Leonards, Pioneer, Maryland, Champion, N.S.W. Boundary, and the Border Star, representing, in the aggregate, about £220,000." (Quart Pot, Sugarloaf, and Ruby Creek Tin Mines, 20 Jul 1872, p.15)

Wilson's Downfall & Sugar Loaf Creek

"During the past few days large areas of land have been taken up, both in this colony and Queensland—in fact the principal portions of the creeks and swamps for something like fourteen miles by eight miles wide, have been pegged off and secured—some of the land being exceedingly rich ... Sugar Loaf Creek ... Ruby Creek, Wilson's Downfall ... Quartpot ... This portion of the colony is awaking to a new life ... A bright and prosperous future awaits it." (News From the Tin Mines, 11 Mar 1872, p.3)

However, in 1874 life was not bright for all. "SUGAR LOAF TIN SELECTION. I own a selection on the Sugar Loaf. It is six feet by two ; a freehold, and anybody is free to hold it for what I care. And I believe you will agree with me when I recount my experience of that claim: 'Believing and fond' in the spring time of youthful tin selections, I was induced by a friend to locate a claim there, but the recent floods brought my neighbour from above down upon me like a thousand bricks without an invitation, depositing without let or license about 100 wheelbarrows, 200 gang planks, forty sluice boxes, to say nothing of the seventeen tons in weight in depth of the most impenetrable and immovable mud that Queensland can afford immediately on top of my selection, to the great annoyance and discomfort of the undersigned.

> *Swearing is of no use. I have long since ceased indulging in violent expletives;*
> *but I think the most fastidious person I ever met would have excused me upon that occasion*
> *for quietly stepping behind a gum tree and giving vent a few remarks*
> *in words calculated to render language emphatic.*

If the gum leaves fell in showers from the branches at my mild eulogy upon tin mines in general, and the 'cussedness' of things in particular—it wasn't my fault.

Well, I told you in my last letter that I would tell you all about tin in my next ... I will give you an idea how the grosser material is obtained. First you locate a selection and sink a lot of holes here and there about the size and shape of a common sized grave. When you strike payable dirt—that is if you get a pound of tin to the dish of wash dirt below from 8 to 10 foot 'stripping'—you conclude you have struck ile. A sham ditch is then opened across tho creek, river, or gully called a face, and the wash dirt, generally from an inch to 2 feet in depth, containing tin in irregular deposits, is thrown or wheeled out on barrows to the sluice boxes. Of these there are two descriptions, one about 1 foot wide by 12 or 14 long, the other 2½ at head and tapering to 1 foot at lower end ...

As the wash is dumped from the barrows into the boxes a sluicer pokes at, in, and through it alternately with a long-handled shovel and a six-tilled pitch fork, tossing it over, raking out the stones, continually shovelling back the heavier material which is being carried down the inclined box by the water, which bubbles, tumbles, and percolates through the sticky dirty wash, until all is clean and nothing left but a few water-worn pebbles, interspersed with black sand, titanic iron, and tin, which is taken in buckets to the streaming box—some using shaking or percussion tables—where the same operation is gone over, but in a more careful manner, until by its specific gravity nothing is left but clean tin ore, some black, generally interspersed with grey ore and ruby tin, containing from 60 to 75 per cent tin.

It is next dried on large shoots of iron under which a fire is built, then cooled, weighed, and placed in bags of 1 cwt. each. Some claims employ steam engines with shifting tramways and winches to elevate stripping dirt, others overshot water wheels for elevating water and keeping tho working-ground dry; others require great lengths of fluming, using tailings boxes, patent separators, etc., while, generally, the work is conducted by the simplest principles of mechanics and hydraulics ...

A telegram announced that an attempt had been made to fire Merry's store, situated between the Joint Stock and National banks, with a view to pillage. The origin of this incendiary report is believed to have no other foundation than the

> *accidental ignition of a lucifer, which had been jammed in the casement*
> *of the door when being shut for the night."* (Stannum Notes, 9 Mar 1874, p.3)

In 1875, "taking Gunn's store, on Cemetery Creek, as centre, and with a five-mile radius can be swept the whole of the tin mines in the most northern part of New South Wales that sends its tin ore through Queensland. By statistics lately taken, the total amount forwarded up to December 31 last amounted to 3099 tons, equal in value to £155,724 15s.; the average price being £50 95; the maximum, £70; and the minimum, £39 13s. 4d. This ore was raised from four different creeks and their tributaries, all having then rise from Sugarloaf. Our working population varied from 500 to 1000.

At present there are employed nearly 700, this number including 210 Chinese; Wylie claiming as her number 155. No information can be obtained of the number of acres applied for, but by running over the different tracings of each creek and summing up the whole, something like 7000 acres have been surveyed for different applicants. Upon this a deposit of £1750 was paid; survey fees, say £400; refused applicants, about £200; making a total of £2350, the first revenue obtained from here for tin land. At present labor is employed on about 2000 acres, the remaining 5000 being the great grievance of the day." (The Tin Mines, 3 Apr 1875, p.6)

Main Range

1874 MAIN RANGE COAL "Recently operations were commenced for tapping the vast seams of coal which are known to exist in the Main Range." (Summary for Europe, 12 Sep 1874, p.3)

Looking back in history, the mineral discoveries sparked a transformative era for the areas surrounding Tenterfield and Stanthorpe. Miners, speculators, and settlers flocked to the area, eager to capitalize on its abundant resources. Despite various challenges, the industry thrived for a time, leaving a significant mark on the local economy. Though the boom eventually waned, its legacy remains deeply embedded in the fabric of the district.

Early resident families

1900 "ROAD CONTRACT – Tenders for road contract 11/001, Amosfield to Acacia Creek, were opened yesterday. John Crisp submitted the lowest bid at £573 7s." (The Tenterfield, 11 Sep 1900, p.2)

1905 "MARYLAND, Buller Co; 499 miles N. from Sydney; rail to Thurlimba (Queensland), hire 3 miles; Bott Conrad, selector; Dailey Fred T., storekeeper & postmaster; Donnelly Jno., selector; Einam Wm., selector; Flint Robt., selector; Greenup Alfd. S., station manager; Hopgood Geo., boarding house; Hunt Thomas W., orchardist; Kemp Chas., selector; Moss George, teacher; Muir Gilbert, selector

WILSON'S DOWNFALL RESIDENTS Buller Co. 503 miles N.; rail Tenterfield, then 28 miles; Bonner Bros., graziers; Bottrell Thomas, farmer; Bryce Jno., dredge master; Christiansen Peter, farmer; Crome Sami., butcher; Diegan M., bootmaker; Dillon Owen, farmer; Gallagher Patrick, farmer; Green Joseph, farmer & grazier; Hendry Jas., farmer; Hosking Anthony, blacksmith; Johansen Carl, farmer; Johansen Carl, jun., farmer & contractor; Knight William, farmer; Lamont Jas., farmer; McAllister Don, farmer; Meston Frank, farmer; Newley Joseph & Jos. J., farmers; Palmer Mrs. A., Co. & H. hotel; Paterson Robert, farmer & butcher; Pillar John & Charles, farmers; Quinlan Denis, butcher; Rebora Louis, farmer; Routledge Thomas, farmer; Smith David G., commission agent; Stelzner Carl, blacksmith; Stonebridge Geo. & Wm., farmers; Turner Mrs. Henry, farmer; Willson M., tick inspector.

TENTERFIELD [& Boonoo Boonoo], Clive; Co. 479 miles N. by rail from Syd.; 2 bks. (Joint Stock & N.S.W.); 2 newspapers; Adams George, carter; Adams J. W., jun., blacksmith; Adams Wm., sen., farmer; Allnutt Robt. H., police magistrate; Alsopp Wm., tanner; Anderson Gustave, farmer; Andrews Jno., farmer; Austin Andw., farmer; Austin Eli, farmer; Bachfield H., agent; Bailey Jno., farmer; Baker Mrs. Benson, dressmaker; Baldey John, baker; Barry Michl., farmer; Bassan Harry H., draper; Bates A. W., farmer; Bates Jas. W., farmer; Bauer Thos., farmer; Beirne Fred T., farmer; Bentley Geoffry W., proprietor "Courier"; Blaker F. C., farmer; Blaker Jno. C., farmer; Blumer C., teacher; Bonhag Jno., farmer, Swamp Oak; Boston Jno., farmer, Telfer's Farm; Boston Jos., farmer; Boston Thos. E., farmer; Boxwell James G., manager, Clifton; Brauer Chas. H., farmer; Brauer Fred, farmer; Brauer Geo., farmer; Brown Fredk., farmer; Brown John E., Commercial Hotel; Burke J. E., farmer; Burrow Bros., Clifton Station; Butler Alfred S., photographer; Butt Arthur J., carpenter; Capponi Mrs., fruiterer; Carolan Geo., telegraph operator; Cavanough Charles I., chemist; Chambers Isaac, farmer; Chambers W. T., farmer; Chapman J. T., farmer; Chick Jno., farmer; Chorley Andw., farmer; Chorley Hy. J., farmer; Chorley Wm., farmer; Clarke Hugh, carrier; Clarke Thomas, carpenter; Clarke Wm., compositor; Claverie Benj., bootmaker; Coghlan Stephen, farmer; Collins Arehd., carrier; Collins Charles, grazier; Collins John H., carrier; Connelly A. E., butcher; Connelly Jno., farmer; Connelly Philip, farmer; Connelly Wm., farmer; Cook Jos., gardener; Cooper Henry, carpenter; Corney David & Wm., coach builders; Corney Jno., wheelwright; Corrin Jno., farmer; Corrin Thos., farmer; Costa Mrs. S., fruiterer; Cowley Percy, stock inspector; Crisp Alf., farmer; Crisp William, jun., butcher; Croft Wm. H., railway examiner; Crosby Rev. E. E. (Methodist); Cubis Edw., farmer; Cubis Edw., jun., farmer; Curry Henry, butcher; Cushion W., chemist; Dalton H., tinsmith; Daly Thomas, carpenter; Dawson Robert, farmer; Day James S., carpenter; Dean Geo., farmer; Dean Jno. A. S., farmer; Deardon George, farmer; Dengate Horace, station master; Dickson Jno., horse breaker; Dickson Samuel, butcher; Dill Macky, Rev. B. (Presbyterian); Donaghey Jno., farmer; Donaghey T. H., farmer; Donaghey W. J., farmer; Donnellan John, contractor; Donnelly Jas., farmer; Donoghue Jno., P.O. Club Hotel; Donoghue Patrick, cordial manufacturer; Donohoe Jas., farmer; Doolin Mrs. J., boarding house; Doohn B. J., produce merchant; Dorrington Thomas, carpenter; Dowe S. H., manager Bank of N.S.W.; Doyle J., constable; Drennert Jno., wheelwright; Driscoll Jno., farmer; Drummond W., surveyor; Durham J. S., farmer; Dutton C. S., Cooredulla station; Dutton Chas., grazier; Dwyer J., boarding house; Dwyer Martin, farmer; Ebert Adam, farmer; Ebert Edw., farmer; Egan Daniel, saddler; Eggert John; Elliott Theo., photographer & fruiterer; Ellis P. N., accountant Bank N.S.W.; Emanuel Hector, guard; England Jno., farmer; Etherden Benj., tanner; Evenis Wm. H., soap manufacturer; Finnerty Patk., carpenter; Fisher Mrs. Mary, fruiterer; Fisher W., blacksmith; Flynn John, dealer; Flynn Thomas, contractor; Forrest F., clerk of petty sessions; French John, hairdresser; Funston Wm., 'bus proprietor; Gallagher J. W.; Gallagher Michael, farmer; Garr Charles L., storekeeper; Geyer Hy., farmer; Geyer Jno., farmer; Geyer W. G., farmer; Glohe August, carrier; Goodrich W., farmer; Gosling W., farmer; Grogan John, farmer; Grogan Jos., farmer; Grogan Michl., farmer; Grogan Patk., farmer; Grogan Wm., farmer; Hake, H. H., accountant A.J.S. Bank; Hall Samuel; Hamilton Walt. W., manager A.J.S. Bank; Hammersley M., farmer; Hamra C. & Co., drapers; Hamra Carl (H. & Co.); Hannay Peter, manager 'Star'; Harmer Alfred, bricklayer; Hars H. E., farmer; Hass Jacob, farmer; Hass Wm., farmer; Hawkins Patk., jun., wheelwright; Hawkins Patk., produce merchant; Hawthorn Michael, farmer; Hayward Thos., farmer; Hearn Rev. Jno. (S.C.); Heiss Andw., bricklayer; Hennessey Michl., farmer; Hewetson T. W., saw mills; Hill Wm. T., carter; Hitchins A., J.P., surveyor; Hodgson Chas., farmer; Hogarth W. V., assistant surveyor; Holly Alex., farmer; Holly Geo., farmer; Holly Hy., farmer; Hope E. S., painter; Hoskin C. Percy, reporter; Hoskin Francis, gardener; Hoskin Thomas, farmer; Hoskins Fredk. Wm., agent; Howard Michl., farmer; Howard Thos., farmer & fruiterer; Howarth A., teacher; Hughes Pat., sen., farmer; Hughes Pat., jun., farmer; Hunting Hy., farmer; Hunting Jno., farmer; Hurtz Chas., farmer; Hurtz Hy., farmer; Hutchings J. T., farmer; Hynes H., Riverton station; Imberger Julius, saw mills; Imberger Pius J., sawyer; Irby Edward; Jeffrey Peter, Mingoola station; Jensen Christen, jeweller; Johnston David, grazier; Jordan Wm., teacher; Judge E., blacksmith; Juergens Emil H.; Kay Robert, bootmaker; Kelly Jas. E., farmer; Kelly Jno., baker; Kelly Mortr. J., carrier; Kelly Mortimer, produce dealer; Kemp Thos. C., wool classer; Kennedy A. A., drover; Kermode George, agent; Kilmister Thomas, librarian; King Thos., teacher; Kline Henry, manager boot factory; Kneipp Fred., saddler; Koch Geo., farmer; Koch Jno., jun., farmer; Krahe Chas. E., letter carrier; Krahe F., tailor; Krahe J. E. L., farmer; Krahe Louis C., blacksmith; Kurtzemberger E., farmer; Kuskey Henry, coachbuilder; Kyburg Gottlieb, carpenter; Lane Chas., farmer; Larracy Michl., farmer; Lawler B. M., farmer; Lee Hon. Chas. A., J.P., M.P.; Lee N. K., mineralogist; Leech Jno., farmer; Leech Wm., farmer, Leech's Gully; Leis C. Louis, farmer; Leis Chas., store, Jennings; Leis Geo., farmer; Leis Thos., Terminus Hotel; Lillicrap Chris., miller; Lillicrap James S., 'bus proprietor; Lillicrap Robt., grazier; Lillie G. G., line repairer; Lobsey G., postmaster; Loder A. C., forester; Lomax John, carter; Lum Gar Charles, store; Lynch Jos., wheelwright; McAllister Robert, farmer; McAskill James, fettler; McDonald D. J., butcher; McDonald Jno., farmer; McKerihan Edw. S., draper; McKerihan Jas., carter; McKerihan James S., grocer; McLean Jas., Royal Hotel; McLennan M., farmer; McNamara Pat., farmer; McNichol Jno., farmer; Manfredi Frank, tobacconist; Manfredi Gaetano, tailor; Manly Thos., harness maker; Manser Stephen, farmer; Mansfield Alfred, clerk & paykeeper; Mansfield Jno., farmer; Mara Jas., carrier; Mara Jno., carrier; Mara Michl., farmer; Mara Wm., farmer; Marsden W. F., farmer; Marsh W. G., farmer; Marstella F. C., farmer; Martin John, hairdresser; Matheson John E., engine driver; Maxwell J. C.; Merrell Edward, inspector of nuisances; Merrell Herbert, blacksmith; Miller Chas. (Hamra & Co.); Miller Thomas, farmer; Mitchell A. Oliver; Mitchell & Co., agents; Palings Pianos (see advt.); Mitchell A. Co., G. H., auctioneers; Mitchell Geo. H. T. (M. & Co.); Moran W., tailor; Morgan C. J. T., carrier; Morley A. H., carrier; Morris Aaron S., baker; Morris Jno., baker; Moylan J. Philip, farmer; Moylan Robert, farmer; Mulhern Dan K., farmer; Mullane Daniel, telegraph operator; Mullins Jas., farmer; Murphy Dan., jun., farmer; Murphy Jno., farmer; Murphy Mrs. D., fruiterer; Murray Jno., farmer, Jennings; Neagle Jno., farmer; Neilson Jno., carpenter, Jennings; Nelmes C., engine driver; New England Sawmilling Co. (A. Robertson, manager); Newt Samuel, farmer; Newton W., medical practitioner; Nowlan Robert, farmer; O'Connor H. A. D., surveyor; O'Leary Daniel, bus proprietor; O'Leary William, farmer; O'Neil Felix, farmer; Parker Edward, carpenter; Paval Charles, farmer; Peberdy Thos. & Son, storekeepers; Peberdy William, bicycle dealer & repairer, gunsmith, picture frame maker, tennis racquets re-strung, Manners-st.; Perkins W., bootmaker; Petherick Edward J., dentist; Petrie Phillip, farmer; Phillips J., fruiterer; Pierce J. H.; Pillar James, farmer; Pillar John, mailman; Pillar Thomas, jun., farmer; Pitkin G. F., sen., farmer; Pitkin Henry, farmer; Pollard J. E., painter; Power Patrick, carrier; Priddle Robert, farmer; Pitkins Walter, farmer; Pritchard Louis J., sen., contractor; Purkiss H. (Wilson & Purkiss); Purvis A., manager Maidenhead Station; Quin Ohee, gardener; Bank James, sergeant police; Readett Charles W., solicitor; Reid & Co., W., storekeepers; Reid John H., J.P., mine manager; Reid Thomas W. F., farmer, Leech's; Reid William, J.P. (Reid & Co.); Richards John R., postmaster; Roach A., compositor; Robertson A., manager New England Sawmilling Co.; Robertson David, tailor; Robinson Joseph, drill instructor; Roche W., hairdresser; Rock George, farmer; Rock John, farmer; Rolph A. E., farmer; Rolph William J., farmer; Roper James H. (Roper & Walker); Roper & Walker, storekeepers; Roper Whitfield, store; Rothe Oscar P., taxidermist; Russell A., constable; Russell Alexander, overseer; Ryan John, farmer; Ryan William, farmer; Scarf F., store; Scarf M. G., store; Schiffman Frederick, farmer; Schroeder Peter, farmer; School of Arts (H. H. Bassan, sec.); Scott Samuel R., stock inspector; Scott William, Criterion Hotel; Scott William E., engineer; Senf Andrew, farmer; Senf Christopher, farmer; Simons Frederick, carpenter; Simons John Walford; Smith A. J., saddler; Smith Fred, farmer; Smith George, farmer; Smith George R., farmer; Smith Henry A., grazier; Smith Rev. H. Granville (E.); Smith Merton, station owner; Smith Robert T., farmer; Sommerlad A., farmer; Sommerlad J. H., farmer; Sommerlad William H., farmer; Stack James, farmer; Stack R. D., farmer; Steed Reuben, farmer; Steed Richard, farmer; Stevenson Mrs. A. C.; Stevenson Robert, stock & station agent; Stewart Charles, farmer; Stone A. Eagles, farmer; Strauss John, contractor; Strong John, farmer; Struck John P., farmer; Sullivan T., hospital warder; Sweeney John J., farmer; Sweeting Robert, grazier; Taylor Abraham, farmer; Taylor Alfred H., carrier; Taylor C. G., miller; Taylor Edward, farmer; Taylor John Ross, farmer; Taylor Matthew, farmer; Telfex H. E., grazier; Telford Edward J., farmer; Telford John, farmer, Leech's Gully; Telford John, farmer; Tenterfield Chilled Meat Works (R. Stevenson, sec.); The Tenterfield and Inter-colonial Courier, W. Bentley, proprietor; Thomas Jas. F., solicitor; Tomkins Burgoyne, grazier; Tomkins Hy. W., manager, Mole Station; Toohey John, farmer; Toohey Michael, farmer; Tooley E., gaoler; Vick R. E., music teacher; Vock Ch. Ludwig, farmer; Vock Jno. M., farmer; Vowell Ed., road superintendent; Wait Thomas, gardener; Walker Thos., manager, Tenterfield; Walters Paul T., tobacconist; Warner W. B. H., surveyor; Watts Thos., farmer; Weir Wm. & Co., butcher; Weir David, farmer; Weir Thos., tinsmith; Welburn Thomas, farmer; Westbury Jas., farmer; Whalan Jas., farmer; Whalan Jno. P., farmer; Whereat E. E. & Co., millers & boot manufacturers; Whereat Ed. Wm., manager, boot factory; Whereat Isaac, J.P., auctioneer & coroner; White Mrs. Dinah, farmer, Leech's; Whittaker Alf., watchmaker & bandmaster; Whitton E. W., grazier; Whitton Jno., jun., farmer; Whitton Jos., farmer; Whitton Luke, farmer; Williams Jno., carpenter & undertaker; Williams Jno., farmer; Williams Richard, farmer; Williams Wm., farmer; Wilke Peter, station overseer; Willis J. G. E., farmer; Wilson & Purkiss, cheese factory; Winser F. E., bailiff; Wilson Stuart (W. & Purkiss); Winterton Geo., farmer; Woolnough Richd. D., station overseer; Wyman Jno. A., blacksmith; Young George." (The New South Wales Post Office directory, Issue 1905, p.637)

1913 MARRIAGE AT LISTON "Feb. 14th. Miss Daisy Glasby, of Killarney, to Mr. Walter S. Armstrong, late of Stanthorpe; at St. John's Church, Liston, Queensland." (Family Notices, 6 Mar 1913, p.13)

1926 "WEDDING Broom—Bottrell. A picturesque wedding was celebrated at St. Paul's Church of England, Stanthorpe (Q.) on August 7, when Mr. William James Broom (youngest son of Alfred Broom of Plymouth, England) married Miss Beatrice Beryl (Dolly) Bottrell (youngest daughter of Thomas Bottrell of 'Broadmeadows,' Amosfield, New South Wales). The Rev. C. D. Gillman officiated, and Miss A. Pierpoint presided at the organ ... Miss Althea Christensen (niece of the bride), who attended as chief bridesmaid, wore a frock of ivory crepe de chine with burnt lace trimmings and a hat of tagel straw. Miss Edie Edwards (niece of the bride), who attended as second bridesmaid, wore a frock of lemon crepe de chine with a georgette hat to match ... As the bridal party left the vestry, the Wedding March was played. At the conclusion of the ceremony, a reception was held at the Wembley Café. The bride's mother, wearing brocaded black morocain with Oriental trimmings, accompanied by a hat to harmonize, received the guests ... As the newlyweds departed by car for Warwick, where they spent their honeymoon, the bride wore a gold-knitted costume with a matching hat." (Wedding, 6 Sep 1926, p.3)

1927 LISTON RESIDENTS. "W. Bonner, Chas Burton, Hy Burton, Miss Crome, R. Crome, W. Gallagher, T. Goodyear, G. Goodyear, R. Mcalister, F. Stonebridge, Mrs C. White, T. Wise." (New South Wales Post Office Directory, 1927)

1930 DISTRICT RESIDENT FAMILIES. "**Amosfield**—Burton, Cameron, Beddow, Bottrell, Brown, Burley, Christensen, Edwards, Gallagher, Goodyear, Harriman, Hume, McCleer, Murphy, Newley, Ross, Smith, Stonebridge, Taylor, Watson, Werner, Winfield, Young; **Liston**—Barnett, Bailey, Beddow, Bonner, Brown, Burton, Cook, Crome, DeCourcy, Dillon, Donaghey, Goodwin, Green, Lochart, Lowien, Morris, Newely, Orchin, Pillar, Reeder, Squelch, Waterson, Smith, Stonebridge, Wise; **Maryland**—Austin, Barnard, Bonner, Butler, Clauson, Cowan, Donnelly, Einam, Fagg, Firmbach, Flood, Games, Greenup, Hopgood, Mann, Shatte, Steele, Waterson; **Wilson's Downfall**—Ayris, Barlow, Batty, Beddow, Bonner, Bottrell, Burton, Butler, Christensen, Cook, Crome, Davidson, Fagg, Fox, Gallagher, Glock, Goodyear, Green, Guiney, Hannon, Harriman, Holloway, Kearney, Lowien, Marsden, Meston, Newley, Owen, Palmer, Paterson, Pillar, Rach, Rutledge, Smith, Stalling, Stonebridge, Strugnell, Turner, Young; **Wylie Creek**—Barlow, Elliott, Firmbach, Fox, Gallagher, Goodyear, Madsen, Martin, Ragh, Smith, Ward, Winfield.

Occupations included: Home duties, blacksmith, labourer, farmer, police constable, carpenter, engineer, engine driver, ambulance officer, plumber, Clerk in Holy Orders, gatekeeper, butcher, station manager, herd tester, teamster, dairyman, bank clerk, school teacher, grazier, nurse, timber faller, tractor driver, sawmiller, bank manager, carrier, timber-hauler, selector, stock inspector, storekeeper, tick inspector, road contractor, ganger, timber worker, stockman, dressmaker, wheelwright, orchardist, housekeeper, sawyer, miner, post-master, orderman, timber-getter, maintenance man, motor-driver, postmistress, grocer, hotelkeeper, shearer, artist, overseer, bush nurse, shop assistant, commercial traveller, civil engineer, farm worker, postal assistant, lorry driver, surveyor." (Australian Electoral Rolls, 1903–1980, Ancestry.com)

Amosfield/Liston War Memorial

1920 "A FINE MEMORIAL TO HONOR AMOSFIELD SOLDIERS ... Amosfield, a small centre, situated about 11 miles from Stanthorpe, is not going to allow the memory of the men who went from there to go uncherished and unperpetuated. The people of the district subscribed the funds for a monument and it is now nearly finished ... On the top of a freestone pedestal stands the figure of an Australian digger, uniformed, and with reversed rifle, paying a tribute to the fallen ... When the work is completed the monument will be placed in the school grounds at Amosfield." (A Fine Memorial, 28 Sep 1920, p.7) See *Appendix E: 1918 Map showing Amosfield new school site*.

1920 "AMOSFIELD'S TRIBUTE. A SPLENDID WAR MEMORIAL. THE DISTRICT'S FINE RECORD ... Though an obscure place on the Australian map, Amosfield loyally did its share for the Empire, for 35 men enlisted from there, eight of whom wore either killed or wounded and the remainder returned uninjured.

Yesterday a 'Gazette' representative inspected a handsome war memorial, which is to be erected at Amosfield in memory of the dead, and a tribute to the living, for their services to King and Country during the recent war. The memorial is an imposing and handsome one, and stands in the monumental yards of Bruce Brothers, in Russell-street … the material is from Queensland and the work was performed by Queenslanders. The Helidon freestone was dug from Millers' Quarry at Helidon, the figure was carved by Mr. Alf Batstone, of South Brisbane, and the designing of and cutting out of the remainder was done by Messrs. Bruce Bros., natives of Toowoomba … the faultless piece of work … 14 feet, and the weight is approximately four tons … the names of the wounded are indicated by a red star (a star for each wound), while a black star denotes the soldiers who were killed … the stone would serve for all time … it will be removed to Amosfield about the second or third week in October." (Amosfield's Tribute—A Splendid War Memorial, 28 Sep 1920, p.4)

1920 "SOLDIERS' MEMORIAL STATUE FOR AMOSFIELD … monument that is to be finally erected at Amosfield … inscribed: Erected by the public of this district in memory of the soldiers who lost their lives, and in recognition of the services of the men who fought in the Great War, 1914-1919 … 7 made the supreme sacrifice, and eighteen were wounded, making a total of 25 casualties. One man was wounded four times, and many of the others were wounded more than once." (Soldiers' Memorial, 9 Oct 1920, p.5) The image of the "hand-coloured photograph was duplicated from an original taken soon after the dedication ceremony, enlarged and hand-coloured and framed in a now-lost oval frame for display. It was displayed in the family home of 2545 Private Ernest Bazen Beddow, 35th Battalion, of Willson's Downfall, who died on 28 January 1917 … Pte Beddow is buried at the Bilston cemetery, Staffordshire, England." (Amosfield - Liston War Memorial at Amosfield, New South Wales, circa 1920)

1920 "BEAUTIFUL MEMORIAL JUST UNVEILED … The monument which stands in the school grounds … Lieut.-Col. Bruxner, M.L.A., performed the ceremony." (News from the Country—Tenterfield, 8 Dec 1920, p.4)

1964 SOLDIERS' MEMORIAL AMOSFIELD RELOCATED "the memorial was moved and rededicated in Liston in 1964." (Australian War Memorial, 2021) "The names of those who served in World War Two were added at a later date." (Liston–Amosfield War Memorial, 2021)

The Troops

1915 "EMPIRE DAY AT AMOSFIELD. Empire Day proved rather a successful one at Amosfield. A picnic and sports were held in the Amosfield Public School grounds, in aid of the Belgian Relief Fund. The school children assembled at their usual time, and were addressed by Mr. Harper, of Stanthorpe, who spoke of the greatness of our Empire and the present crisis in Europe. By this time a large gathering of people had assembled. The remainder of the day was spent in sports and sale of gifts, which comprised stock, poultry, farm produce, fancy work, and sundry articles. Mr. J. Barlow acted as auctioneer, and seemed the right man in the right place. Mr. M. Alcorn, teacher of the Public School at Amosfield acted as secretary and treasurer to the movement. At night a concert and dance were held in the schoolroom and over £20 was taken at the door. The total for the day amounted to £163 5s 4d, expenses £7 13s 6d, leaving a balance of £155 13s 6d to swell the fund. The people, of Amosfield deserve special praise for their liberal support to this grand cause." (Empire Day at Amosfield, 8 Jun 1915, p.2)

1915 "TENTERFIELD, August 9. The Australia Day Fund now totals over £800, and there is more to come. A number of farmers at Homestead have just completed sowing 20 acres of oats on land provided by Mr. W. Hordan, with the proceeds going to the Australian Wounded Fund. The district celebrations raised £230 in Urbenville and £286 in Wilson's Downfall." (Country Movements, 10 Aug 1915, p.7)

1916 DANCE "A dance was held at Mr. Thos. Bottrell's residence in Amosfield to provide tobacco for the troops in the trenches. Misses Schaeffer and Stalling supervised the arrangements, and £6/3/ was raised." (Country Movements, 14 Jun 1916, p.8)

1916 PRESENTATIONS "There was a large gathering of residents at the Methodist Church, Amosfield, to bid farewell to Private Charles Crome … a happy speech, made reference to the solider's popularity both as a churchman and a citizen … Ted Stalling arrived home yesterday." (Presentations, 14 Jul 1916, p.7)

1917 "THREE NEW ENGLANDERS: THE STALLING FAMILY [PTE. R. J. Stalling, PTE. E. R. Stalling, PTE. W. A. Stalling] are sons of the late Mr. and Mrs. F. A. Stalling of Wilson's Downfall, New England district and are crack rifle shots and thorough bushmen. They are grandsons of the late Surgeon Michael Kelley, who served under Sir John Moore (prior to Wellington assuming command on the Continent) and was thrice wounded. He was also wounded in the Battle of New Orleans, taken prisoner, escaped, and finally served under Lord Gough in the Army of the Punjab. He held three medals and clasps for Indian campaigns and two Peninsula medals. He was one of the famous Light Brigade in the Battle of Balaclava, having three horses shot from under him. Seven cousins of these lads are also in the firing line." (Three New Englanders, 7 Feb 1917, p.26)

1918 "WILSON'S DOWNFALL. Soldier Wounded. Mr. C. Turner, of Wilson's Downfall, has been notified that his brother, Private H. J. Turner, has been wounded in the right shoulder and left hand." (Wilson's Downfall, 28 Aug 1918, p.17)

1919 WELCOME HOME "A welcome home was tendered to Pte. Bern Turner in the Wilson's Downfall hall. Corn. William Holies returned from the front during the Christmas holidays. He was welcomed in the Liston hall, Wilson's Downfall." (Soldiers of the North, 6 Feb 1919, p.1)

Local schools

1880 "PUBLIC SCHOOL INSPECTION—Mr. William Thompson, Inspector of Public Schools for the Northern district, has just paid his customary visit to the Public Schools in this neighbourhood. These include Tenterfield, Bryan's Gap, and Amosfield Schools, and from what we can learn, although the attendance has scarcely been as satisfactory as previously, the Inspector was generally satisfied with the progress made since his last visit. Of the Tenterfield School, Mr. Thompson, we hear, speaks highly of the assiduity of Mr. Studdy, the headmaster, and of his well-sustained efforts to promote the efficiency of the school. At Amosfield, it is in contemplation, we are informed, to remove the school to a more central position, where it could be more generally availed of." (Tenterfield, 26 Mar 1880, p.6)

1881 ATTENDANCE "There is a large, though scattered, population in the district, as may be seen by the number of children attending the schools. The school at Sugarloaf (proper) has over 100 names on the roll, with an average attendance of over 70, while Amosfield (Herding Yard) has over 50 on the roll, with an average attendance of over 30. The rosy cheeks, sturdy limbs, and general appearance of these children as they tramp to school offer convincing proof of the healthiness of the climate." (Mines and Mining, 24 Sep 1881, p.22)

1890 "BOONOO BOONOO Provisional School." (Armidale Circuit Court, 31 Oct 1890, p.4)

1894 "TENDERS ACCEPTED PUBLIC SCHOOLS The following tenders in connection with public schools have been accepted by the Government ... Amosfield – Improvements and repairs John Wilson – £69 10s." (Tenders Accepted, 22 Dec 1894, p.18)

1906 FIRE AT AMOSFIELD. Public School Destroyed. A little after 10 a.m. Wednesday, a fire broke out at the School ... Mr. Court, the School Master smelt a peculiar, smoky smell in School, and on going outside to ascertain the cause he found the roof of the building on fire. The school was dismissed at once, the children being much alarmed. Assistance was quickly in attendance, but very little could be done from the rapid spread of the fire ...

The building is an old, of weatherboards, pine shingle roof, covered with iron, and much ant eaten, and decayed. Some time ago it was condemned by the Government Inspector, and money voted by Parliament for a new school.

The fire it is believed started from a spark from the kitchen chimney (it being lower than the main building) which it is supposed to have been blown by a chopping wind, between the shingles and the iron roofing, fanning the spark into a blaze. The kitchen fire was the only one on the premises. The fire is no doubt accidental, and the building is uninsured." (Fire at Amosfield—Public School Destroyed, 27 Apr 1906, p.2)

1906 TEACHER "The resignations of Miss Ruby Eather, pupil teacher at Emmaville School, and Mr. Oliver J. Atkinson, teacher at Boonoo Boonoo School, have been accepted." (Gazette Notices, 8 May 1906, p.2)

1912 AMOSFIELD TEACHER "Mr. W. McKnight ... recently was promoted to Amosfield near the Queensland border. The value of Mr. McKnight, whose unostentatious manner, and ready and obliging disposition was much appreciated by his friends." (Stroud, 27 Feb 1912, p.2)

1913 POLLING PLACES "The polling-places in the electorate at which the local option poll will be taken are .... Boonoo Boonoo, school ... Tenterfield, School of Arts ... Wilson's Downfall, Courthouse." (Tomorrow's Vote, 5 Dec 1913, p.4)

When war is near and dangers high, God and soldier is all the cry;
When war is o'er and all things righted, God's forgotten and the soldier slighted.

1916 "Mr. Kellett of the Boonoo Boonoo school (Tenterfield) proceeded to Armidale last week for final acceptance in the military forces. In response to the request for offers of motor vehicles for the use of the Tenterfield Recruiting Sergeant, Mr. Cotton has offered his motor, and Mr. Jordan his sulky. There is a lot of travelling to be done, and the Secretary, Mr. J. Iddon, will be pleased to hear from others willing to help." (War Items, 28 Mar 1916, p.8)

1927 AMOSFIELD TEACHER "Miss Eva Glasby (teacher) passed away after a serious operation, said Mr. Eric Pearson. Randal Young was also school teacher who lived at Amosfield in 1930." (Source unknown)

1929 A WARWICK RETROSPECT "September 6. The recent function at the Warwick East State School had more than ordinary significance to at least three of those present—the Mayor (Alderman D. Connolly) and Alderman Sterne, who attended the school 47 years ago, and Mrs. Catherine Newcombe, who was one of the original scholars. Mrs. Newcombe is now approaching her 77th birthday, and has the honour of claiming acquaintance with the first school established in Warwick. Interesting facts relative to Warwick's first school are given by Mr. H. Sterne. He stated that in 1855 (before the separation of Queensland from New South Wales), Mr. Jonathan Harris was appointed by the Education Board of New South Wales to take charge of the first national school in Warwick. An adventurous trip by steamer from Sydney, and by bullock waggon and horseback from Brisbane, landed the new teacher, his wife, and two children at their destination. Mr. and Mrs. Harris remained in their position for a number of years, and amongst other schools opened by them was that at Maryland. After a long residence in Warwick the family removed to Brisbane, where Mr. Harris died in 1894.

The first school was a wooden building, standing on the western side of the present East Warwick School. The teacher and his family were in residence in half of the building, and the school was in the other half. Between 1855 and 1874 the present brick building was erected, and the old wooden school was still utilised. The brick building was divided by a partition, one half of the school being for boys and the other for girls. The wooden school was used for the smaller children. At the official inspection in March, 1874, there was 143 boys present out of an enrolment of 193, and 85 girls out of an enrolment of 128. The staff of the boys' school was as follows :-Joseph Canny (h.t., admitted June, 1870), Peter McDermott (p.t, July, 1872), Thos. Spencely (a.t., May, 1872), Joseph McKinley (p.t., April, 1670), John Hutcheon (p.t., October, 1870). The personnel of the staff of the girls' school was :—Mrs. Canny (h.t. admitted September, 1864), Fanny Thorn (p.t., July, 1870), Eliza Longwill (p.t., October, 1871). Later in the same year Mary Fleming and Sarah Magary were appointed pupil teachers.

About 1874 the Church of England nonvested school was opened, and it took a good number of pupils from the East School. On June 25, 1874, the foundation stone of the Warwick West Boys', Girls', and Infants' School was laid. The event was marked by a public demonstration, and the largest gathering ever known up to that date assembled in Warwick In July, 1875, the building was completed, and Mr. and Mrs. Canny were appointed master and mistress of the new school. Mr. Canny's salary was £277 per annum, and he taught a fifth class of four boys, and a fourth class of 27 boys. Mr. A. J. Haswell was junior assistant teacher, being in charge of a third class of 18 boys. His salary was £85 per annum. Other teachers were Messrs. J. Hutcheon (£85 per annum), P. McDermott (£55 per annum), S. Spencer (£47 per annum), J. McKinley (£40). The salary of Mrs. Canny, head mistress of the Warwick West Girls' School, was £205. Other teachers were Miss Mary Fleming (£20), Miss Eliza Longwill (£30), Miss S. Magary (£20). Mr. Sterne recalls that the frame that now supports the school bell is identical with the one in existence 47 years ago. The grounds were then much smaller, and bore no comparison with their appearance at the present time so far as beauty is concerned, the garden plots established by the head master (Mr. T. Garland) being a feature of the school to-day." (Early School Days, 11 Sep 1929, p.10)

1940s AMOSFIELD & WYLIE CREEK TEACHERS "I was associated with him (Eric Pearson) in the early 1940s. At the time I was teacher-in-charge at Amosfield on the new England Highway not far from Stanthorpe, Queensland and Eric was in charge at Wylie Creek that had no school so Eric taught in the local hall … Eric married a local girl, Evelyn Crome. My wife and I decorated the Liston Methodist Church for the wedding and the bride wore my wife's wedding dress. Unfortunately Evelyn become ill when they went to London and after a short illness died. I did not see Eric again … What an outstanding career this man had … E. J. Parker Retired" (Eric remembered, 1 Sep 2003, p.10)

1968 LISTON SCHOOL CLOSED May 1968; Mr Terry Parsons was the last teacher; school bus to Stanthorpe … "In spite of the cold weather prevailing a gathering of more than 80 people attended in the Liston Hall on June 8 last to bid farewell to the last teacher at Liston (Mr. Terry Parsons) … While everyone regretted the closure of the Liston school, the last and only school in this area, they all realised the children must benefit.

Many schools had opened and closed in the district over the years mainly due to movement of population which often occurred in districts where mining had once been a prominent industry … In these days, he (Mr. Madsen) said it was extremely desirable all children should have the benefit of higher education (busing to Stanthorpe school) … In olden days stamina and the ability to swing an axe and such like counted for a lot but today with this country entering an industrial and commercial era, education was imperative" (The Stanthorpe Border Post, Issue unknown, 1968)

Local Schools 1876-1968

1875 Herding Yard Creek Provisional School opened at Amosfield
1876 Herding Yard Creek Provisional School closed in June
1876 Amosfield Public School opened July
1953 Amosfield Public School closed August
1953 Liston School opened
1968 Liston School closed — students bused to Stanthorpe

2020 Mrs Val White recalled "the beautiful old pear tree at the Amosfield school. Her late husband Tim White's brother Jack White was a teacher there." While John C. Burton recalls "there were 120 children at the Amosfield School before WW2, maybe in 1939. Mr Parker was a teacher at the school. Rose Burton also was a teacher, as was Ted Burton's wife Mabel. Rose Burton rode in a Cobb and Co. coach."

1911 Sheahan's Hotel, Maryland Street, Stanthorpe (First load of tin from Blue Mountain Creek workings) – Courtesy State Library of Queensland

ca. 1872 Examiner and Times Newspaper office
Warwick – Courtesy State Library of Queensland

Small timber dwelling of Walter C. Hume (Mineral Land Commissioner from 8 Nov 1872 to 1 Jul, 1875) at the Land Commissioners Camp at Stanthorpe – Courtesy State Library of Queensland

Tin escorts – Liston Hall Committee,
courtesy of local residents

ca. 1873 Miners working at St. Leonard's Tin Mine, Sugarloaf Creek near Stanthorpe – Courtesy State Library of Queensland

ca. 1910 Race and Sluicing Equipment at Boonoo Boonoo Gold Mine, Tenterfield – Courtesy State Library of New South Wales

ca. 1895 Gold mining at Boonoo Boonoo, Tenterfield area, NSW – Courtesy State Library of New South Wales

ca. 1910 Water wheel at Boonoo Boonoo Gold Mine, Tenterfield – Courtesy State Library of New South Wales

ca. 1875 Man working at a sluice possibly relating to tin mining near Stanthorpe
(William Boag) – Courtesy State Library of Queensland

ca. 1872 Patrons outside the Miners Refuge Hotel, Broadwater, proprietor of the hotel was Peter Connell (William Boag) – Courtesy State Library of Queensland

ca. 1872 Tin miners with sluice boxes in Stanthorpe district (William Boag) – Courtesy State Library of Queensland

Bucket Dredge at Herding Yard – Liston Hall Committee, courtesy of local residents

1872 Offices of the new Banca Tin Mining Company, Stanthorpe (William Boag) – Courtesy State Library of Queensland

Christensen Family – Liston Hall Committee, courtesy of local residents

Bottrell Family – Liston Hall Committee, courtesy of local residents

ca. 1872 Henry Hillinger, butcher, Stanthorpe district (William Boag) – Courtesy State Library of Queensland

ca. 1890s Clifford Family of Stanthorpe – Courtesy State Library of Queensland

Border Baker, Stanthorpe, Qld (William Boag) – Courtesy State Library of Queensland

Blacksmith shop, John Burton recalls three blacksmith shops in Amosfield area – Liston Hall Committee, courtesy of local residents

J. M. Deacon, Watchmaker & Jeweller, Wilson's Downfall – Liston Hall Committee, courtesy of local residents

Cheese Factory, Liston – Liston Hall Committee, courtesy of local residents

ca. 1870 Making hay on Green Hills Farm, Warwick – Courtesy State Library of Queensland

ca. 1899 Anderson's General Store, Stanthorpe (Mr and Mrs Anderson standing outside their store) – Courtesy State Library of Queensland

Crome Christmas Party, Grange, Liston – Liston Hall Committee, courtesy of local residents

Maypole girls at Milford, Liston – Liston Hall Committee, courtesy of local residents

The Church of England, Ladies Guild, Liston – Liston Hall Committee, courtesy of local residents

Tennis group – Liston Hall Committee, courtesy of local residents

Snow at Salisbury, Tenterfield (Whereat Family) – Courtesy Tenterfield Information Centre

1925 Original Liston Hall Committee – Liston Hall Committee, courtesy of local residents

ca. 1928 Swimming group – Liston Hall Committee, courtesy of local residents

ca. 1905 Amosfield School – Liston Hall Committee, courtesy of local residents

Cricket match, Amosfield – Liston Hall Committee, courtesy of local residents

Cricket – Liston Hall Committee, courtesy of local residents

Amosfield cricket team – Liston Hall Committee, courtesy of local residents

ca. 1897 Glengallan Homestead – Courtesy State Library of Queensland

ca. 1900 Children on bicycles in front of H. Weynand's blacksmith business, Allora – Courtesy State Library of Queensland

1904 Amosfield Footy Club – Liston Hall Committee, courtesy of local residents

ca. 1898 Group of golf players (A. B. Butler), Tenterfield – Courtesy State Library of New South Wales

Sandy Flat Rifle Club (A. B. Butler), via Tenterfield – Courtesy State Library of New South Wales

Picnic at Bottrell's Flat, Amosfield – Liston Hall Committee, courtesy of local residents

ca. 1920s Nine Mile Race Day – Liston Hall Committee, courtesy of local residents

Amosfield Saleyards – Liston Hall Committee, courtesy of local residents

Below left ca. 1905 Group photo of team members in Tug of War game, Amosfield "Identified in the photo: front row left, Mr. Beddow, and third from the left, Mr. Charlie Turner" – Courtesy State Library of Queensland; Below right – Courtesy Liston Hall Committee, courtesy of local residents

Amosfield Band – Courtesy Mrs Lynette Reay, 81 years, 2020 "My great uncles are in the photo: 2nd row on right is Edwin Rupert Stalling, next to him with the hat, I believe is Alby Knight, and 3rd in the front row I believe is my Great Uncle William Aaron Stalling. Both of these uncles were killed in WW1."

The Church of England, Liston – Liston Hall Committee, courtesy of local residents

The Catholic Church – Liston Hall Committee, courtesy of local residents

ca. St. Mark's Church of England under construction, Warwick – Courtesy State Library of Queensland
ca. 1865 First St. Mary's Roman Catholic Church, Warwick (the new church was opened in 1926)
– Courtesy State Library of Queensland

Below right: Joss House located on Wylie Creek down Cemetery Creek Lane (Chinese priest, Chas Crome, Ethel Stokoe, Evelyn Michael, Clas Glass or Clem Pillar) – Liston Hall Committee, courtesy of local residents;
Below left - ca. Early 1900s The Methodist Church, Amosfield – Liston Hall Committee, courtesy of local residents

Wylie Creek Hall – Liston Hall Committee, courtesy of local residents

June 1914 Salvaging fire damaged articles after fire destroyed part of the town of Stanthorpe
– Courtesy State Library of Queensland

Derrick Burton – Courtesy John C. Burton

Jim Newley WWI – Liston Hall Committee, courtesy of local residents

Jack Newley WWII – Liston Hall Committee, courtesy of local residents

Pte Edwin Rupert Stalling – Courtesy Mrs Lynette Reay

Pte Ernest Bazen Beddow – Courtesy Australian War Memorial

1920 Amosfield, Hand coloured and mounted black and white print – Courtesy Australian War Memorial

Allan Crome WWII – Liston Hall Committee, courtesy of local residents

Charles Crome WWI – Liston Hall Committee, courtesy of local residents

Joseph Newley WWI – Liston Hall Committee, courtesy of local residents

William Aaron Stalling – Courtesy Mrs Lynette Reay

Boonoo Boonoo School – Liston Hall Committee, courtesy of local residents

Buggy in front of Wylie Creek State School – Courtesy State Library of Queensland

ca. 1873 Public School, High Street Tenterfield (J. Paine), J. J. Walsh Headmaster
in foreground – Courtesy State Library of New South Wales

Local school, possibly Amosfield School – Liston Hall Committee, courtesy of local residents

1873 School children outside Stanthorpe State School (William Boag) – Courtesy State Library of Queensland

1900 Amosfield School "The school photo I have no idea of the children. The more I look at it, the girl 6th from left in the back row could be my Mum, Elsie Marjorie Stalling. It is hard as there are no old photos of her as a child." – Courtesy Mrs Lynette Reay, 81 years, 2020

ca. 1875 Warwick Central State School – Courtesy State Library Queensland

ca. 1911 Foundation pupils and teachers of St. Catherine's School, Stanthorpe
(Nun is Sister Evelyn) – Courtesy State Library of Queensland

Amosfield School – Liston Hall Committee, courtesy of local residents

10/4/1929 Amosfield School students – Liston Hall Committee, courtesy of local residents

1935 Amosfield - Back, 2nd and 3rd rows: Names supplied with photo; 1st row names supplied by John Burton Back row: Joan Kiehne, Elva Stonebridge, Neta Einam, Dorothy Newley, Rona Cook, Elva Beddow, Mary Goodwin, Roma Scott, Celia Kienhne, May Wise, Lillian Betteridge, Jane Sullivan 3rd row: Alieen Newley, Joan Smith, Bobby Ross, Boysen Burton, Len Marsden, Toddy Einam, Bruce Marsden, Neville Butler, Harold Scott, John Lowein, Lorna Green, Beryl Goodyear 2nd row: Nola Werner, Alma Butler, unknown, May Newley, Joan unknown, Mavis Werner, Jean Butler, Joan Lowien, Elaine Burton 1st row: Jeff Lowein, John Burton, unknown Goodwin, Ray Einam, Brian Einam, Balfa Morgan, unknown, unknown, unknown – Courtesy Veronica Mason, Ancestry.com

ca. 1905 Students on the verandah of Stanthorpe State School – Courtesy State Library of Queensland

1915 Amosfield School- Back row: Barbara Hendry (holding doll), Jack Turner, Gordon Palmer, Norman Crisp, Audrey Palmer, Violet Potts, Olga Newley, Alf Burton Four girls: Grace Stonebridge, Marion Bottrell, Doris Harriman (bow tie), Harriet Turner Next row: Eva Stonebridge, Daisy Bottrell, Mary Sullivan, Annie Palmer (little lower), Gladys Goodyear, Eva Burton, Rachel Palmer, George Bottrell, Kathleen Turner, unknown Five standing on left: Eva Palmer (dark hair), Kathleen Stonebridge (ribbon hair), George Palmer, Stanley Gibson, Alice Gallagher Seated: Jack Burton, Cecil Lawer, Jack Lawer, Hugh Newley, Percy Banks, Don Bonner, Alf Harriman, Eric Goodyear, Clyde Banks, Charlie Turner, Ted Burton Kneeling: Sid Turner, Ida Banks, Livinia Beddow, Pearl Lawer, unknown, Brendon Palmer, unknown Gibson, Doris Gibson (white collar), Dolly Bottrell, Eva Onglee, Della Lanagan, Billy Clifford, Gordon Bonner On grass: Maisie White, Carrie White, unknown, Edna Bonner, Sinclair White, Reg Lawer, unknown Goodyear (kneeling behind girl with plaits), unknown, Dickie Turner (kneeling back), John Gallagher (white collar) - Courtesy Kerry Johnson (nee Burton)

LISTON SCHOOL CLOSURE

"in spite of the cold wind prevailing a gathering of more than 80 people attended in the Liston Hall on June 8 last to bid farewell to the last school teacher at Liston and also to give pupils of Amosfield and Liston School an opportunity for re-union ... bus service now conveyed their children to the Stanthorpe schools, where the benefits of higher education could be obtained ... while everybody generally regretted the closure of the Liston School, the last and only school in the area, they all realised the children must benefit ... The Amosfield School which had opened in 1878 had survived the longest period but was closed when the Liston School had been erected ... In olden days stamina and the ability to swing an axe and such like counted for a lot but today with this country entering an industrial and commercial era, education was imperative and the first part of it began at school ... the Chairman then called on Mr. Parker, who had been a teacher at the Amosfield School in the 1940s ... In the Tenterfield district alone no fewer than 22 small schools had been closed ... The younger folks then enjoyed themselves playing games and the older folk a really good time chatting about ancient days. Thus ended a memorable gathering." (The Stanthorpe Border Post, Issue unknown, 1968)

Above right: Circa 1960s Liston School - Back row: Carolyn Crome, unknown, Heather Beddow, unknown 3rd row: Gary Hurtz, Terry Crome, Peter Crossman, Rodney Crome, Janelle Burton 2nd row: Christine Beddow, Daryl Beddow, Tony Hurtz 1st row: Glen Crossman, Kay Crossman, Robyn Burton, Greg Burton - Courtesy John C. Burton
Right: Offices of the Border Post and Stannum Miner (William Boag) - Courtesy State Library of Queensland

Chapter Ten

Cobb & Co.'s Coach and Collectables Museum
Liston, N.S.W.

THE DAYS OF COBB & CO.
by William Muggridge

I dream of the good old coaching days, Of the grand old long-ago;
Of the joyful ride — a seat outside — On the coach of Cobb & Co.;
Of the music of the swingle-bars And the merry hoof-taps, too;
When the leather springs were wonder things, And the year-old things were new.

When the emu and the kangaroo Fled across the unmade track,
As we went along; and the driver's song Awakened the old out-back.
Ah, the horses then blazed coaching ways, And carried the pioneer.
Then the bush was wide. The far outside Nowadays is brought too near.

The railway train and the motor car Have hustled the coach away
To Phantom Land, where, I understand, All the good things will stay;
Away at the end of life's mirage, In that far-off promised land,
Where swingle-bars — not motor cars — Give joy to the happy band.

To the happy band of good old days, To the days of Cobb & Co.,
I lift my glass as I toast The Pass Into which the old days go.
Ah, soon I shall see the phantom coach, And secure a seat outside;
Then through The Gate, Where old friends wait, On a Cobb & Co. I'll ride.

(The Days of Cobb & Co., 8 Feb 1924, p.3)

Liston—a country mountain village with crisp, frosty mornings and a past well remembered …

From memories of Cobb and Co. in the district, horse and buggies, bush tracks, Shank's pony, local dances, sports days, picnics, Tug-of-War Teams, Amosfield Bands, wild blackberry & mushroom picking, fresh vegetables, homemade preserves, jams & ginger beer, kerosene fridges, buckets made from kerosene tins, drinking from condensed milk cans, castor oil, outhouses, 'Joe Blakes', rabbit trapping, panning the creeks, working the dredges and the memory of our fallen soldiers … to generators for electricity and finally access to higher education (1968) and power at the flick of a switch (1977). Liston and the surrounding area has a rich and very personal history for many of the families who have been a part of the locality for generations.

Liston—with its echoes of cracking whips and cricket games from the good old days—is situated in New South Wales, on the eastern fall of the Great Dividing Range. Surrounding places include Amosfield, Boonoo Boonoo, Maryland, Rivertree, Sugarloaf, Wilson's Downfall and Wylie Creek. The area was on the Cobb and Co. route from Tenterfield to Warwick, and beyond. The Great Northern Road that joined Sydney to Brisbane in the 1800s, travelled through Tenterfield, Boonoo Boonoo, Wilson's Downfall, Liston and Maryland.

Nowadays, Liston is in the Tenterfield Shire local government area and relies on cattle farming and tourism. Stanthorpe, across the New South Wales/Queensland border, is the closest town for other employment and services. In the Tenterfield Shire, areas "identified as having nature conservation values include ten National Parks (Koreelah, Mt. Clunie, Tooloom, Mt. Nothofagus, Maryland, Bald Rock, Boonoo Boonoo, Basket Swamp, Timbarra and Washpool), 16 State Forests (Koreelah, Beaury, Yabbra, Bookookoorara, Wilson's Downfall, Boonoo, Gilgurry, Girard, Malara, Ewingar, Billirimba, Speribo, Forestland, Capoompeta, Donnybrook and Torrington), seven Nature Reserves (Captain's Creek, Demon, Tracing the Natural Evolution of Australia [AHT] Environment-Naturally Evolved [SHT] 9 Bolivia Hill, Bluff River, Mt. MacKenzie, Doonybrook and Torrington), seven Nature Reserves (Captain's Creek, Demon, Tracing the Natural Evolution of Australia (AHT) Environment-Naturally Evolved [SHT] 9 Bolivia Hill, Bluff River, Mt. MacKenzie, Doonybrook and Gibralter) and two State Conservation Areas (Torrington and Curry's Gap)." (A Thematic History of Tenterfield Shire, 2004, pp.8-9)

Cobb and Co. Coach & Collectables Museum

In the heart of Liston, the Cobb and Co. Coach & Collectables Museum can be found. You are able to view the broad spectrum of change in the village and the surrounding areas, from the recrafted Cobb and Co. coach by John C. Burton, Junior, to the old Herding Yard Creek/Amosfield/Liston school bell, circa 1875.

2017 The beginnings of the museum—Local Liston resident, John C. Burton, was taken aback when the Seven Mile Lane that runs past his residence near Liston Creek, New South Wales, was renamed Herding Yard Creek Road. This jolted him, in 2017, into wanting to acknowledge the history of the village, and to share with the community and visitors some heritage of the Liston area, in which he has lived all his life. This desire led John, in his late 80s, to build a replica Cobb and Co. stage coach, a nod to the coach service from a bygone era. John's journey continued with the restoration of a dray, culminating in the establishment of a bush museum in 2020, to remember the good old days.

At 91 years of age, John with his supporters, designed and constructed a building that houses the coach, dray, old harnesses and other collectables. John donated many of his old tools and items of interest to the museum, aptly named Cobb and Co. Coach & Collectables. John Charles Burton, Junior—John was a carpenter by trade and his hobbies included collecting antiques and the restoration of old things. In 2017, he joined 'The Guild of Model Wheelwrights' for whom His Royal Highness Prince Philip, Duke of Edinburgh was patron.

When John was born on 27 April 1929, at the Pines Hospital in Stanthorpe, his father Henry William Burton (21/7/1892) was 36 years old, and his mother Dorris A'Del Burton (nee Glasby, 24/12/1895) was 33 years old. The family lived at 'Pine Croft', Amosfield. Dorris was born and spent her childhood at Rivertree, during the silver mining days. Henry was born at the Sandy Waterholes, along the Seven Mile or Herding Yard Creek, near Maryland, where his father, Charles Wiliam Burton, was a landowner.

ca. 1853 Records show that the Burton family has been in the Liston district since Charles Burton, John's great grandfather, arrived in Australia from England, possibly in 1853—"Burton, Charles, M, 26 years, gentleman, English, arrived Port Philip, Sydney. Calphurissa, 5 May 1853." (Victoria, Australia, Assisted and Unassisted Passenger Lists [1839-1923], 1853)

1856 Charles' first marriage to Margaret Francis, 1 October 1856, occurred in Warwick; their children were Johannah, Charles William and John George.

John with his dog Skeeta
at Pine Croft, Amosfield

They were living in Warwick when they married, and at Maryland when Margaret died; Charles' second marriage was to Mercy (Mary) Francis in Stanthorpe, their child was Rose Ann. (Charles Burton's Death Certificate, 1893)

1882 Charles Burton, address Green Hills, Maryland. (Charles Burton's Marriage Certificate, 1882)

1889 On 20 August, son Charles William Burton (Chas) married Emily Rebecca Francis. (born 18/6/1868). (Australia Marriage Index, 1788-1950)

1891 New South Wales, Australia Census Tenterfield, Buller, Bookookoorara—Township or village Wilson's Downfall, Ruby Creek ... Charles Burton and Chas W. Burton both listed. (New South Wales Australia Census, 1891)

1892 Charles William Burton, Maryland, applied for and was granted 300 acres. (Land District of Tenterfield, Sept-Oct 1892, p.85)

1913 Charles W. Burton, address Herding Yard Creek, Maryland. (Tenterfield—Tenterfield Pastures Protection Board, 1913, p.175) Charles and Emily's children were Henry William (Harry), Ethel, Mary, Charles Samuel, Edward Richmond, Eva Francis, Alfred Norman, John Clarence, Emily Kathleen and Freda Mary, some of whom lived and raised their families in the Liston District, including Amosfield.

From his mother taking a horse and sulky to travel from Amosfield to Tenterfield for local dances, to riding his push bike to Rural School from Amosfield to Stanthorpe, to the smart technology of today—John Charles Burton Junior has heard about or seen it all.

1949 John at Liston

John's workshop

2019 Dray restored by John and his recrafted coach

2019 The Hon. Barnaby Joyce MP and John

Liston – Liston Hall Committee, courtesy of local residents

Appendices

Appendix A: Map Reference List

- 1842 MAP OF MORETON BAY – National Library of Australia
- 1859 MAP OF THE AUSTRALIAN COLONIES, Printed London 1859 University, Stanford & California 94305, The Barry Lawrence Ruderman Map Collection – Spotlight at Stanford
- 1866 MAP OF QUEENSLAND WITH SQUATTING RUNS, by W. Owen, Main and Mail Roads (thick black line, part of the Great Northern Road identifiable – National Library of Australia
- 1894 MAP SHEWING THE POSTAL STATIONS, MAIL ROADS & TELEGRAPH OFFICES IN NEW SOUTH WALES – National Library of Australia
- 1895 MAP OF NEW SOUTH WALES RAILWAYS, SHOWING COACH AND OTHER ROUTES FROM THE VARIOUS STATIONS : together with mileage from Sydney, with diagrams of North Coast, South Coast, and parts of southern and western lines – National Library of Australia
- 1902 MAP OF PARISH OF WYLIE (County of Buller, 'Old Mail Track from Warwick' to Liston, via Herding Yard/Seven Mile Creek road identifiable on map) – Courtesy State Library of New South Wales
- 1910 MAP OF PARISH OF RUBY, County of Buller (Road from Warwick to Liston along Herding Yard/Seven Mile Creek shown) – Courtesy State Library of New South Wales
- 1918 MAP SHOWING AMOSFIELD NEW SCHOOL SITE, Amos, Stalling, Christensen blocks – Courtesy of Lynette Reay
- 1920 MAP OF THE NORTH EASTERN TOURIST DISTRICT: including New England tableland and showing principal fishing streams New South Wales, Australia – Department of Lands, S.G. Miller, Sydney

Appendix B: 1860s & 1870s Telegraphic Communication

- 1860 Feb. 7.—Publication of first message sent by telegraph from Sydney to Newcastle, thence by steamer to Brisbane
- 1861 April 13—Telegraphic communication established between Ipswich and Brisbane …July 9.— Telegraph line from Sydney to Tenterfield completed … Aug. 17.—Telegraphic communication established between Brisbane and Toowoomba … Nov. 6.—Communication (telegraphic) between Brisbane and Sydney established … Nov. 9.—First public telegram sent from Sydney to Brisbane
- 1862 Communications from England Jan. 14.—Telegram received Brisbane contents which were dated London, December 2, news being only 40 days old
- 1872 "Telegraph line being built between Maryland and Stanthorpe (opened in June) … Communications with Europe Oct. 21.—Direct telegraphic communication with Europe established
- 1873 Telegraph N.S.W.—The telegraph lines now in operation throughout the Colony of New South Wales … The wires at the Border connect the colony with Queensland

(Tenterfield To Stanthorpe, 20 July 1872, p.9 & Queensland's half century 1859 to 1909 notable events, 8 Dec 1909, p.25-29)

Appendix C: 1860s & 1870s Rail Development

- 1864 Queensland railway April 22.—First trip on the first railway in Queensland; run from Ipswich 8 miles towards Toowoomba; attempt made to wreck it … July 31.—First railway Qld formally opened
- 1865 First Qld locomotive Jan. 11.— First locomotive ever started in Queensland made trial trip at Ipswich
- 1867 Toowoomba train April 12.— Arrival of first train in Toowoomba (from Ipswich) … April 30.— Line between Ipswich and Toowoomba formally opened (Two passenger trains daily goods train when required)
- 1869 Allora's rail March 11.— Opening of railway to Allora
- 1878 Rail line April 17.—Contract first section Warwick and Stanthorpe railway (20 miles 28 chains) let Overend and Co., £178,683
- 1881 Stanthorpe railway May 3.— Stanthorpe Railway declared open
- 1884 Border railway April 30.— First sod Stanthorpe Border Railway turned by Mrs J. F. G. Foxton, wife of the member for Carnarvon

(Early History—The Stanthorpe Line, 2 Apr 1930, p.6 & Queensland's half century 1859 to 1909 notable events, 8 Dec 1909, p.25-32)

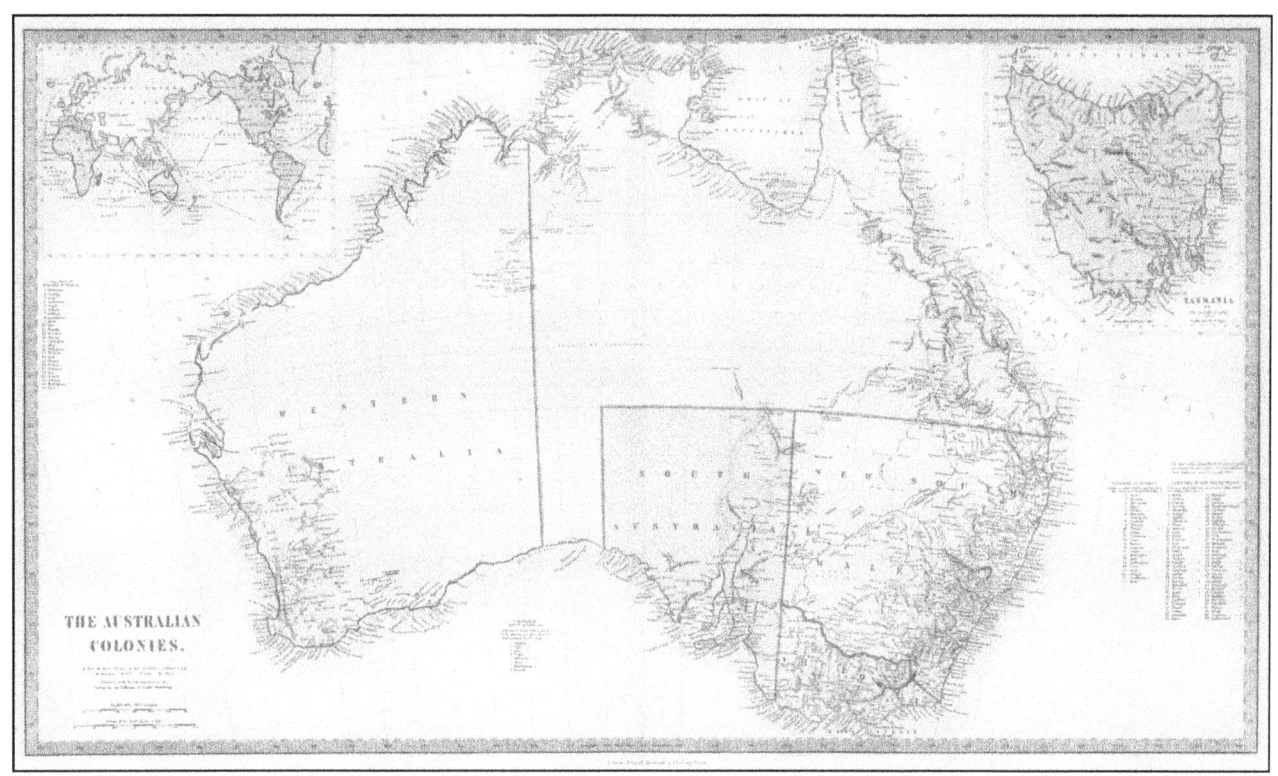

APPENDIX D: 1859 Map of The Australian Colonies –
Printed London 1859

APPENDIX E: 1918 Map showing Amosfield new school site, Amos, Stalling, Christensen blocks –
Courtesy of Lynette Reay

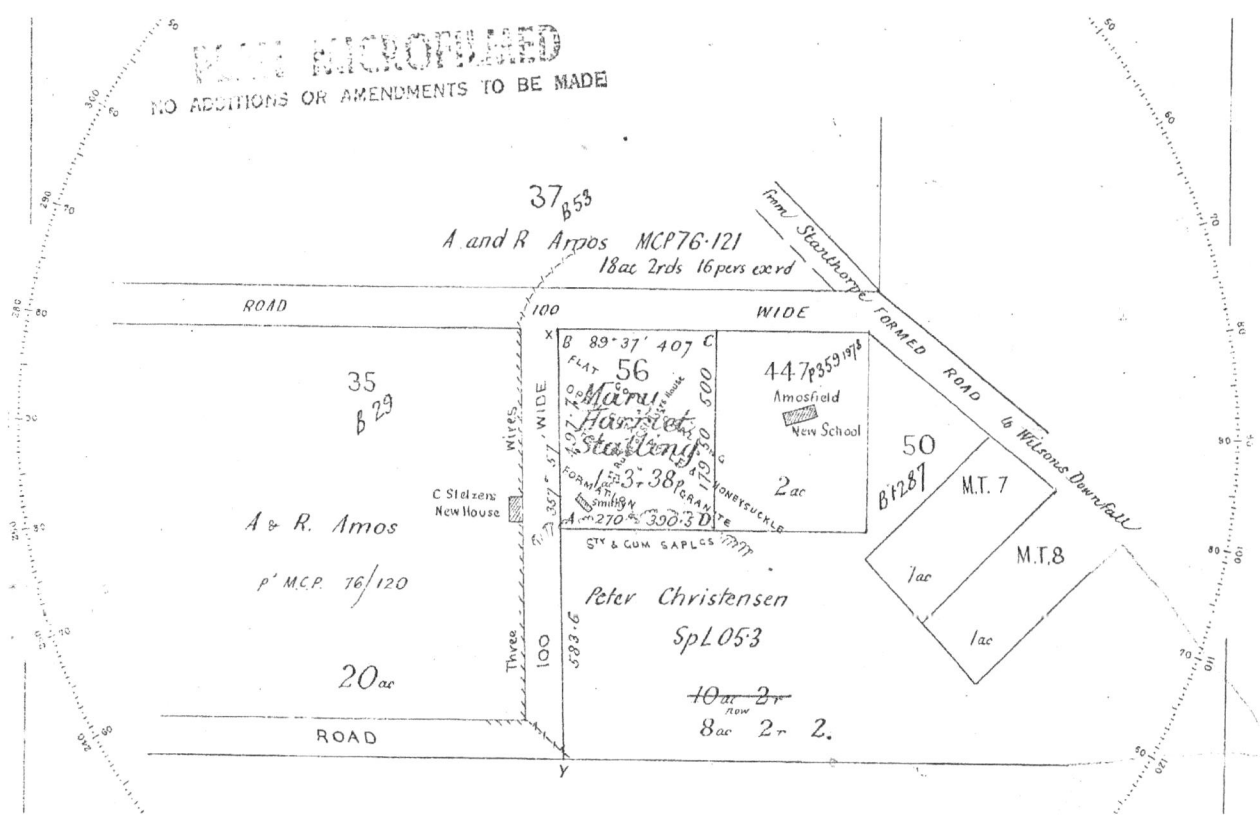

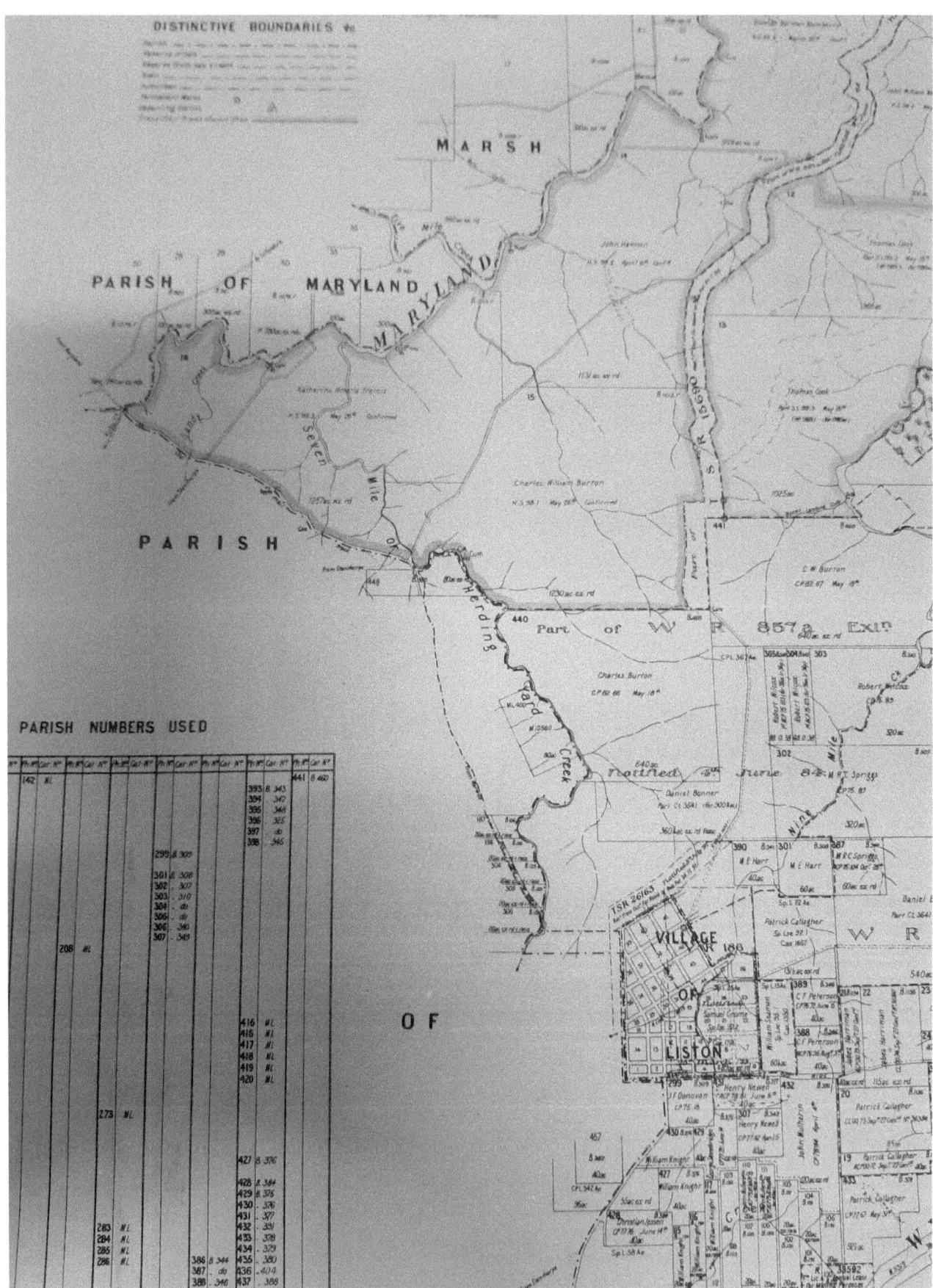

APPENDIX F: 1902 Map of Parish of Wylie (County of Buller, 'Old Mail Track from Warwick' to Liston, via Herding Yard/Seven Mile Creek road identifiable on map) – Courtesy State Library of New South Wales

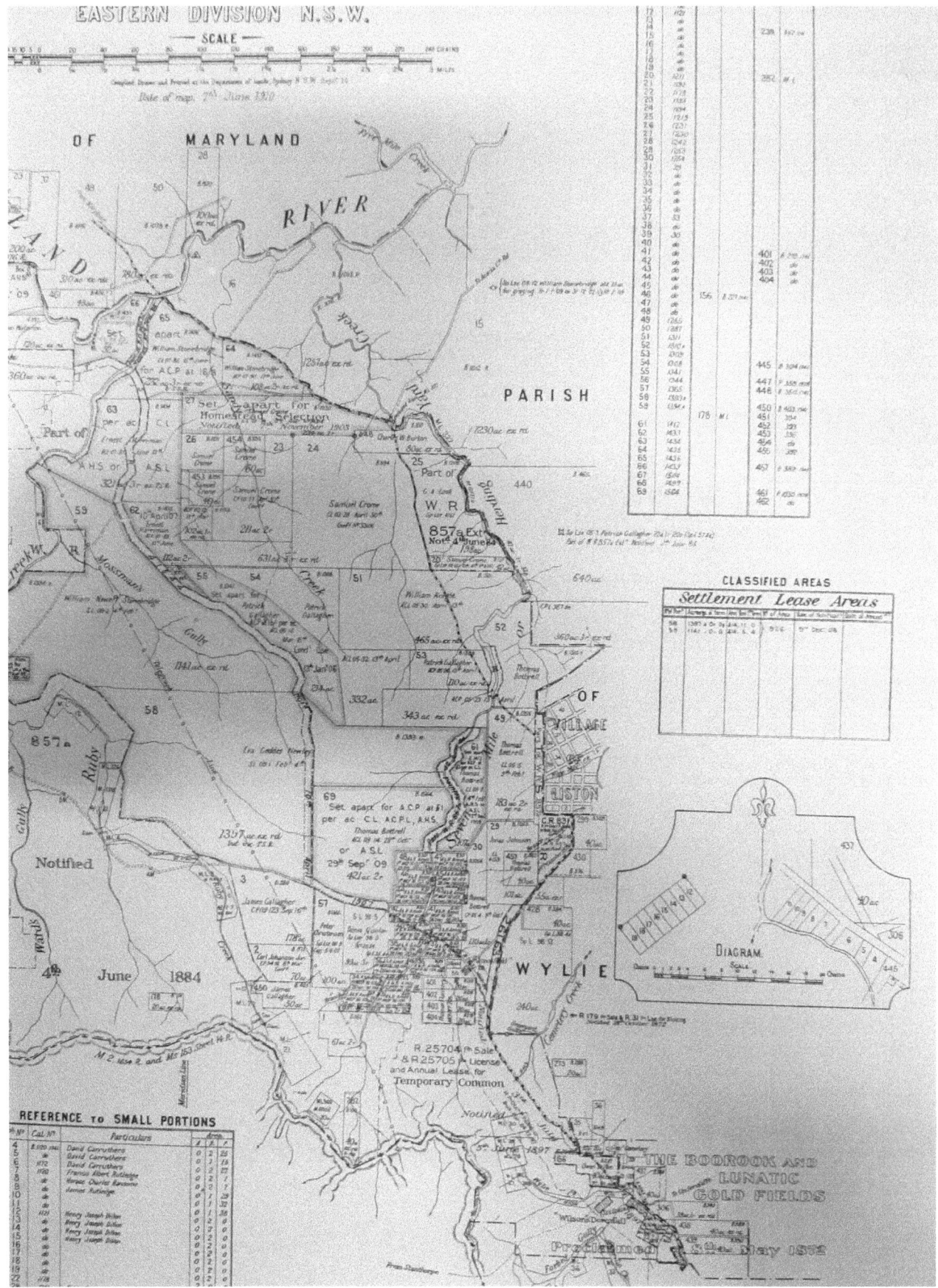

APPENDIX G: 1910 Map of Parish of Ruby, County of Buller (Road from Warwick to Liston along Herding Yard/Seven Mile Creek shown) – Courtesy State Library of New South Wales

APPENDIX H: Mail Tenders, Contractors & Routes

Year	Route	Warwick	Maryland	Stanthorpe	Sugarloaf	Amosfield	Wilson's Downfall	Bookookoorara	Boonoo Boonoo	Undercliff	Tenterfield	Deepwater	Dundee	Glenn Innes	Armidale
1841	Mail conveyance								●	●	●				●
1848	Incl. Brisbane Ipswich Drayton	●													●
1850	Horseback, Once a week, John Gill Gayndah, incl. Drayton	●									●				●
1862	Twice a week, Charles Tuckwood		●						●	●	●				●
1862	Horseback, John Aspinall, Toowoomba	●	●												
1862	Calling for tenders No. 41		●						●	●	●				●
1862	Calling for tenders No. 10		●							●	●				
1865	Calling for Tenders, Twice a week, No. 50		●							●	●				
1866	Horseback, Once a week, 1 or 2 years, John Aspinall, Qld Service, incl. Toowoomba	●	●												
1867	James Fox	●	●												
1867	**Cobb and Co.,** Toowoomba	●													
1868	Calling for Tenders, Twice a week, No. 42		●						●	●	●				
1868	**Cobb and Co.,** Toowoomba	●													
1868	Horseback, J. Aspinall	●	●												
1868	Calling for Tenders 1 or 3 years		●						●	●	●				
1868	Horseback, Twice a week, M. Curry		●						●	●	●				●
1869	Mail conveyance		●						●	●	●				
1870	Horseback, Twice a week, M. Curry		●						●	●	●				
1870	Calling for Tenders, Twice a week, Horse, 1 or 2 years	●	●												
1870	Calling for Tenders, Twice a week, Coach, 2 years	●	●												
1870	Twice a week, Two years, Coach **Cobb and Co.** No. 44, Qld Service, incl. Brisbane	●	●								●				
1870	Qld Service, Sun and Wed 5am, **Cobb and Co.**	●	●								●				
1871	Twice a week, Two years, Coach, **Cobb and Co.** No. 44, Qld Service, incl. Brisbane	●	●								●				
1872	Twice a week, **Cobb and Co.** Coach	●	●								●				
1873	Twice a week, **Cobb and Co.** Coach	●	●								●				
1872	Charles Tuckwood	●	●						●	●	●				
1872/73	Horse, Twice a week, 7 miles E. M. McLeod, No.119, incl. Ruby Creek		●												
1873	**Cobb and Co.** Coach		●				●				●	●	●		●
1873	Charles Tuckwood	●	●						●	●	●				
1873	**Cobb and Co.** plus other coaches	●	●	●											
1873	Three to six times a week, Not yet decided	●	●								●		●	●	
1874	Calling for tenders, 3 a week, July1874-1875/6		●								●	●	●	●	
1874	Twice a week, **Cobb and Co.** Coach	●	●								●				
1874	**Cobb and Co. & Cobb and Co.,** incl Ballandean	●		●			●								

1874	**Cobb and Co.**	•		•			•							
1874	2 or 4 horse coach, Three times a week, 119 miles, **Cobb and Co.** Coach		•					•			•	•	•	•
1874	Horseback, Twice a week, T. W. Simms, incl. Ruby Creek		•											
1875	Three times a week, **Cobb and Co.** Coach		•				•				•	•	•	•
1875	Calling for tenders, 3 times a week for two years		•								•	•	•	•
1875	Calling for tenders, Coach, Six times a week	•	•	•										
1875	Calling for tenders, Coach, Three times a week	•	•	•										
1875	Calling for tenders, Coach, Three times a week				•		•							
1875	Calling for tenders, Horseback, Three times a week				•		•							
1875	Horseback, To and from twice a week, 7 miles, F. Mossmann No. 132, incl. Ruby Creek		•											
1876	Calling for tenders, Twice a week No. 54, incl. Ruby Creek		•											
1876	Mail conveyance		•								•	•	•	•
1876	Coach, 3 times a week	•	•	•										
1876	Coach, 6 times a week	•	•	•										
1876	Coach, 3 times a week				•		•							
1876	Horse, 3 times a week				•		•							
1877	Mon Wed Sat 5.30am, **Cobb and Co.** coach service	•									•			
1877	3 times a week, **Cobb and Co.** Coach		•				•				•	•	•	•
1877	Daily except Sun 5.30am, **Cobb and Co.** coach service	•		•										
1877	Mon Wed Sat 12 noon returning Tues Thurs Sun 10am, **Cobb and Co.** coach service				•		•							
1877	Sun and Warwick Tues Thurs, **Cobb and Co.** coach service	•	•								•			
1878	Horseback, 2 or 4 horse coach, Three times a week—119 miles, **Cobb and Co.** Coach, No. 151		•			•	•				•	•	•	•
1878	Six times a week, **Cobb and Co.** Coach		•	•	•						•			
1878	Horse, Three times a week, **Cobb and Co.**					•	•							
1879	2 or 4 horse coach, Three times a week—119 miles, **Cobb and Co.** Coach, No. 159		•			•	•				•	•	•	•
1879	Horseback, 2 or 4 horse coach, Three times a week—119 miles **Cobb and Co.** Coach, No. 151		•			•	•				•	•	•	•
1879	Six times a week, Three years, **Cobb and Co.** (Combined tender) No. 77		•			•	•				•			
1880	Three or six times a week, Cobb and Co. (Combined tender,) No. 77		•			•	•				•			
1880	2 or 4 horse coach, Six times a week—52 miles, Cobb and Co., No. 1		•	•		•	•				•			
1880	COBB & CO.'s Telegraph Lines of ROYAL MAIL COACHES (no mention of mail): From WARWICK to MARYLAND and STANTHORPE Daily (Sundays excepted), at 5.30 From STANTHORPE to TENTERFIELD Daily (Thursdays excepted), at 12 noon From STANTHORPE to WARWICK Daily (Sundays excepted), at 1 p.m. From TENTERFIELD to STANTHORPE, MARYLAND, & WARWICK Daily (Thurs excepted), at 5 a.m.													
1880	Horseback, Three times a week—3 miles, Cobb and Co., No. 1					•	•							

Year	Description	Maryland	North Killarney	Acacia Creek	Cullendore	Liston	Rivertree	Wilson's Downfall	Boonoo Boonoo	Jennings	Tenterfield	Bryan's
1881	Horseback, Three times a week—3 miles, **Cobb and Co.**, No. 1					•	•					
1881	2 or 4 horse coach, Six times a week—52 miles, **Cobb and Co.**, No.1		•	•	•		•				•	
1881	Six times a week, Three years, **Cobb and Co.** (Combined tender)		•			•	•				•	
1881	Royal Mail Coach Daily (No mention of mail contract)	•	•	•							•	
1882	Three times a week—3 miles, Horseback, **Cobb and Co.**, No. 1					•	•					
1882	2 or 4 horse coach, Six times a week—52 miles, **Cobb and Co.**, No.1		•	•	•		•				•	
1883	Three times a week		•	•								
1883	Three times a week					•	•					
1883	Coach, Six times a week			•	•		•	•			•	
1884	Horseback, Three times a week—3 miles No. 218, Robert Paterson					•	•					
1884	Six times a week, **Cobb and Co.**			•	•		•				•	
1885	3 or 4 horse coach, Six times a week—44 miles, **Cobb and Co.**, No.1			•	•		•				•	
1885	Horseback, Three times a week—3 miles No. 218, Robert Paterson					•	•					
1885	Horseback, Three times a week—3 miles No. 223, Robert Paterson					•	•					
1886	Calling for tenders, Horseback, Three times a week, No. 87					•	•					
1886	Calling for tenders, Six times a week (Contract to terminate on the opening of the Railway line in New South Wales or Queensland, as may be required.), No. 82 incl. Kyoomba			•	•		•				•	
1886	6 times a week, 2 or 4 horse coach (Contract to terminate on opening of Railway line in New South Wales or Qld, as may be required.) **Cobb and Co.** Coach, No. 82, incl. Kyoomba (Qld)			•	•		•				•	
1886	Horseback 3 times a week, Hugh Grant, £36					•	•					
1890	Calling for Tenders Twice a week, No. 98							•	•		•	
1891	Mail conveyance			•	•		•					
1892	Horseback, Once a week, No. 101, David G. Smith			•	•		•					
1893	Calling for Tenders, Twice a week, No. 90							•	•		•	
1898	Coach Service (No mention of mail contract)	•				•				•		
1898	Mail conveyance							•	•		•	•
1898	Mail conveyance			•				•	•		•	•
1899	C. Pillar		•	•			•					

Year	Description	North Killarney	Acacia/Acacia Creek	Stanthorpe	Sugarloaf	Amosfield	South Rivertree	Rivertree	Wilson's Downfall	Boonoo Boonoo	Tenterfield	Leech's Gully
1900	Mail conveyance		•								•	
1900	Mail conveyance	•							•			
1902	Coach Service (No mention of mail), P.M. Charles Shoblom								•		•	
1902	Sulky, one horse, Three times per week—27 miles, No. 298, John H. Collins								•	•	•	•
1902	Horseback, Twice a week via surveyed road—37 miles, No. 300, John Dillon, incl. Mountain View (Qld)	•	•						•			
1903	Horseback, Twice a week via surveyed road—37 miles, No. 300, John Dillon, incl. Mountain View (Qld)	•	•						•			
1904	Horseback, Twice a week via surveyed road—37 miles, No. 300, John Dillon, incl. Mountain View (Qld)	•	•						•			
1902	Horseback, Twice a week—17 miles, No. 301, William Goodyear						•	•	•			
1903	Horseback, Twice a week—17 miles, No. 301, William Goodyear						•	•	•			
1912	Twice a week, (Qld Service)—16 miles			•					•			
1912	Horseback, Four times a week, W. Goodyear				•				•			
1912	Sulky and one horse, Twice a week, W. Goodyear, incl. Wylie Creek, Legume				•				•			
1912	Sulky and one horse, James Morris						•	•	•			
1912	Qld Service, Twice a week and thereafter at 3 Months notice, William Goodyear, incl. Kyoomba (Qld)			•		•			•			
1912	Sulky and one horse, Twice a week, David Merchant, incl. Bookookoorara								•	•	•	•
1916	Twice a week, No. 169, incl. Bookookoorara								•	•	•	•
1916	Twice a week, Vehicle, horse, No. 358 William Goodyear, incl. Wylie Creek, Windaroo, Lower Acacia Creek, Legume					•			•			
1916	Six times a week, Sulky, horse, No. 369, Samual Beddow, incl. Kyoomba (Qld)			•	•				•			
1916	Twice a week, Vehicle horse, No. 359, Thomas Goodyear						•	•	•			
1917	Twice a week Vehicle horse No. 358, William Goodyear, incl. Wylie Creek, Windaroo, Lower Acacia Creek, Legume					•			•			
1917	Six times a week Sulky horse, No. 369, Samual Beddow, incl. Kyoomba (Qld)			•	•				•			
1917	Twice a week, Vehicle or horseback, No. 359, Thomas Goodyear						•	•	•			
1918	Six times a week, Sulky horse, No. 369, Samual Beddow, incl. Kyoomba (Qld)			•	•				•			
1918	Twice a week, Vehicle horse, No. 359, Thomas Goodyear						•	•	•			

Reference List

1816 'CLASSIFIED ADVERTISING,' The Sydney Gazette and New South Wales Advertiser (NSW: 1803 - 1842), 18 May, p. 2, viewed 08 Apr 2021, http://nla.gov.au/nla.news-page493045

1831 'CLASSIFIED ADVERTISING,' The Sydney Gazette and New South Wales Advertiser (NSW: 1803 - 1842), 24 September, p. 4, viewed 14 Nov 2020, http://nla.gov.au/nla.news-article2202719

1831 'CLASSIFIED ADVERTISING,' The Sydney Gazette and New South Wales Advertiser (NSW: 1803 - 1842), 29 December, p. 2, viewed 14 Nov 2020, http://nla.gov.au/nla.news-article2204232

1832 'CLASSIFIED ADVERTISING,' The Sydney Gazette and New South Wales Advertiser (NSW: 1803 - 1842), 14 January, p. 4, viewed 14 Nov 2020, http://nla.gov.au/nla.news-article2204456

1842 'LEASE OF BUILDINGS AT MORETON BAY.', New South Wales Government Gazette (Sydney, NSW : 1832 - 1900), 12 April, p. 551. , viewed 17 May 2025, http://nla.gov.au/nla.news-article230661841

1842 'SALE OF TOWN ALLOTMENTS.', The Sydney Herald (NSW : 1831 - 1842), 22 April, p. 3. , viewed 17 May 2025, http://nla.gov.au/nla.news-article28651979

1846 'CLASSIFIED ADVERTISING', The Moreton Bay Courier (Brisbane, Qld. : 1846 - 1861), 12 September, p. 1. , viewed 18 May 2025, http://nla.gov.au/nla.news-article3716336

1846 'ORIGINAL POETRY.', The Moreton Bay Courier (Brisbane, Qld. : 1846 - 1861), 31 October, p. 4. , viewed 20 May 2025, http://nla.gov.au/nla.news-article3714799

1848 'GOVERNMENT GAZETTE,' The Maitland Mercury and Hunter River General Advertiser (NSW: 1843 - 1893), 2 February, p. 4, viewed 8 Nov 2020, http://nla.gov.au/nla.news-article713436

1849 'CLASSIFIED ADVERTISING', The Moreton Bay Courier (Brisbane, Qld. : 1846 - 1861), 8 September, p. 1. , viewed 17 May 2025, http://nla.gov.au/nla.news-article3715404

1850 'CLASSIFIED ADVERTISING', The Moreton Bay Courier (Brisbane, Qld. : 1846 - 1861), 12 January, p. 1. , viewed 18 May 2025, http://nla.gov.au/nla.news-article3709236

1850 'CLASSIFIED ADVERTISING', The Moreton Bay Courier (Brisbane, Qld. : 1846 - 1861), 10 August, p. 1. , viewed 01 June 2025, http://nla.gov.au/nla.news-article3714983

1850 'CONVEYANCE OF POST OFFICE MAILS,' People's Advocate and New South Wales Vindicator (Sydney, NSW: 1848 - 1856), 26 January, p. 5, viewed 10 March 2021, https://trove.nla.gov.au/newspaper/article/251537973

1850 'DOMESTIC INTELLIGENCE,' The Sydney Morning Herald (NSW: 1842 - 1954), 23 January, p. 2, viewed 1 Oct 2020, http://nla.gov.au/nla.news-article12915197

1853 'ADVERTISING', Empire (Sydney, NSW : 1850 - 1875), 19 February, p. 1. , viewed 01 June 2025, http://nla.gov.au/nla.news-article60137946

1853 'VICTORIA, AUSTRALIA, ASSISTED AND UNASSISTED PASSENGER LISTS, 1839-1923,' Ancestry.com [online], https://www.ancestry.com.au/imageviewer/collections/1635/images/30796_1254480047-00608?pId=2647876 [Accessed 7 Dec 2020]

1854 'ADVERTISING,' The Argus (Melbourne, Vic.: 1848 - 1957), 16 October, p. 7, viewed 14 Nov 2020, http://nla.gov.au/nla.news-article4799000

1854 'ADVERTISING,' The Argus (Melbourne, Vic.: 1848 - 1957), 28 November, p. 9, viewed 09 Dec 2020, http://nla.gov.au/nla.news-article4800950

1854 'ADVERTISING,' The Argus (Melbourne, Vic.: 1848 - 1957), 31 January, p. 3, viewed 09 Dec 2020, http://nla.gov.au/nla.news-article4802637

1854 'LAND CARRIAGE COMPANIES FOR THE NORTHERN, SOUTHERN, AND WESTERN INTERIOR, 24 Jun 1854, p.4)

1855 'FAMILY NOTICES', The Moreton Bay Courier (Brisbane, Qld. : 1846 - 1861), 10 March, p. 2. , viewed 18 June 2025, http://nla.gov.au/nla.news-article3708878

1856 'ADVERTISING,' Bendigo Advertiser (Vic.: 1855 - 1918), 23 May, p. 3, viewed 14 Nov 2020, http://nla.gov.au/nla.news-article88050197

1856 'ADVERTISING,' The Age (Melbourne, Vic.: 1854 - 1954), 21 November, p. 1, viewed 10 Dec 2020, http://nla.gov.au/nla.news-article154872805

1856 'ADVERTISING,' The Argus (Melbourne, Vic.: 1848 - 1957), 19 May, p. 2, viewed 14 Nov 2020, http://nla.gov.au/nla.news-article4838201

1856 'DOMESTIC INTELLIGENCE.', The Moreton Bay Courier (Brisbane, Qld. : 1846 - 1861), 24 May, p. 2. , viewed 18 May 2025, http://nla.gov.au/nla.news-article3710397

1856 'IMPOUNDED AT TENTERFIELD,' NSW Government Gazette (Sydney, NSW: 1832 - 1900), 15 February, p. 540, viewed 17 Mar 2021, https://trove.nla.gov.au/newspaper/article/228681246

1857 'ADVERTISING,' The Age (Melbourne, Vic.: 1854 - 1954), 23 February, p. 3, viewed 12 Nov 2020, http://nla.gov.au/nla.news-article154824523. State Library of Victoria.

1857 'LOCAL AND DOMESTIC.', The North Australian, Ipswich and General Advertiser (Ipswich, Qld. : 1856 - 1862), 3 February, p. 3. , viewed 01 June 2025, http://nla.gov.au/nla.news-article78849329

1858 'BOONOO BOONOO.', Northern Times (Newcastle, NSW : 1857 - 1918), 27 March, p. 4. , viewed 08 June 2025, http://nla.gov.au/nla.news-article128753406

1858 'TENTERFIELD,' Empire (Sydney, NSW: 1850 - 1875), 19 February, p. 5, viewed 11 Nov 2020, http://nla.gov.au/nla.news-article60428636

1858 'THE NEW ENGLAND GOLD FIELDS—THE ROCKY RIVER,' The Armidale Express and New England General Advertiser (NSW.: 1856 - 1954), 3 April, p. 2, viewed 11 Apr 2021, http://nla.gov.au/nla.news-article188980841

1859 'ADVERTISING', The Armidale Express and New England General Advertiser (NSW : 1856 - 1861; 1863 - 1889; 1891 - 1954), 10 September, p. 1. , viewed 18 May 2025, http://nla.gov.au/nla.news-article189984143

1859 'INDEX PAGE', New South Wales Government Gazette (Sydney, NSW : 1832 - 1900), 31 December, p. ix. , viewed 18 May 2025, http://nla.gov.au/nla.news-article226214597

1859 'LOCAL AND GENERAL.', Maryborough and Dunolly Advertiser (Vic. : 1857 - 1867 ; 1914 - 1918), 19 September, p. 3. , viewed 18 June 2025, http://nla.gov.au/nla.news-article253600669

1859 'PROCLAMATION OF QUEENSLAND,' Empire (Sydney, NSW: 1850 - 1875), 8 August, p. 5, viewed 7 Dec 2020, http://nla.gov.au/nla.news-article60399557

1859 'TENTERFIELD,' The Moreton Bay Courier (Brisbane, Qld.: 1846 - 1861), 22 January, p. 2, viewed 11 Apr 2021, http://nla.gov.au/nla.news-article3720488

1860 'ADVERTISING', The Armidale Express and New England General Advertiser (NSW : 1856 - 1861; 1863 - 1889; 1891 - 1954), 7 January, p. 1. , viewed 18 May 2025, http://nla.gov.au/nla.news-article188961205

1860 'COUNTRY NEWS.', The Armidale Express and New England General Advertiser (NSW : 1856 - 1861; 1863 - 1889; 1891 - 1954), 7 April, p. 2. , viewed 09 June 2025, http://nla.gov.au/nla.news-article188961458

1860 'LOCAL AND DOMESTIC.', The Darling Downs Gazette and General Advertiser (Toowoomba, Qld. : 1858 - 1880), 19 January, p. 3. , viewed 18 June 2025, http://nla.gov.au/nla.news-article75525737

1861 'BOONOO BOONOO DIGGINGS,' Sydney Mail (NSW: 1860 - 1871), 14 September, p. 3, viewed 20 Mar 2021, http://nla.gov.au/nla.news-article166694377

1861 'CLEVER CAPTURE OF TWO SWINDLERS.', Goulburn Herald (NSW : 1860 - 1864), 3 July, p. 4. , viewed 08 June 2025, http://nla.gov.au/nla.news-article105778817

1861 'CONVEYANCE OF MAILS,' New South Wales Government Gazette (Sydney, NSW: 1832 - 1900), 27 September, pp. 2055–2056, viewed 7 Nov 2020, http://nla.gov.au/nla.news-article225138106

1861 'CONVEYANCE OF MAILS,' New South Wales Government Gazette (Sydney, NSW: 1832 - 1900), 6 December, p. 2612, viewed 10 Dec 2020, http://nla.gov.au/nla.news-article225140118

1861 'IPSWICH POST OFFICE.', The North Australian, Ipswich and General Advertiser (Ipswich, Qld. : 1856 - 1862), 8 March, p. 2. , viewed 18 May 2025, http://nla.gov.au/nla.news-article77432542

1862 'ADVERTISING,' Bathurst Free Press and Mining Journal (NSW: 1851 - 1904), 20 August, p. 1, viewed 10 Dec 2020, http://nla.gov.au/nla.news-article62720942 State Library of New South Wales.

1862 'ADVERTISING', The Sydney Morning Herald (NSW : 1842 - 1954), 21 March, p. 2. , viewed 18 June 2025, http://nla.gov.au/nla.news-article13226119

1862 'LEGISLATIVE ASSEMBLY.', The Courier (Brisbane, Qld. : 1861 - 1864), 29 May, p. 2. , viewed 17 May 2025, http://nla.gov.au/nla.news-article4605941

1862 'MAIL CONTRACTS,' The Maitland Mercury and Hunter River General Advertiser (NSW: 1843 - 1893), 7 January, p. 3, viewed 7 Nov 2020, http://nla.gov.au/nla.news-article18685988

1862 'MODERN COLONIAL COACHING.', Maryborough and Dunolly Advertiser (Vic. : 1857 - 1867 ; 1914 - 1918), 13 June, p. 6. , viewed 18 June 2025, http://nla.gov.au/nla.news-article253513563

1863 'NOTES AND NEWS,' North Australian and Queensland General Advertiser (Ipswich, Qld.: 1862 - 1863), 15 August, p. 3, viewed 14 Nov 2020, http://nla.gov.au/nla.news-article77294025

1864 'ADVERTISING,' The Argus (Melbourne, Vic.: 1848 - 1957), 30 January, p. 7, viewed 10 Dec 2020, http://nla.gov.au/nla.news-article5743396

1864 'CONVEYANCE OF MAILS,' New South Wales Government Gazette (Sydney, NSW: 1832 - 1900), 11 October, p. 2273, viewed 7 Nov 2020, http://nla.gov.au/nla.news-article225359666

1864 'MISCELLANEOUS.', Queensland Times, Ipswich Herald and General Advertiser (Qld. : 1861 - 1908), 16 July, p. 4. , viewed 17 May 2025, http://nla.gov.au/nla.news-article123607200

1864 'TENDERS. CONVEYANCE OF MAILS,' New South Wales Government Gazette (Sydney, NSW: 1832 - 1900), 2 September, p. 1969, viewed 14 Nov 2020

1865 'ADVERTISING,' The Darling Downs Gazette and General Advertiser (Toowoomba, Qld.: 1858 - 1880), 23 September, p. 3, viewed 27 Nov 2020, http://nla.gov.au/nla.news-article75513027

1865 'CONVEYANCE OF MAILS 1866,' The Darling Downs Gazette and General Advertiser (Toowoomba, Qld.: 1858 - 1880), 8 November, p. 3, viewed 7 Nov 2020, http://nla.gov.au/nla.news-article75513119

1865 'TELEGRAPHIC', 21 Oct 1865, p.4 – Source currently not accessible

1865 'THE QUEENSLAND TELEGRAPH LINES,' The Darling Downs Gazette and General Advertiser (Toowoomba, Qld.: 1858 - 1880), 25 January, p. 4, viewed 1 Oct 2020, http://nla.gov.au/nla.news-article75513998

1866 'ADVERTISING,' Warwick Argus and Tenterfield Chronicle (Qld.: 1866 - 1879), 28 March, pp. 3-4, viewed 08 Apr 2021, http://nla.gov.au/nla.news-article75666774

1866 'CAPT. THUNDERBOLT, ALIAS WARD, THE BUSHRANGER.', The Maitland Mercury and Hunter River General Advertiser (NSW : 1843 - 1893), 29 March, p. 2. , viewed 18 June 2025, http://nla.gov.au/nla.news-article18712031

1866 'GOVERNMENT NOTIFICATIONS.', The Queenslander (Brisbane, Qld. : 1866 - 1939), 15 December, p. 7. , viewed 15 May 2025, http://nla.gov.au/nla.news-article20310900

1866 'TENDERS ACCEPTED FOR CARRYING MAILS,' The Toowoomba Chronicle and Queensland Advertiser (Qld.: 1861 - 1875), 12 December, p. 3, viewed 14 Nov 2020, http://nla.gov.au/nla.news-article212785519

1866 'THE LINE FROM HELIDON TO BIGGE'S CAMP.', The Queenslander (Brisbane, Qld. : 1866 - 1939), 7 April, p. 11. , viewed 03 June 2025, http://nla.gov.au/nla.news-article20307059

1866 'THE SKETCHER,' The Queenslander (Brisbane, Qld.: 1866 - 1939), 19 May, p. 12, viewed 18 Mar 2021, http://nla.gov.au/nla.news-article20307621

1866 'WARWICK,' Brisbane Courier (Qld.: 1864 - 1933), 6 July, p. 4, viewed 15 Mar 2021, https://trove.nla.gov.au/newspaper/article/1270518

1866 'WARWICK—COACHING,' The Queenslander (Brisbane, Qld.: 1866 - 1939), 7 July, p. 8, viewed 8 Apr 2021, http://nla.gov.au/nla.news-article20308488

1867 'CONVEYANCE OF MAILS,' New South Wales Government Gazette (Sydney, NSW: 1832 - 1900), 16 August, p. 1927, viewed 10 Dec 2020, http://nla.gov.au/nla.news-article225478251

1867 'PUGH'S QUEENSLAND ALMANAC, directory and law calendar'

1867 'TENTERFIELD,' The Armidale Express and New England General Advertiser (NSW: 1856 - 1861; 1863 - 1889; 1891 - 1954), 28 December, p. 3, viewed 17 Apr 2021, http://nla.gov.au/nla.news-article187932638

1867 'TENTERFIELD.', Clarence and Richmond Examiner and New England Advertiser (Grafton, NSW : 1859 - 1889), 26 February, p. 2. (Edition 2), viewed 21 May 2025, http://nla.gov.au/nla.news-article61887709

1867 'THE GERMAN BUSHRANGER.', Warwick Argus and Tenterfield Chronicle (Qld. : 1866 - 1879), 8 March, p. 2. , viewed 16 May 2025, http://nla.gov.au/nla.news-article75667427

1868 'JENKINS THE BUSHRANGER.', Warwick Examiner and Times (Qld. : 1867 - 1919), 4 July, p. 4. , viewed 16 May 2025, http://nla.gov.au/nla.news-article82096635

1868 'MONDAY, APRIL 13, 1868,' The Argus (Melbourne, Vic.: 1848 - 1957), 13 April, p. 4, viewed 8 Apr 2021, http://nla.gov.au/nla.news-article5813399

1868 'TENTERFIELD,' The Armidale Express and New England General Advertiser (NSW: 1856 - 1861; 1863 - 1889; 1891 - 1954), 27 June, p. 3, viewed 7 Nov 2020, http://nla.gov.au/nla.news-article187998671

1869 'CLASSIFIED ADVERTISING,' The Queenslander (Brisbane, Qld.: 1866 - 1939), 21 August, p. 12, viewed 7 Nov 2020, http://nla.gov.au/nla.news-article20325448

1869 'CONSEYANCE OF MALIS FOR 1870.', Warwick Examiner and Times (Qld. : 1867 - 1919), , viewed 11 Nov 2020, http://nla.gov.au/nla.news-article82098758

1869 'COUNTRY NEWS.', The Armidale Express and New England General Advertiser (NSW : 1856 - 1861; 1863 - 1889; 1891 - 1954), 4 December, p. 3. , viewed 16 June 2025, http://nla.gov.au/nla.news-article189960844

1869 'MAIL CONTRACTS.', Dalby Herald and Western Queensland Advertiser (Qld. : 1866 - 1879), 11 December, p. 2. , viewed 08 Nov 2024, http://nla.gov.au/nla.news-article215450543

1870 'ADVERTISING,' Warwick Examiner and Times (Qld.: 1867 - 1919), 20 August, p. 1, viewed 1 Oct 2020, http://nla.gov.au/nla.news-article82099789

1870 'CHRONICLE OF OCCURRENCES,' The Sydney Morning Herald (NSW: 1842 - 1954), 31 December, p. 4, viewed 26 Mar 2021, http://nla.gov.au/nla.news-page1457486

1870 'CLASSIFIED ADVERTISING', The Brisbane Courier (Qld. : 1864 - 1933), 31 January, p. 1. , viewed 19 June 2025, http://nla.gov.au/nla.news-article1308293

1870 'CLASSIFIED ADVERTISING,' The Brisbane Courier (Qld.: 1864 - 1933), 25 July, p. 1, viewed 14 Nov 2020, http://nla.gov.au/nla.news-article1324252

1870 'CLASSIFIED ADVERTISING,' The Brisbane Courier (Qld.: 1864 - 1933), 18 November, p. 1, viewed 14 Nov 2020, http://nla.gov.au/nla.news-article1334553

1870 'FROM GOVERNMENT GAZETTE, 18TH OCTOBER, 1870.', New South Wales Police Gazette and Weekly Record of Crime (Sydney : 1860 - 1930), 26 October, p. 288. , viewed 21 May 2025, http://nla.gov.au/nla.news-article252049728

1870 'GOVERNMENT GAZETTE NOTICES,' New South Wales Government Gazette (Sydney, NSW: 1832 - 1900), 17 January, p. 116, viewed 7 Nov 2020, http://nla.gov.au/nla.news-article223285182

1870 'TENTERFIELD,' The Armidale Express and New England General Advertiser (NSW: 1856 - 1861; 1863 - 1889; 1891 - 1954), 21 May, p. 2, viewed 25 Nov 2020, http://nla.gov.au/nla.news-article189961243

1870 'THE COURIER.', The Brisbane Courier (Qld. : 1864 - 1933), 28 January, p. 2. , viewed 16 June 2025, http://nla.gov.au/nla.news-article1308088

1871 'ADVERTISING,' The Sydney Morning Herald (NSW: 1842 - 1954), 30 December, p. 8, viewed 10 Dec 2020, http://nla.gov.au/nla.news-article28417108

1871 'BRISBANE,' Maryborough Chronicle, Wide Bay and Burnett Advertiser (Qld.: 1860 - 1947), 21 January, p. 2, viewed 18 Mar 2021, http://nla.gov.au/nla.news-article148035851

1871 'GOULBURN POLICE COURT—DECREASE OF CRIME IN THE COLONY,' The Goulburn Herald and Chronicle (NSW: 1864 - 1881), 14 October, p. 3, http://nla.gov.au/nla.news-article101096942

1871 'RUNS OF CROWN LANDS.', New South Wales Government Gazette (Sydney, NSW : 1832 - 1900), 31 October, p. 2495. , viewed 26 Jul 2023, http://nla.gov.au/nla.news-article223718575

1871 'TENTERFIELD,' Clarence and Richmond Examiner and New England Advertiser (Grafton, NSW: 1859 - 1889), 21 November, p. 2, viewed 7 Nov 2020, http://nla.gov.au/nla.news-article61878368

1871 'THE MAIL SERVICE,' The Brisbane Courier (Qld.: 1864 - 1933), 13 November, p. 3, viewed 11 Dec 2020, http://nla.gov.au/nla.news-article1320712

1871 'THE TENTERFIELD ROAD,' The Brisbane Courier (Qld.: 1864 - 1933), 27 January, p. 3, viewed 25 Nov 2020, http://nla.gov.au/nla.news-article1303410

1872 TIN MINING AT QUART POT CREEK.' Warwick Examiner and Times (Qld. : 1867 - 1919), 30 March, p. 2. , viewed 17 May 2025, http://nla.gov.au/nla.news-article82102136

1872 'A TRIP TO THE TIN MINES,' Clarence and Richmond Examiner and New England Advertiser (Grafton, NSW: 1859 - 1889), 3 December, p. 3, viewed 8 Nov 2020, http://nla.gov.au/nla.news-article61880091

1872 'A TRIP TO THE TIN MINES.', The Armidale Express and New England General Advertiser (NSW : 1856 - 1861; 1863 - 1889; 1891 - 1954), 23 November, p. 3. , viewed 19 June 2025, http://nla.gov.au/nla.news-article188988565

1872 'ADVERTISING,' Empire (Sydney, NSW: 1850 - 1875), 19 October, p. 1, viewed 7 Nov 2020, http://nla.gov.au/nla.news-article60866979. State Library of New South Wales.

1872 'ANSWERS TO CORRESPONDENTS.', Australian Town and Country Journal (Sydney, NSW : 1870 - 1919), 28 December, p. 8. , viewed 21 May 2025, http://nla.gov.au/nla.news-article70499336

1872 'AT THE TIN MINES—WARWICK TO STANTHORPE,' The Brisbane Courier (Qld.: 1864 - 1933), 11 November, p. 3, viewed 27 Nov 2020, http://nla.gov.au/nla.news-article1300982

1872 'AUSTRALIAN TIN.', The Queenslander (Brisbane, Qld. : 1866 - 1939), 27 April, p. 6. , viewed 09 June 2025, http://nla.gov.au/nla.news-article27270710

1872 'EPITOME OF NEWS,' The Armidale Express and New England General Advertiser (NSW: 1856 - 1861; 1863 - 1889; 1891 - 1954), 23 November, p. 2, viewed 7 Nov 2020, http://nla.gov.au/nla.news-article188988566

1872 'MINING.', Empire (Sydney, NSW : 1850 - 1875), 30 December, p. 3. , viewed 24 May 2025, http://nla.gov.au/nla.news-article60869847

1872 'NEW ENGLAND.', The Maitland Mercury and Hunter River General Advertiser (NSW : 1843 - 1893), 11 April, p. 4. , viewed 03 June 2025, http://nla.gov.au/nla.news-article18762658

1872 'NEWS FROM THE TIN MINES,' The Brisbane Courier (Qld.: 1864 - 1933), 11 March, p. 3, viewed 15 Nov 2020, http://nla.gov.au/nla.news-article1315836

1872 'QUART POT, SUGARLOAF, AND RUBY CREEK TIN MINES.', Australian Town and Country Journal (Sydney, NSW : 1870 - 1919), 20 July, p. 15. , viewed 24 May 2025, http://nla.gov.au/nla.news-article70495955

1872 'QUARTPOT AND RUBY CREEKS REVISITED,' The Armidale Express and New England General Advertiser (NSW: 1856 - 1861; 1863 - 1889; 1891 - 1954), 9 November, p. 2, viewed 7 Nov 2020, http://nla.gov.au/nla.news-article188988465

1872 'QUEENSLAND JOTTINGS,' Australian Town and Country Journal (Sydney, NSW: 1870 - 1907), 21 December, p. 18, viewed 1 Oct 2020, http://nla.gov.au/nla.news-article70499222

1872 'STANNUM-CUM-STANTHORPE.', The Darling Downs Gazette and General Advertiser (Toowoomba, Qld. : 1858 - 1880), 3 July, p. 3. , viewed 24 May 2025, http://nla.gov.au/nla.news-article75528796

1872 'STANTHORPE,' The Darling Downs Gazette and General Advertiser (Toowoomba, Qld.: 1858 - 1880), 7 August, p. 3, viewed 16 Nov 2020, http://nla.gov.au/nla.news-article75527904

1872 'STANTHORPE,' Toowoomba Chronicle and Queensland Advertiser (Qld.: 1861 - 1875), 30 November, p. 3, viewed 30 Mar 2021, https://trove.nla.gov.au/newspaper/article/212792014

1872 'STANTHORPE.', The Darling Downs Gazette and General Advertiser (Toowoomba, Qld. : 1858 - 1880), 26 June, p. 3. , viewed 19 June 2025, http://nla.gov.au/nla.news-article75527943

1872 'STANTHORPE.', The Toowoomba Chronicle and Queensland Advertiser (Qld. : 1861 - 1875), 7 September, p. 2. , viewed 18 May 2025, http://nla.gov.au/nla.news-article212789736

1872 'STANTHORPE.', Dalby Herald and Western Queensland Advertiser (Qld. : 1866 - 1879), 10 August, p. 3. , viewed 05 June 2025, http://nla.gov.au/nla.news-article215604102

1872 'STANTHORPE.', Queensland Times, Ipswich Herald and General Advertiser (Qld. : 1861 - 1908), 27 June, p. 3. , viewed 24 May 2025, http://nla.gov.au/nla.news-article123618507

1872 'TENTERFIELD TO STANTHORPE,' The Sydney Mail and New South Wales Advertiser (NSW: 1871 - 1912), 20 July, p. 74, viewed 13 Apr 2021, http://nla.gov.au/nla.news-article162668606

1872 'TENTERFIELD TO STANTHORPE,' The Sydney Morning Herald (NSW: 1842 - 1954), 17 July, p. 9, viewed 11 Dec 2020, http://nla.gov.au/nla.news-article13260663

1872 'TENTERFIELD TO STANTHORPE.', The Maitland Mercury and Hunter River General Advertiser (NSW : 1843 - 1893), 20 July, p. 5. , viewed 18 June 2025, http://nla.gov.au/nla.news-article18765285

1872 'TENTERFIELD,' The Armidale Express and New England General Advertiser (NSW: 1856 - 1861; 1863 - 1889; 1891 - 1954), 31 August, p. 6, viewed 11 Dec 2020, http://nla.gov.au/nla.news-article188988020

1872 'TENTERFIELD,' The Armidale Express and New England General Advertiser (NSW: 1856 - 1861; 1863 - 1889; 1891 - 1954), 28 September, p. 6, viewed 7 Nov 2020, http://nla.gov.au/nla.news-article188988192

1872 'TENTERFIELD,' The Goulburn Herald and Chronicle (NSW: 1864 - 1881), 17 February, p. 3, viewed 7 Nov 2020, http://nla.gov.au/nla.news-article101094498

1872 'TENTERFIELD.', The Armidale Express and New England General Advertiser (NSW : 1856 - 1861; 1863 - 1889; 1891 - 1954), 9 November, p. 6. , viewed 21 May 2025, http://nla.gov.au/nla.news-article188988456

1872 'TENTERFIELD.', The Armidale Express and New England General Advertiser (NSW : 1856 - 1861; 1863 - 1889; 1891 - 1954), 24 August, p. 6. , viewed 11 Dec 2020, http://nla.gov.au/nla.news-article188987987

1872 'THE MARYLAND TIN DISCOVERIES,' Queensland Times, Ipswich Herald and General Advertiser (Qld.: 1861 - 1908), 19 March, p. 3, viewed 7 Nov 2020, http://nla.gov.au/nla.news-article123622027

1872 'THE TIN COUNTRY.', The Brisbane Courier (Qld. : 1864 - 1933), 4 May, p. 6. , viewed 21 May 2025, http://nla.gov.au/nla.news-article1306297

1872 'THE TIN MINES,' The Maitland Mercury and Hunter River General Advertiser (NSW: 1843 - 1893), 22 February, p. 3, viewed 16 Nov 2020, http://nla.gov.au/nla.news-article18761416

1872 'THE TIN MINES.', The Brisbane Courier (Qld. : 1864 - 1933), 28 May, p. 3. , viewed 05 June 2025, http://nla.gov.au/nla.news-article1332827

1872 'TIN AND COPPER MINING,' The Maitland Mercury and Hunter River General Advertiser (NSW.: 1843 - 1893), 9 July, p. 3, viewed 15 Nov 2020, http://nla.gov.au/nla.news-article18764991

1872 'TIN MINING AT QUART POT CREEK.', Warwick Examiner and Times (Qld. : 1867 - 1919), 30 March, p. 2. , viewed 17 May 2025, http://nla.gov.au/nla.news-article82102136

1872 'VISIT OF THE PREMIER TO THE NORTHERN DISTRICTS.', The Sydney Morning Herald (NSW : 1842 - 1954), 23 October, p. 5. , viewed 08 June 2025, http://nla.gov.au/nla.news-article13265282

1872 'WARWICK,' The Brisbane Courier (Qld.: 1864 - 1933), 1 November, p. 3, viewed 9 Apr 2021, http://nla.gov.au/nla.news-article1300140

1873 'A SCAMPER OVER THE TIN MINES NEAR TENTERFIELD,' The Sydney Morning Herald (NSW: 1842 - 1954), 24 February, p. 12, viewed 10 Dec 2020, http://nla.gov.au/nla.news-article13321817

1873 'CHRISTMAS EVE IN A CHURCH, AND WHAT CAME OF IT,' South Australian Register (Adelaide, SA: 1839 - 1900), 26 Dec, p. 6, viewed 25 Jan 2023, http://nla.gov.au/nla.news-article39297288

1873 'COUNTRY NEWS.', The Armidale Express and New England General Advertiser (NSW : 1856 - 1861; 1863 - 1889; 1891 - 1954), 24 May, p. 6. , viewed 24 May 2025, http://nla.gov.au/nla.news-article189987298

1873 'GOVERNMENT GAZETTE TENDERS AND CONTRACTS,' New South Wales Government Gazette (Sydney, NSW: 1832 - 1900), 16 January, p. 151, http://nla.gov.au/nla.news-article230046802

1873 'MY FIRST VISIT TO QUEENSLAND,' Empire (Sydney, NSW.: 1850 - 1875), 8 September, p. 4, viewed 11 Dec 2020, http://nla.gov.au/nla.news-article63234758

1873 'NEW ENGLAND,' The Maitland Mercury and Hunter River General Advertiser (NSW.: 1843 - 1893), 24 April, p. 3, viewed 27 Nov 2020, http://nla.gov.au/nla.news-article18773021

1873 'PUGH'S ALMANACS 1862-1866', Issue 1873

1873 'STANTHORPE.', The Toowoomba Chronicle and Queensland Advertiser (Qld. : 1861 - 1875), 29 March, p. 3. , viewed 12 June 2025, http://nla.gov.au/nla.news-article212789405

1873 'TENTERFIELD.', The Armidale Express and New England General Advertiser (NSW : 1856 - 1861; 1863 - 1889; 1891 - 1954), 1 February, p. 3. , viewed 21 May 2025, http://nla.gov.au/nla.news-article189986701

1874 'ADVERTISING,' The Sydney Morning Herald (NSW: 1842 - 1954), 21 November, p. 2, viewed 7 Nov 2020, http://nla.gov.au/nla.news-article13335823

1874 'AFFAIRS AT STANTHORPE.', Warwick Examiner and Times (Qld. : 1867 - 1919), 7 March, p. 2. , viewed 19 June 2025, http://nla.gov.au/nla.news-article82104434

1874 'CONVEYANCE OF MAILS,' New South Wales Government Gazette (Sydney, NSW: 1832 - 1900), 8 May, p. 1415, viewed 7 Nov 2020, http://nla.gov.au/nla.news-article224724801

1874 'GOVERNMENT GAZETTE TENDERS AND CONTRACTS,' New South Wales Government Gazette (Sydney, NSW: 1832 - 1900), 19 January, p. 174-176, http://nla.gov.au/nla.news-article223691545

1874 'PUGH'S ALMANACS, 1862-1866', Issue 1874

1874 'STANNUM NOTES.', The Telegraph (Brisbane, Qld. : 1872 - 1947), 9 March, p. 3. , viewed 24 May 2025, http://nla.gov.au/nla.news-article169517240

1874 'STANTHORPE.', The Telegraph (Brisbane, Qld. : 1872 - 1947), 3 January, p. 2. , viewed 19 June 2025, http://nla.gov.au/nla.news-article169519469

1874 'STANTHORPE.', The Queenslander (Brisbane, Qld. : 1866 - 1939), 28 February, p. 10. , viewed 24 May 2025, http://nla.gov.au/nla.news-article18329827

1874 'STANTHORPE.', The Telegraph (Brisbane, Qld. : 1872 - 1947), 4 June, p. 3. , viewed 05 June 2025, http://nla.gov.au/nla.news-article169519714

1874 'SUMMARY FOR EUROPE,' The Darling Downs Gazette and General Advertiser (Toowoomba, Qld.: 1858 - 1880), 12 September, p. 3, viewed 11 Apr 2021, http://nla.gov.au/nla.news-article75469122

1874 'THE COURIER.', Brisbane Courier (Qld. : 1864 - 1933) 1874, 24 February, Qld., p. 2. https://trove.nla.gov.au/newspaper/article/1379624?searchTerm=1874%20cobb%20and%20co.%20warwick

1874 'THE TOURIST,' The Sydney Mail and New South Wales Advertiser (NSW: 1871 - 1912), 27 June, p. 816, viewed 7 Nov 2020, http://nla.gov.au/nla.news-article162479958

1875 'ADVERTISING,' Queensland Times, Ipswich Herald and General Advertiser (Qld.: 1861 - 1908), 7 August, p. 2, viewed 14 Nov 2020, http://nla.gov.au/nla.news-article122071084

1875 'CLASSIFIED ADVERTISING,' The Brisbane Courier (Qld.: 1864 - 1933), 7 August, p. 7, viewed 7 Nov 2020, http://nla.gov.au/nla.news-article1379942

1875 'COBB & CO.,' Gympie Times and Mary River Mining Gazette (Qld.: 1868 - 1919), 5 May, p. 4, viewed 10 Dec 2020, http://nla.gov.au/nla.news-article168911735

1875 'COBB'S BOX,' Wagga Wagga Advertiser and Riverine Reporter (NSW: 1868 - 1875), 6 February, p. 4, viewed 18 Jan 2023, http://nla.gov.au/nla.news-article104117694

1875 'COBB'S BOX,' Whitworth, R.P. (and Percy Robert), Collection – State Library of NSW. Call numbers MJ 2 S 37, DSM/A823/W [online] https://collection.sl.nsw.gov.au/digital/oxxPKjDooXWvE [Accessed 17 Nov 2020]

1875 'CONVEYANCE OF MAILS,' New South Wales Government Gazette (Sydney, NSW: 1832 - 1900), 13 January, p. 97, viewed 10 Dec 2020, http://nla.gov.au/nla.news-article223652288

1875 'CONVEYANCE OF MAILS,' New South Wales Government Gazette (Sydney, NSW: 1832 - 1900), 1 October, p. 3057, viewed 10 Dec 2020, http://nla.gov.au/nla.news-article223585248

1875 'GOVERNMENT GAZETTE TENDERS AND CONTRACTS,' New South Wales Government Gazette (Sydney, NSW: 1832 - 1900), 13 January, p. 97, viewed 11 Dec 2020, http://nla.gov.au/nla.news-article223652288

1875 'LATEST EUROPEAN INTELLIGENCE,' The Gundagai Times and Tumut, Adelong and Murrumbidgee District Advertiser (NSW: 1868 - 1931), 12 June, p. 3, viewed 14 Nov 2020, http://nla.gov.au/nla.news-article122757530

1875 'STANTHORPE,' The Queenslander (Brisbane, Qld.: 1866 - 1939), 31 July, p. 3, viewed 14 Apr 2021, https://trove.nla.gov.au/newspaper/article/18337221

1875 'TENTERFIELD,' Glen Innes Examiner and General Advertiser (NSW: 1874 - 1908), 30 June, p. 2, viewed 1 Oct 2020, http://nla.gov.au/nla.news-article217833322

1875 'TENTERFIELD,' Glen Innes Examiner and General Advertiser (NSW: 1874 - 1908), 25 August, pp. 2-3, viewed 1 Oct 2020, http://nla.gov.au/nla.news-article217834526

1875 'THE TIN MINES.', The Queenslander (Brisbane, Qld. : 1866 - 1939), 3 April, p. 6. , viewed 24 May 2025, http://nla.gov.au/nla.news-article18335468

1876 'GOVERNMENT GAZETTE NOTICES,' New South Wales Government Gazette (Sydney, NSW: 1832 - 1900), 13 September, p. 3659, viewed 18 Mar 2021, https://trove.nla.gov.au/newspaper/article/224731349

1876 'LOCAL AND GENERAL ITEMS.', Warwick Argus and Tenterfield Chronicle (Qld. : 1866 - 1879), 20 April, p. 2. , viewed 20 May 2025, http://nla.gov.au/nla.news-article75830180

1876 'TIN MINING.', The Week (Brisbane, Qld. : 1876 - 1934), 10 June, p. 18. , viewed 19 June 2025, http://nla.gov.au/nla.news-article184999972

1877 'CLASSIFIED ADVERTISING,' The Brisbane Courier (Qld.: 1864 - 1933), 7 July, p. 8, viewed 8 Nov 2020, http://nla.gov.au/nla.news-article1364871

1877 'GOVERNMENT GAZETTE TENDERS AND CONTRACTS,' New South Wales Government Gazette (Sydney, NSW: 1832 - 1900), 20 January, p. 315, viewed 18 Mar 2021, https://trove.nla.gov.au/newspaper/article/223126946

1877 'LOCAL NEWS', The Maitland Mercury and Hunter River General Advertiser (NSW : 1843 - 1893), 6 March, p. 5. , viewed 20 May 2025, http://nla.gov.au/nla.news-article18816262

1877 'TENTERFIELD,' The Armidale Express and New England General Advertiser (NSW: 1856 - 1861; 1863 - 1889; 1891 - 1954), 5 January, p. 6, viewed 11 Dec 2020, http://nla.gov.au/nla.news-article188959464

1877 'WARWICK.', The Ipswich Observer and West Moreton Advocate (Qld. : 1870 - 1879), 24 April, p. 2. , viewed 18 May 2025, http://nla.gov.au/nla.news-article285133058

1878 'COUNTRY NEWS,' The Sydney Mail and New South Wales Advertiser (NSW: 1871 - 1912), 19 October, p. 633, viewed 10 Dec 2020, http://nla.gov.au/nla.news-article162694897

1878 'DEATH OF THE FOUNDER OF COBB AND Co.', The Goulburn Herald and Chronicle (NSW : 1864 - 1881), 28 September, p. 3. , viewed 18 June 2025, http://nla.gov.au/nla.news-article100879416

1878 'GENERAL INTELLIGENCE.', Glen Innes Examiner and General Advertiser (NSW : 1874 - 1908), 10 December, p. 2. , viewed 08 June 2025, http://nla.gov.au/nla.news-article217825871

1878 'GOVERNMENT GAZETTE TENDERS AND CONTRACTS—CONVEYANCE OF MAILS,' NSW Government Gazette (Sydney, NSW: 1832 - 1900), 23 January, p. 328, viewed 8 Nov 2020, http://nla.gov.au/nla.news-article224593283

1878 'MARSUPIAL BILL; OR THE BAD BOY, THE GOOD DOG, AND THE OLD MAN KANGAROO.', The Queenslander (Brisbane, Qld. : 1866 - 1939), 21 December, p. 20. (Unknown), viewed 09 June 2025, http://nla.gov.au/nla.news-article19778053

1878 'MARYLAND,' The Sydney Mail and New South Wales Advertiser (NSW: 1871 - 1912), 1 June, p. 780, viewed 1 Oct 2020, http://nla.gov.au/nla.news-article162690995 State Library of New South Wales.

1878 'SITE FOR A VILLAGE AT LISTON,' New South Wales Government Gazette (Sydney, NSW: 1832 - 1900), 8 July, p. 2654, viewed 18 Mar 2021

1878 'TALK ON 'CHANGE,' The Australasian (Melbourne, Vic.: 1864 - 1946), 21 September, p. 17, viewed 27 Nov 2020, http://nla.gov.au/nla.news-article143001218

1878 'TENTERFIELD', The Week (Brisbane, Qld. : 1876 - 1934), 2 March, p. 21. , viewed 14 Apr 2021, http://nla.gov.au/nla.news-article181817870

1878 'THE SILVER MINES NEAR TENTERFIELD.', The Sydney Morning Herald (NSW : 1842 - 1954), 27 June, p. 6. , viewed 08 June 2025, http://nla.gov.au/nla.news-article13411685

1878 'WARWICK POST OFFICE.', Warwick Examiner and Times (Qld. : 1867 - 1919), 20 July, p. 6. , viewed 16 May 2025, http://nla.gov.au/nla.news-article82121285

1879 'CONVEYANCE OF MAILS.', New South Wales Government Gazette (Sydney, NSW : 1832 - 1900), 17 October, p. 4592. , viewed 20 May 2025, http://nla.gov.au/nla.news-article223122408

1879 'DESTRUCTIVE FIRE AT MARYLAND STATION,' Evening News (Sydney, NSW: 1869 - 1931), 11 July, p. 4, viewed 10 Dec 2020, http://nla.gov.au/nla.news-article107165893

1879 'GOVERNMENT GAZETTE NOTICES,' New South Wales Government Gazette (Sydney, NSW: 1832 - 1900), 31 October, pp. 4873–4877, viewed 10 Dec 2020, http://nla.gov.au/nla.news-article223123215

1879 'GOVERNMENT GAZETTE TENDERS AND CONTRACTS,' New South Wales Government Gazette (Sydney, NSW: 1832 - 1900), 13 January, p. 181, viewed 9 Nov 2020, http://nla.gov.au/nla.news-article223657040

1879 'GOVERNOR BRISBANE.', The Sydney Mail and New South Wales Advertiser (NSW : 1871 - 1912), 25 January, p. 133. , viewed 16 May 2025, http://nla.gov.au/nla.news-article162809789

1879 'LOCAL AND GENERAL NEWS,' Warwick Examiner and Times (Qld.: 1867 - 1919), 30 August, p. 2, viewed 3 Oct 2020, http://nla.gov.au/nla.news-article82115480

1879 'THE IRON ROAD TO STANTHORPE,' Warwick Argus (Qld.: 1879 - 1901), 18 October, p. 2, viewed 5 Nov 2020, http://nla.news-article82293913

1879 'WEDNESDAY, OCTOBER 15, 1879,' The Morning Bulletin (Rockhampton, Qld.: 1878 - 1954), 15 October, p. 2, viewed 9 Apr 2021, http://nla.gov.au/nla.news-article51981449. The National Library of Australia.

1880 'ADVERTISING', Warwick Examiner and Times (Qld. : 1867 - 1919), 3 January, p. 1. , viewed 03 June 2025, http://nla.gov.au/nla.news-article82116328

1880 'CLASSIFIED ADVERTISING,' The Brisbane Courier (Qld.: 1864 - 1933), 25 February, p. 4, viewed 10 Dec 2020, http://nla.gov.au/nla.news-article902998

1880 'GOVERNMENT GAZETTE TENDERS AND CONTRACTS,' New South Wales Government Gazette (Sydney, NSW: 1832 - 1900), 13 January, p. 202, viewed 23 Nov 2020, http://nla.gov.au/nla.news-article224186825

1880 'OFFICIAL NOTIFICATIONS.', The Brisbane Courier (Qld. : 1864 - 1933), 10 July, p. 6. , viewed 17 May 2025, http://nla.gov.au/nla.news-article884025

1880 'POST-OFFICE ROBBERY.', Evening News (Sydney, NSW : 1869 - 1931), 19 May, p. 2. , viewed 16 May 2025, http://nla.gov.au/nla.news-article108746261

1880 'TENTERFIELD.', The Armidale Express and New England General Advertiser (NSW : 1856 - 1861; 1863 - 1889; 1891 - 1954), 26 March, p. 6. , viewed 01 June 2025, http://nla.gov.au/nla.news-article192876865

1880 'THE WARWICK ARGUS.', Warwick Argus (Qld. : 1879 - 1901), 1 June, p. 2. , viewed 29 May 2025, http://nla.gov.au/nla.news-article82295355

1881 'ADVERTISING', The Telegraph (Brisbane, Qld. : 1872 - 1947), 28 March, p. 4. , viewed 11 Jan 2025, http://nla.gov.au/nla.news-article183375794

1881 'MINES AND MINING.', Australian Town and Country Journal (Sydney, NSW : 1870 - 1919), 24 September, p. 22. , viewed 09 June 2025, http://nla.gov.au/nla.news-article70960510

1881 'OPENING OF THE STANTHORPE RAILWAY.', The Telegraph (Brisbane, Qld. : 1872 - 1947), 3 May, p. 2. , viewed 18 June 2025, http://nla.gov.au/nla.news-article183374031

1882 'ADVERTISING,' The Sydney Morning Herald (NSW: 1842 - 1954), 9 September, p. 3, viewed 8 Nov 2020, http://nla.gov.au/nla.news-article13526187

1882 'FATAL AFFRAY AT WILSON'S DOWNFALL,' The Brisbane Courier (Qld.: 1864 - 1933), 12 September, p. 3, viewed 1 Oct 2020, http://nla.gov.au/nla.news-article3402801

1882 'FROM BRISBANE TO SYDNEY OVERLAND,' The Queenslander (Brisbane, Qld.: 1866 - 1939), 6 May, p. 556, viewed 7 Nov 2020, http://nla.gov.au/nla.news-article19784015

1882 'TENTERFIELD.', The Armidale Express and New England General Advertiser (NSW : 1856 - 1861; 1863 - 1889; 1891 - 1954), 15

September, p. 4. , viewed 07 June 2025, http://nla.gov.au/nla.news-article192856602

1882 'THE FATAL FRACAS AT WILLSON'S DOWNFALL.', Warwick Argus (Qld. : 1879 - 1901), 9 September, p. 3. , viewed 05 June 2025, http://nla.gov.au/nla.news-article75665234

1882 'THUNDERBOLT,' Evening News (Sydney, NSW: 1869 - 1931), 10 November, p. 2, viewed 19 Mar 2021, http://nla.gov.au/nla.news-article107994884

1882 'THUNDERBOLT,' Evening News (Sydney, NSW: 1869 - 1931), 15 November, p. 5, viewed 19 Mar 2021

1883 'BRISBANE TO MELBOURNE,' The Queenslander (Brisbane, Qld.: 1866 - 1939), 24 March, p. 453, viewed 8 Nov 2020, http://nla.gov.au/nla.news-article19790166

1883 'FISTIANA.', Queensland Figaro (Brisbane, Qld. : 1883 - 1885), 5 May, p. 7. , viewed 05 June 2025, http://nla.gov.au/nla.news-article83677229

1883 'GOVERNMENT NOTICES,' The Sydney Morning Herald (NSW: 1842 - 1954), 20 September, p. 3, viewed 8 Nov 2020, http://nla.gov.au/nla.news-article13545108

1883 'NO TITLE', The Sydney Daily Telegraph (NSW : 1879 -1883), 23 February, p. 2. , viewed 17 May 2025, http://nla.gov.au/nla.news-article238488811

1883 'OUR PURE MERINO STUD FLOCKS.', The Queenslander (Brisbane, Qld. : 1866 - 1939), 7 April, p. 551. , viewed 18 June 2025, http://nla.gov.au/nla.news-article19790413

1883 'TELEGRAPHIC INTELLIGENCE.', The Maitland Mercury and Hunter River General Advertiser (NSW : 1843 - 1893), 5 June, p. 3. , viewed 20 May 2025, http://nla.gov.au/nla.news-article904947

1884 'GOVERNMENT GAZETTE TENDERS AND CONTRACTS,' New South Wales Government Gazette (Sydney, NSW: 1832 - 1900), 21 January, p. 504, viewed 23 Nov 2020, http://nla.gov.au/nla.news-article222086121

1885 'ADVERTISING,' Darling Downs Gazette (Qld.: 1881 - 1922), 8 June, p. 2, viewed 2 Dec 2020, http://nla.gov.au/nla.news-article170829623 State Library of Queensland.

1885 'CONVEYANCE OF MAILS,' New South Wales Government Gazette (Sydney, NSW: 1832 - 1900), 22 September, p. 6164, viewed 23 Nov 2020, http://nla.gov.au/nla.news-article219878207

1885 'CONVEYANCE OF MAILS,' New South Wales Government Gazette (Sydney, NSW: 1832 - 1900), 7 November, p. 7214, viewed 10 Dec 2020, http://nla.gov.au/nla.news-article223762671

1885 'GEOGRAPHIC HISTORY OF QUEENSLAND', 1895, p.35

1885 'GOVERNMENT GAZETTE NOTICES,' New South Wales Government Gazette (Sydney, NSW: 1832 - 1900), 20 January, p. 621, viewed 11 Dec 2020, http://nla.gov.au/nla.news-article221623501

1885 'TELEGRAPH STATION AT DALVEEN.', Warwick Examiner and Times (Qld. : 1867 - 1919), 15 April, p. 2. , viewed 07 June 2025, http://nla.gov.au/nla.news-article82092569

1885 'THE STANTHORPE-BORDER EXTENSION.', The Telegraph (Brisbane, Qld. : 1872 - 1947), 28 May, p. 2. , viewed 19 June 2025, http://nla.gov.au/nla.news-article174159846

1885 'THE WARWICK ARGUS.', Warwick Argus (Qld. : 1879 - 1901), 22 December, p. 2. , viewed 07 June 2025, http://nla.gov.au/nla.news-article75845802

1886 'GOVERNMENT GAZETTE NOTICES,' New South Wales Government Gazette (Sydney, NSW: 1832 - 1900), 3 September, p. 6024, viewed 18 Mar 2021, https://trove.nla.gov.au/newspaper/article/222436364

1886 'OPENING OF THE GREAT NORTHERN (N.S.W.) RAILWAY TO TENTERFIELD.', Queensland Times, Ipswich Herald and General Advertiser (Qld. : 1861 - 1908), 21 October, p. 5. , viewed 07 June 2025, http://nla.gov.au/nla.news-article122555696

1886 'TENTERFIELD', Newcastle Morning Herald and Miners' Advocate (NSW : 1876 - 1954), 10 April, p. 2. , viewed 14 Apr 2021, http://nla.gov.au/nla.news-article138797899

1887 'A TRIP TO MARYLAND,' Warwick Argus (Qld.: 1879 - 1901), 15 January, p. 2, viewed 18 Mar 2021, http://nla.gov.au/nla.news-article76652871

1887 'CONVEYANCE OF MAILS,' New South Wales Government Gazette (Sydney, NSW: 1832 - 1900), 12 November, p. 7641, viewed 10 Dec 2020, http://nla.gov.au/nla.news-article219929208

1887 'NEWS IN BRIEF.', The Riverine Herald (Echuca, Vic. : Moama, NSW : 1869 - 1954; 1998 - 2002), 4 February, p. 2. , viewed 17 May 2025, http://nla.gov.au/nla.news-article114649750

1888 'CONFIRMATION OF PARISH ROADS,' New South Wales Government Gazette (Sydney, NSW: 1832 - 1900), 11 May, p. 3296, viewed 10 Dec 2020, http://nla.gov.au/nla.news-article222761219

1888 'COUNTRY NEWS.', The Queenslander (Brisbane, Qld. : 1866 - 1939), 24 November, p. 935. , viewed 20 May 2025, http://nla.gov.au/nla.news-article19937267

1888 'QUEENSLAND NEWS.', The Brisbane Courier (Qld. : 1864 - 1933), 23 February, p. 5. , viewed 29 May 2025, http://nla.gov.au/nla.news-article3468499

1889 'CONVEYANCE OF MAILS,' New South Wales Government Gazette (Sydney, NSW: 1832 - 1900), 1 October, p. 6854, viewed 10 Dec 2020, http://nla.gov.au/nla.news-article222100182

1889 'HISTORY OF NEW SOUTH WALES,' Balmain Observer and Western Suburbs Advertiser (NSW: 1884 - 1907), 5 October, p. 8, viewed 9 Nov 2020, http://nla.gov.au/nla.news-article132308080

1890 'ARMIDALE CIRCUIT COURT.', The Richmond River Herald and Northern Districts Advertiser (NSW : 1886 - 1942), 31 October, p. 4. , viewed 31 May 2025, http://nla.gov.au/nla.news-article127726606

1890 'CONVEYANCE OF MAILS,' New South Wales Government Gazette (Sydney, NSW: 1832 - 1900), 8 November, p. 8724, viewed 10 Dec 2020, http://nla.gov.au/nla.news-article221645722

1890 'GOULBURN RIVER.', The Maitland Mercury and Hunter River General Advertiser (NSW : 1843 - 1893), 11 December, p. 6. , viewed 19 June 2025, http://nla.gov.au/nla.news-article18990825

1890 'THUNDERBOLT,' The Richmond River Herald and Northern Districts Advertiser (NSW: 1886 - 1942), 26 September, p. 6, viewed 19 Mar 2021, http://nla.gov.au/nla.news-article127722828

1891 'CLASSIFIED ADVERTISING', The Queenslander (Brisbane, Qld. : 1866 - 1939), 29 August, p. 387. , viewed 16 Oct 2024, http://nla.gov.au/nla.news-article20295649

1891 'CONVEYANCE OF MAILS,' New South Wales Government Gazette (Sydney, NSW: 1832 - 1900), 6 November, p. 8861, viewed 10 Dec 2020, http://nla.gov.au/nla.news-article219923859

1891 'ECHOES AND OPINIONS.', Clarence and Richmond Examiner (Grafton, NSW : 1889 - 1915), 12 May, p. 2. , viewed 16 June 2025, http://nla.gov.au/nla.news-article61238087

1891 'NEW SOUTH WALES, AUSTRALIA CENSUS,' Ancestry.com [online] https://www.ancestry.com.au [Accessed 7 Dec. 2020]. (New South Wales, Australia Census, 1891)

1891 'THE INFLUENZA EPIDEMIC.', Evening News (Sydney, NSW : 1869 - 1931), 18 November, p. 5. , viewed 21 May 2025, http://nla.gov.au/nla.news-article111996909

1892 'CONVEYANCE OF MAILS,' New South Wales Government Gazette (Sydney, NSW: 1832 - 1900), 16 September, p. 7505, viewed 10 Dec 2020, http://nla.gov.au/nla.news-article222204850

1892 'LAND DISTRICT OF TENTERFIELD,' Government Gazette Sept–Oct. [online] https://www.ancestry.com.au, NSW Government [Accessed 7 Dec 2020]

1892 'NEWS OF THE DAY.', The Armidale Express and New England General Advertiser (NSW : 1856 - 1861; 1863 - 1889; 1891 - 1954), 25 October, p. 5. , viewed 20 May 2025, http://nla.gov.au/nla.news-article189977622

1892 'TENTERFIELD.', Australian Town and Country Journal (Sydney, NSW : 1870 - 1919), 19 March, p. 16. , viewed 07 June 2025, http://nla.gov.au/nla.news-article71235392

1893 'BATHURST FREE PRESS,' Magna [?] at [?]. Monday, July 17, 1893, Bathurst Free Press and Mining Journal (NSW: 1851 - 1904), 17 July, p. 2, viewed 18 Mar 2021, http://nla.gov.au/nla.news-article62183930

1893 'FATAL ACCIDENT AT STANTHORPE.', The Brisbane Courier (Qld. : 1864 - 1933), 28 February, p. 6. , viewed 19 June 2025, http://nla.gov.au/nla.news-article3556248

1894 'LOCAL AND GENERAL NEWS.', Queensland Times, Ipswich Herald and General Advertiser (Qld. : 1861 - 1908), 15 November, p. 4. , viewed 29 May 2025, http://nla.gov.au/nla.news-article123754008

1894 'TENDERS ACCEPTED.', Australian Town and Country Journal (Sydney, NSW : 1870 - 1919), 22 December, p. 18. , viewed 09 June 2025, http://nla.gov.au/nla.news-article71267683

1894 'TENTERFIELD' https://trove.nla.gov.au/newspaper/article/71213087/5240938

1895 'COBB And CO.,' Warwick Argus (Qld.: 1879 - 1901), 30 March, p. 4, viewed 18 Nov 2020, http://nla.gov.au/nla.news-article76649248

1895 'COUNTRY NOTES.', Evening News (Sydney, NSW : 1869 - 1931), 12 July, p. 3. , viewed 24 May 2025, http://nla.gov.au/nla.news-article109886204

1895 'DOWN THE DARLING IN A CANOE.', The Brisbane Courier (Qld. : 1864 - 1933), 7 December, p. 8. , viewed 05 June 2025, http://nla.gov.au/nla.news-article3614383

1895 'GEOGRAPHIC HISTORY OF QUEENSLAND,' Meston, Archibald. [online] Edmund Gregory, Government Printer, Brisbane. Available at: https://espace.library.uq.edu.au [Accessed 7 Dec 2020]. The University of Queensland.

1896 'THE BUSHRANGER.', Australian Town and Country Journal (Sydney, NSW : 1870 - 1919), 8 February, p. 10. , viewed 27 May 2025, http://nla.gov.au/nla.news-article71241687

1897 'COBB & CO.'S CATALOGUE OF HIGH CLASS VEHICLES,' One Search, State Library of Queensland, pp. 1–28, Record number 997321704702061. Available at: bishop.slq.qld.gov.au

1897 'QUEENSLAND', Newcastle Morning Herald and Miners' Advocate (NSW : 1876 - 1954), 4 June, p. 5. , viewed 16 May 2025, http://nla.gov.au/nla.news-article134884526

1897 'TOUR OF THE MINISTER FOR WORKS,' The Sydney Morning Herald (NSW.: 1842 - 1954), 25 September, p. 5, viewed 26 Mar 2021, http://nla.gov.au/nla.news-article28253189

1898 'WARD ALIAS THUNDERBOLT[?]', The Walcha Witness and Vernon County Record (NSW : 1895 - 1906), 1 January, p. 2. , viewed 19 June 2025, http://nla.gov.au/nla.news-article194098135

1899 'IPSWICH POST OFFICE TENDER', The Week (Brisbane, Qld. : 1876 - 1934), 22 September, p. 4. , viewed 18 May 2025, http://nla.gov.au/nla.news-article182875540

1899 'N.S.W. MAIL CONTRACTS,' Warwick Examiner and Times (Qld.: 1867 - 1919), 25 October, p. 2, viewed 7 Nov 2020, http://nla.gov.au/nla.news-article82144873

1899 'QUEENSLAND', Daily Telegraph (Launceston, Tas. : 1883 - 1928), 14 September, p. 2. , viewed 16 May 2025, http://nla.gov.au/nla.news-article154070896

1899 'THE IPSWICH POST-OFFICE.', Queensland Times, Ipswich Herald and General Advertiser (Qld. : 1861 - 1908), 23 May, p. 4. , viewed 18 May 2025, http://nla.gov.au/nla.news-article123161061

1899 'THE POST OFFICE BURGLARY.', The Age (Melbourne, Vic. : 1854 - 1954), 14 September, p. 6. , viewed 16 May 2025, http://nla.gov.au/nla.news-article188669842

1900 'QUEEN'S BIRTHDAY.', The Tenterfield Intercolonial Courier and Fairfield and Wallangarra Advocate (NSW : 1900 - 1914), 22 May, p. 2. , viewed 21 May 2025, http://nla.gov.au/nla.news-article108697020

1900 'THE TENTERFIELD.', The Tenterfield Intercolonial Courier and Fairfield and Wallangarra Advocate (NSW : 1900 - 1914), 11 September, p. 2. , viewed 09 June 2025, http://nla.gov.au/nla.news-article108698048

1900 'WILSON'S DOWNFALL,' The Tenterfield Intercolonial Courier and Fairfield and Wallangarra Advocate (NSW.: 1900 - 1914), 10 July, p. 2, viewed 12 Dec 2020, http://nla.gov.au/nla.news-article108697416

1901 'ADVERTISING', The Tenterfield Intercolonial Courier and Fairfield and Wallangarra Advocate (NSW : 1900 - 1914), 26 February, p. 3. , viewed 07 June 2025, http://nla.gov.au/nla.news-article108699476

1901 'LAND SALES.', Government Gazette of the State of New South Wales (Sydney, NSW : 1901 - 2001), 20 February, p. 1337. , viewed 19 June 2025, http://nla.gov.au/nla.news-article226375908

1901 'PUBLIC WORKS TENDER.', The Telegraph (Brisbane, Qld. : 1872 - 1947), 28 February, p. 4. (SECOND EDITION), viewed 16 May 2025, http://nla.gov.au/nla.news-article174946014

1901 'WILSON'S DOWNFALL—ANNUAL RACES,' The Tenterfield Intercolonial Courier and Fairfield and Wallangarra Advocate (NSW.: 1900 - 1914), 16 August, p. 2, viewed 6 Dec 2020, http://nla.gov.au/nla.news-article108701139

1902 'AN EVIDENCE OF THE DROUGHT,' Molong Express and Western District Advertiser (NSW: 1887 - 1954), 27 September, p. 1 (Supplement to the Molong Express), http://nla.gov.au/nla.news-article139545310

1902 'COBB AND CO.,' The Daily Telegraph (Sydney, NSW: 1883 - 1930), 15 May, p. 4, viewed 10 Dec 2020, http://nla.gov.au/nla.news-article237619124

1902 'CONTRACTS FOR THE CONVEYANCE OF MAILS IN THE STATE OF NEW SOUTH WALES,' Commonwealth of Australia Gazette (National: 1901 - 1973), 13 March, p. 113, viewed 10 Dec 2020, http://nla.gov.au/nla.news-article232346059 Office of Parliamentary Counsel.

1902 'MY LIFE IN MANY STATES AND IN FOREIGN LANDS,' Train, George Francis, pp. xxi. 340, D. Appleton, New York, SR 910.4 T768. The National Library of Australia (My Life in Many States and in Foreign Lands, 1902, pp.133–134)

1902 'STOPPAGE OF THE MAIL COACHES,' The Brisbane Courier (Qld.: 1864 - 1933), 14 May, p. 4, viewed 6 Dec 2020, http://nla.gov.au/nla.news-article19173709

1902 'THE EARLY DAYS. PIONEERS AND PIONEERING ON THE DARLING DOWNS.', The Toowoomba Chronicle (Qld. : 1902 - 1922), 10 July, p. 6. , viewed 18 May 2025, http://nla.gov.au/nla.news-article283946469

1902 'WILSON'S DOWNFALL,' The Tenterfield Intercolonial Courier and Fairfield and Wallangarra Advocate (NSW.: 1900 - 1914), 11 February, p. 2, viewed 6 Dec 2020, http://nla.gov.au/nla.news-article108702814

1903 'AUSTRALIAN ELECTORAL ROLLS', Ancestry.com

1903 'LICENSING COURT,' The Tenterfield Intercolonial Courier and Fairfield and Wallangarra Advocate (NSW: 1900 - 1914), 23 October, p. 2, viewed 18 Mar 2021, http://nla.gov.au/nla.news-article108691734

1903 'MAIL CONTRACTS,' The Tenterfield Intercolonial Courier and Fairfield and Wallangarra Advocate (NSW: 1900 - 1914), 27 October, p. 2, viewed 6 Nov 2020, http://nla.gov.au/nla.news-article108691769

1904 'BRISBANE POST OFFICE.', The Brisbane Courier (Qld. : 1864 - 1933), 19 April, p. 4. , viewed 16 May 2025, http://nla.gov.au/nla.news-article19276242

1904 'GEORGE FRANCIS TRAIN,' Daily News (Perth, WA: 1882 - 1950), 15 March, p. 3, viewed 10 Mar 2021, https://trove.nla.gov.au/newspaper/article/82412811

1904 'NO TITLE', The Toowoomba Chronicle (Qld. : 1902 - 1922), 25 October, p. 3. , viewed 07 June 2025, http://nla.gov.au/nla.news-article284222814

1904 'THE ARMIDALE CHRONICLE, 27 Aug 1904, p.8 – Source no longer accessible

1904 'THE DAYS OF COBB & CO.', The Hillston Spectator and Lachlan River Advertiser (NSW : 1898 - 1952), 4 March, p. 4. , viewed 18 June 2025, http://nla.gov.au/nla.news-article131373737 1925 'Cobb and Company's Coaches.', Country Life Stock and Station Journal (Sydney, NSW : 1924 - 1925), 10 April, p. 28. , viewed 20 May 2025, http://nla.gov.au/nla.news-article128647626

1904 'THE DAYS OF COBB & CO.', Nepean Times (Penrith, NSW : 1882 - 1962), 23 April, p. 2. , viewed 28 May 2025, http://nla.gov.au/nla.news-article100950588

1904 'WILSON'S DOWNFALL,' The Tenterfield Intercolonial Courier and Fairfield and Wallangarra Advocate (NSW.: 1900 - 1914), 14 October, p. 2, viewed 2 Oct 2020, http://nla.gov.au/nla.news-article108694481

1905 'IN AND AROUND TENTERFIELD,' Australian Town and Country Journal (Sydney, NSW: 1870 - 1919), 8 November, pp. 28–33, viewed 18 Mar 2021, http://nla.gov.au/nla.news-article71536544

1905 'OUR INDUSTRIES.', The Sydney Morning Herald (NSW : 1842 - 1954), 11 February, p. 12. , viewed 07 June 2025, http://nla.gov.au/nla.news-article14691324

1905 'THE INTERFIELD Intercolonial Courier. And Fairfield & Wallangarra Advocate', The Tenterfield Intercolonial Courier and Fairfield and Wallangarra Advocate (NSW : 1900 - 1914), 1 August, p. 2. , viewed 07 June 2025, http://nla.gov.au/nla.news-article108705803

1905 'THE NEW SOUTH WALES POST OFFICE DIRECTORY,' Call Number N 919.44 WIS Created/Published Sydney. Available at: http://nla.gov.au/nla.obj-518308191, Sydney: Wise's Directories, 1887-1908, Call Number N 919.44 WIS

1905 'WILSON'S DOWNFALL,' The Tenterfield Intercolonial Courier and Fairfield and Wallangarra Advocate (NSW.: 1900 - 1914), 3 October, p. 2, viewed 6 Dec 2020, http://nla.gov.au/nla.news-article108706370

1906 'BOONOO BOONOO.', The Tenterfield Intercolonial Courier and Fairfield and Wallangarra Advocate (NSW : 1900 - 1914), 2 October, p. 3. , viewed 21 May 2025, http://nla.gov.au/nla.news-article108709215

1906 'CONVEYANCE OF MAILS IN QUEENSLAND.', Commonwealth of Australia Gazette (National : 1901 - 1973), 8 December, p. 1518. , viewed 09 Jan 2025, http://nla.gov.au/nla.news-article232352630

1906 'FIRE AT AMOSFIELD—PUBLIC SCHOOL DESTROYED,' The Tenterfield Intercolonial Courier and Fairfield and Wallangarra Advocate (NSW: 1900 - 1914), 27 April, p. 2, http://nla.gov.au/nla.news-article108707951

1906 'GAZETTE NOTICES.', The Tenterfield Intercolonial Courier and Fairfield and Wallangarra Advocate (NSW : 1900 - 1914), 8 May, p. 2. , viewed 31 May 2025, http://nla.gov.au/nla.news-article108708021

1906 'LONGREACH.', Morning Bulletin (Rockhampton, Qld. : 1878 - 1954), 25 September, p. 3. , viewed 29 May 2025, http://nla.gov.au/nla.news-article53077961

1906 'WILSON'S DOWNFALL—BANQUET TO MR. T. OLVER AND MR. T. A. CAMPION,' The Tenterfield Intercolonial Courier and Fairfield and Wallangarra Advocate (NSW: 1900 - 1914), 14 December, p. 3, viewed 12 Dec 2020, http://nla.gov.au/nla.news-article108709721

1907 'A NOVEL STORM.', The Walcha News and Southern New England Advocate (NSW : 1904 - 1907; 1927), 16 February, p. 6. , viewed 21 May 2025, http://nla.gov.au/nla.news-article191216331

1907 'LOCAL AND GENERAL NEWS.', The Richmond River Herald and Northern Districts Advertiser (NSW : 1886 - 1942), 11 January, p. 9. , viewed 25 May 2025, http://nla.gov.au/nla.news-article12/869331

1907 'MESSES. COBB AND CO.,' The Capricornian (Rockhampton, Qld.: 1875 - 1929), 23 March, p. 34, viewed 1 Feb 2023, http://nla.gov.au/nla.news-article71898945

1907 'MESSRS. COBB AND CO.,' Morning Bulletin (Rockhampton, Qld.: 1878 - 1954), 18 March, p. 4, viewed 19 Mar 2021, http://nla.gov.

au/nla.news-article53093071

1907 'OUR SYDNEY LETTER.', Newcastle Morning Herald and Miners' Advocate (NSW : 1876 - 1954), 30 May, p. 5. , viewed 06 June 2025, http://nla.gov.au/nla.news-article133870301

1908 'ACTA POPULI.', Freeman's Journal (Sydney, NSW : 1850 - 1932), 21 May, p. 32. , viewed 08 June 2025, http://nla.gov.au/nla.news-article109866478

1908 'ADVERTISING', Freeman's Journal (Sydney, NSW : 1850 - 1932), 21 May, p. 5. , viewed 07 June 2025, http://nla.gov.au/nla.news-article109866395

1908 'ORANGE BLOSSOMS,', The Tenterfield Intercolonial Courier and Fairfield and Wallangarra Advocate (NSW : 1900 - 1914), 2 October, p. 2. , viewed 19 June 2025, http://nla.gov.au/nla.news-article128234545

1908 'SPECIAL LICENSING COURT,' The Richmond River Express and Casino Kyogle Advertiser (NSW: 1904 - 1929), 26 June, p. 8, viewed 18 Mar 2021, http://nla.gov.au/nla.news-article123975203 State Library of New South Wales.

1908 'SPECIAL LICENSING COURT,' The Tenterfield Intercolonial Courier and Fairfield and Wallangarra Advocate (NSW: 1900 - 1914), 23 June, p. 2, viewed 11 Apr 2021, http://nla.gov.au/nla.news-article128233507

1908 'THE CONTRIBUTOR', The Sydney Mail and New South Wales Advertiser (NSW : 1871 - 1912), 25 November, p. 1405. , viewed 26 Jul 2023, http://nla.gov.au/nla.news-article163229756

1909 'CONVEYANCE OF MAIL IN NEW SOUTH WALES,' Commonwealth of Australia Gazette (National: 1901 - 1973), 8 May, p. 1094, http://trove.nla.gov.au/newspaper/article/232353864/24990994

1909 'HOLSMAN MOTOR BUGGY,' The Maitland Daily Mercury (NSW: 1894 - 1939), 23 March, p. 5, viewed 18 Mar 2021, http://nla.gov.au/nla.news-article124462464

1909 'QUEENSLAND'S HALF CENTURY 1859 TO 1909 NOTABLE EVENTS', The Brisbane Courier (Qld. : 1864 - 1933), 8 December, p. 23. (Queensland's Half Century), viewed 20 May 2025, http://nla.gov.au/nla.news-article19579953

1909 'STANTHORPE NEWS.', The Brisbane Courier (Qld. : 1864 - 1933), 10 April, p. 5. , viewed 07 June 2025, http://nla.gov.au/nla.news-article19572342

1910 'ADVERTISING', The Tenterfield Intercolonial Courier and Fairfield and Wallangarra Advocate (NSW : 1900 - 1914), 30 December, p. 3. , viewed 19 June 2025, http://nla.gov.au/nla.news-article128298019

1910 'BONNER FAMILY IN FRONT OF THEIR HOME,' State Library of Queensland https://digital.slq.qld.gov.au/delivery/DeliveryManagerServlet?dps_pid=IE123429 [Accessed 5 Dec 2020]

1910 'CORDUROY ROAD.', The Argus (Melbourne, Vic. : 1848 - 1957), 31 May, p. 9. , viewed 21 May 2025, http://nla.gov.au/nla.news-article10860264

1910 'TENNIS.', The Tenterfield Intercolonial Courier and Fairfield and Wallangarra Advocate (NSW : 1900 - 1914), 12 July, p. 3. , viewed 24 May 2025, http://nla.gov.au/nla.news-article128295632

1910 'TENTERFIELD DEVELOPMENTS.', The Sydney Mail and New South Wales Advertiser (NSW : 1871 - 1912), 23 February, p. 14. , viewed 07 June 2025, http://nla.gov.au/nla.news-article164289737

1911 'AN HISTORICAL MAGAZINE,' The Age (Melbourne, Vic.: 1854 - 1954), 4 March 1911: 19. Web. Viewed 10 Dec 2020, http://nla.gov.au/nla.news-article196187750

1911 'IN COACHING DAYS.', The Sydney Mail and New South Wales Advertiser (NSW : 1871 - 1912), 1 November, p. 46. , viewed 31 May 2025, http://nla.gov.au/nla.news-article164332157

1911 'JAMES RUTHERFORD', The Bathurst Times (NSW : 1909 - 1925), 16 October, p. 2. , viewed 21 May 2025, http://nla.gov.au/nla.news-article110016022

1911 'LATE JAMES RUTHERFORD', National Advocate (Bathurst, NSW : 1889 - 1954), 11 November, p. 2. , viewed 18 June 2025, http://nla.gov.au/nla.news-article157791340

1911 'THE SKETCHER,' The Sydney Mail and New South Wales Advertiser (NSW: 1871 - 1912), 25 October, p. 2, viewed 2 Feb 2023, http://nla.gov.au/nla.news-article164332245

1912 'BRAVE YOUNG AUSTRALIAN.', Darling Downs Gazette (Qld. : 1881 - 1922), 28 May, p. 5. , viewed 24 May 2025, http://nla.gov.au/nla.news-article179982653

1912 'CONVEYANCE OF MAIL—COMMONWEALTH OF AUSTRALIA,' Commonwealth of Australia Gazette (National: 1901 - 1973), 18 April, pp. 601–605, viewed 8 Nov 2020, http://nla.gov.au/nla.news-article232362819 Office of Parliamentary Counsel.

1912 'FAMILY NOTICES', The Sydney Morning Herald (NSW : 1842 - 1954), 11 May, p. 16. , viewed 07 June 2025, http://nla.gov.au/nla.news-article15355322

1912 'STROUD,' Dungog Chronicle: Durham and Gloucester Advertiser (NSW: 1894 - 1954), 27 February, p. 2, viewed 18 Mar 2021, http://nla.gov.au/nla.news-article136135461

1912 'TENTERFIELD LICENSING COURT.', The Richmond River Express and Casino Kyogle Advertiser (NSW : 1904 - 1929), 23 January, p. 4. , http://nla.gov.au/nla.news-article124215211 State Library of New South Wales.

1912 'VILLAGE AND SUBURBAN LANDS AT LISTON,' Government Gazette of the State of NSW (Sydney, NSW.: 1901 - 2001), 24 January, p. 458, http://nla.gov.au/nla.news-article226770186

1913 'FAMILY NOTICES,' Queensland Figaro (Brisbane, Qld.: 1901 - 1936), 6 March, p. 13, viewed 18 Apr 2021, http://nla.gov.au/nla.news-article84396449

1913 'TENTERFIELD—TENTERFIELD PASTURES PROTECTION BOARD.', Sands Directories: Sydney and New South Wales, Australia [1858-1933] P.175 [online] (Tenterfield—Tenterfield Pastures Protection Board, 1913, p.175)

1913 'TO-MORROW'S VOTE.', The Richmond River Express and Casino Kyogle Advertiser (NSW : 1904 - 1929), 5 December, p. 4. , viewed 31 May 2025, http://nla.gov.au/nla.news-article123882381

1914 'AMOSFIELD. ANNUAL PUBLIC PICNIC,' The Richmond River Express and Casino Kyogle Advertiser (NSW: 1904 - 1929), 4 December, p. 7, viewed 18 Mar 2021, http://nla.gov.au/nla.news-article124716927

1914 'INDUSTRIAL COURT" The Tenterfield Courier and District Advocate (NSW : 1914) 4 June 1914: 5. Web. 7 June 2025 <http://nla.gov.au/nla.news-article135792715>

1914 'NO TITLE', Darling Downs Gazette (Qld. : 1881 - 1922), 27 June, p. 9. , viewed 17 May 2025, http://nla.gov.au/nla.news-article186864935

1914 'PERSONAL', The Tenterfield Courier and District Advocate (NSW : 1914), 18 June, p. 2. , viewed 07 June 2025, http://nla.gov.au/nla.news-article135792854

1914 'SPORTING NOTES. TENNIS,' The Tenterfield Courier and District Advocate (NSW: 1914), 26 October, p. 2, viewed 18 Mar 2021, http://nla.gov.au/nla.news-article135794232

1914 'TENTERFIELD SHIRE COUNCIL.', The Kyogle Examiner (NSW : 1912; 1914 - 1915; 1917 - 1954), 19 September, p. 1. , viewed 05 June 2025, http://nla.gov.au/nla.news-article234303970

1915 'COUNTRY MOVEMENTS.', The Brisbane Courier (Qld. : 1864 - 1933), 10 August, p. 7. , viewed 12 June 2025, http://nla.gov.au/nla.news-article20036041

1915 'EMPIRE DAY AT AMOSFIELD,' The Richmond River Express and Casino Kyogle Advertiser (NSW: 1904 - 1929), 8 June, p. 2, viewed 18 Mar 2021, https://trove.nla.gov.au/newspaper/article/128581300

1915 'PROPOSED ALTERATION OF DESIGN OF THE VILLAGE OF LISTON,' Government Gazette of the State of NSW (Sydney, NSW: 1901 - 2001), 10 November, p. 6656, viewed 6 Dec 2020, http://nla.gov.au/nla.news-article226921760

1916 'ALTERATION OF DESIGN OF THE VILLAGE OF LISTON,' Government Gazette of the State of NSW (Sydney, NSW: 1901 - 2001), 7 Apr 1916, p. 2082, http://nla.gov.au/nla.news-article225858600

1916 'BRISBANE'S FIRST POST OFFICE.', The Brisbane Courier (Qld. : 1864 - 1933), 4 November, p. 12. , viewed 16 May 2025, http://nla.gov.au/nla.news-article20130099

1916 'CONVEYANCE OF MAILS,' Commonwealth of Australia Gazette (National: 1901 - 1973), 23 June, p.1413, viewed 10 Dec 2020, http://nla.gov.au/nla.news-article232469371 Office of Parliamentary Counsel.

1916 'COUNTRY MOVEMENTS.', The Brisbane Courier (Qld. : 1864 - 1933), 14 June, p. 8. , viewed 09 June 2025, http://nla.gov.au/nla.news-article20122244

1916 'PRESENTATIONS,' Brisbane Courier (Qld.: 1864 - 1933), 14 July, p. 7, viewed 23 Apr 2021. The State Library of Qld.

1916 'WAR ITEMS.', The Armidale Express and New England General Advertiser (NSW : 1856 - 1861; 1863 - 1889; 1891 - 1954), 28 March, p. 8. , viewed 31 May 2025, http://nla.gov.au/nla.news-article191873761

1917 'COACHING IN AUSTRALIA : a history of the coaching firm of Cobb & Co. with guide to the present coaching routes in Queensland.', Lees, William. Brisbane: Carter-Watson Co., Record Number 996938111702061, 21111329569000 2061 Available at: http://onesearch.slq.qld.gov.au [Accessed 1 Oct. 2020]. Print. State Library South Bank Collection. (Coaching in Australia : a history of the coaching firm of Cobb & Co. with guide to the present coaching routes in Queensland, 1917)

1917 'COBB AND CO.,' The Queenslander (Brisbane, Qld.: 1866 - 1939), 1 September, p. 3, viewed 1 Oct 2020, http://nla.gov.au/nla.news-article22341918

1917 'PERSONAL NOTES.', The Queenslander (Brisbane, Qld. : 1866 - 1939), 3 March, p. 13. , viewed 07 June 2025, http://nla.gov.au/nla.news-article22336445

1917 'THREE NEW ENGLANDERS : THE STALLING FAMILY.', Sydney Mail (NSW : 1912 - 1938), 7 February, p. 26. , viewed

12 June 2025, http://nla.gov.au/nla.news-article160387275

1918 'WILSON'S DOWNFALL.', Australian Town and Country Journal (Sydney, NSW : 1870 - 1919), 28 August, p. 17. , viewed 12 June 2025, http://nla.gov.au/nla.news-article263627655

1919 'ADVERTISING', Warwick Daily News (Qld. : 1919 -1954), 18 December, p. 1. , viewed 07 June 2025, http://nla.gov.au/nla.news-article175750235

1919 'OUR HISTORY QANTAS AU', 2019. https://www.qantas.com/au/en/about-us/our-company/our-history.html

1919 'SOLDIERS OF THE NORTH', Daily Observer (Tamworth, NSW : 1917 - 1920), 6 February, p. 1. , viewed 12 June 2025, http://nla.gov.au/nla.news-article105062146

1919 'THE HISTORY OF QUEENSLAND, its people and industries : an historical and commercial review, descriptive and biographical facts figures and illustrations, an epitome of progress' / compiled by Matt. J. Fox Call Number N 994.3 F793 Created/Published Brisbane : States Publishing Co., Brisbane, 1919-1923 Images 999 https://nla.gov.au/nla.obj-268958630/w?searchTerm=%22Cobb+Co%22+%22Brisbane%22+1870&partId=nla.obj-268964903#page/n17/mode/1up

1920 'A FINE MEMORIAL,' Toowoomba Chronicle (Qld.: 1917 - 1922), 28 September, p. 7, viewed 10 Dec 2020, http://nla.gov.au/nla.news-article253171402

1920 'A RETROSPECT.', Warwick Daily News (Qld. : 1919 -1954), 31 May, p. 6. , viewed 21 May 2025, http://nla.gov.au/nla.news-article175762117

1920 'AERIAL MAIL,' Warwick Daily News (Qld.: 1919- 1954), 28 June, p. 6, viewed 6 Dec 2020, http://nla.gov.au/nla.news-article175764273

1920 'AMOSFIELD - Liston War Memorial at Amosfield', New South Wales, circa 1920

1920 'AMOSFIELD'S TRIBUTE—A SPLENDID WAR MEMORIAL,' Darling Downs Gazette (Qld.: 1881 - 1922), 28 September, p. 4, viewed 27 Mar 2021, http://nla.gov.au/nla.news-article174098889

1920 'COBB & CO.'S SERVICE,' The Daily Mail (Brisbane, Qld.: 1903 - 1926), 31 July, p. 4, viewed 21 Apr 2021, http://nla.gov.au/nla.news-article213230116. State Library of Queensland.

1920 'COBB AND CO.'S FACTORY,' Darling Downs Gazette (Qld.: 1881 - 1922), 20 December, p. 2, viewed 18 Mar 2021, http://nla.gov.au/nla.news-article174105965

1920 'MAIL BY PLANE,' Goulburn Evening Penny Post (NSW: 1881 - 1940), 17 August, p. 4 (Evening), viewed 4 Dec 2020, http://nla.gov.au/nla.news-article99218553

1920 'NEWS FROM THE COUNTRY,' The Daily Mail (Brisbane, Qld.: 1903 - 1926), 8 December, p. 4, viewed 2 Oct 2020, http://nla.gov.au/nla.news-article212826826

1920 'SOLDIER'S MEMORIAL,' Warwick Daily News (Qld.: 1919- 1954), 9 October, p. 5, viewed 27 Mar 2021, http://nla.gov.au/nla.news-article175771733

1920 'TENTERFIELD', The Armidale Express and New England General Advertiser (NSW : 1856 - 1861; 1863 - 1889; 1891 - 1954), 24 September, p. 6. , viewed 16 June 2025, http://nla.gov.au/nla.news-article192010308

1921 'AIR TRAVEL IN QUEENSLAND', 2021, p.1, https://www.qhatlas.com.au/content/air-travel-queensland

1921 'FIFTY YEARS AGO,' Darling Downs Gazette (Qld.: 1881 - 1922), 19 November, p. 7,
viewed 7 Nov 2020, http://nla.gov.au/nla.news-article174194203

1921 'IN THE DAYS OF COBB & CO.,' Sydney Mail (NSW: 1912 - 1938), 20 April, p. 8, viewed 5 Dec 2020, http://nla.gov.au/nla.news-article159037714

1921 'THE PASSING OF THE COACH,' The Sun (Sydney, NSW.: 1910 - 1954), 27 February, p. 5, viewed 25 Jan 2023, http://nla.gov.au/nla.news-article221441214

1922 'FIRE AT WILSON'S DOWNFALL,' Warwick Daily News (Qld.: 1919 - 1954), 30 January, p. 2, viewed 1 Oct 2020, http://nla.gov.au/nla.news-article177228349

1922 'HOTEL BURNT DOWN,' Casino and Kyogle Courier and North Coast Advertiser (NSW: 1904 - 1932), 4 February, p. 5, viewed 18 Mar 2021, http://nla.gov.au/nla.news-article234045165

1922 'JUBILEE OF STANTHORPE.', The Telegraph (Brisbane, Qld. : 1872 - 1947), 2 February, p. 3. , viewed 09 June 2025, http://nla.gov.au/nla.news-article168429240

1922 'OLD COACHING DAYS.', The Argus (Melbourne, Vic. : 1848 - 1957), 10 June, p. 7. , viewed 18 June 2025, http://nla.gov.au/nla.news-article4629678

1922 'STORY OF COBB AND CO.', The Argus (Melbourne, Vic. : 1848 - 1957), 20 May, p. 5. , viewed 18 June 2025, http://nla.gov.au/nla.news-article4643657

1922 'TIN AT STANTHORPE—SOME RICH CLAIMS,' The Daily Mail (Brisbane, Qld.: 1903 - 1926), 30 January, p. 11, viewed 13 Nov 2020, http://nla.gov.au/nla.news-article220533228

1922 'TIN DREDGING PLANT AT THE FOUR MILE,' The Daily Mail (Brisbane, Qld.: 1903 - 1926), 30 January, p.11. [online] http://nla.gov.au/nla.news-page23387526. The National Library of Australia acknowledges lenders & donors of collection material: State Library of Qld. [Accessed 4 Dec 2020]

1923 'ADVERTISING,' Leader (Orange, NSW: 1899 - 1945), 9 March, p. 2, viewed 27 Mar 2021, http://nla.gov.au/nla.news-page28100017

1923 'SNAKE IN CANARY CAGE.', Warwick Daily News (Qld. : 1919 -1954), 15 March, p. 4. , viewed 06 June 2025, http://nla.gov.au/nla.news-article177279743

1924 'BACK TO THE SYDNEY OF YEARS AGO - SOME BEAUTY CORNERS AT VAUCLUSE HOUSE,' The Newcastle Sun (NSW: 1918 - 1954), 6 Feb, p. 3, http://nla.gov.au/nla.news-article163216183

1924 'FIRE DESTROYS HOTEL', The Telegraph (Brisbane, Qld. : 1872 - 1947), 27 February, p. 2. (SECOND EDITION), viewed 16 May 2025, http://nla.gov.au/nla.news-article180041086

1924 'LAST COBB AND CO. COACH.', The Capricornian (Rockhampton, Qld. : 1875 - 1929), 4 October, p. 27. , viewed 19 June 2025, http://nla.gov.au/nla.news-article69747104

1924 'MARYLAND. THE BORDER gate between Maryland and Stanthorpe,' Brisbane Courier (Qld.: 1864 - 1933), 1 March, p. 15, viewed 17 Nov 2020, http://nla.gov.au/nla.news-article20666414

1924 'OBITUARY—MRS. A. PALMER,' The Armidale Express and New England General Advertiser (NSW: 1856 - 1861; 1863 - 1889; 1891 - 1954), 10 June, p. 4, viewed 1 Oct 2020, http://nla.gov.au/nla.news-article192002412

1924 'OLD GLEN INNES.', Glen Innes Examiner (NSW : 1908 - 1954), 18 December, p. 2. , viewed 20 May 2025, http://nla.gov.au/nla.news-article184458265

1924 'THE DAYS OF COBB & CO.,' Macleay Argus (Kempsey, NSW.: 1885 - 1954), 8 February, p. 3, viewed 1 Oct 2020, http://nla.gov.au/nla.news-article234452157

1924 'THE LAST COACH,' Western Star and Roma Advertiser (Toowoomba, Qld.: 1875 - 1948), 6 September, p. 4, viewed 18 Nov 2020, http://nla.gov.au/nla.news-article98032727

1925 'BOONOO BOONOO FALLS.', The Sydney Morning Herald (NSW : 1842 - 1954), 15 July, p. 16. , viewed 21 May 2025, http://nla.gov.au/nla.news-article16210390

1925 'COBB AND COMPANY'S COACHES.', Country Life Stock and Station Journal (Sydney, NSW : 1924 - 1925), 10 April, p. 28. , viewed 20 May 2025, http://nla.gov.au/nla.news-article128647626

1925 'GRAFTON-BORDER RAILWAY,' Warwick Daily News (Qld.: 1919 - 1954), 2 July, p. 4, viewed 11 Dec 2020, http://nla.gov.au/nla.news-article175717461

1925 'OVERLAND BY COBB AND CO.,' The World's News (Sydney, NSW: 1901 - 1955), 18 April, p. 8, viewed 1 Oct 2020, http://nla.gov.au/nla.news-article130619835

1925 'PERIODICAL ATTENTION—NORTHERN RIVERS TRIP,' The Queenslander (Brisbane, Qld.: 1866 - 1939), 26 December, p. 8, viewed 1 Oct 2020, http://nla.gov.au/nla.news-article25109542

1925 'RHYMES AND REMARKS,' The Mail (Adelaide, SA: 1912 - 1954), 3 January, p. 3, viewed 25 Jan 2023, http://nla.gov.au/nla.news-article59711043

1926 'A POST OFFICE DESTROYED', Daily Examiner (Grafton, NSW : 1915 - 1954), 28 December, p. 4. , viewed 16 June 2025, http://nla.gov.au/nla.news-article195439398

1926 'OBITUARY—MRS. MARY ASPINALL,' The Queenslander (Brisbane, Qld.: 1866 - 1939), 30 January, p. 15, viewed 27 Nov 2020, https://trove.nla.gov.au/newspaper/article/22751259

1926 'QUIET IN THE STREET.', Glen Innes Examiner (NSW : 1908 - 1954), 27 November, p. 4. , viewed 07 June 2025, http://nla.gov.au/nla.news-article184218742

1926 'THE ROARING DAYS,' Evening News (Sydney, NSW: 1869 - 1931), 17 June, p. 15, viewed 3 Feb 2023, http://nla.gov.au/nla.news-article114389410

1926 'WEDDING', Daily Examiner (Grafton, NSW : 1915 - 1954), 6 September, p. 3. , viewed 09 June 2025, http://nla.gov.au/nla.news-article195434263

1927 'FLOODS IN NORTH', The Sun (Sydney, NSW : 1910 - 1954), 28 January, p. 9. , viewed 21 May 2025, http://nla.gov.au/nla.news-article223468218

1927 'NEW SOUTH WALES POST OFFICE DIRECTORY,' 1927

1927 'THE FIRST MOTOR BUGGY IN AUSTRALIA,' The Sun (Kalgoorlie, WA.: 1898 - 1929), 10 April, p. 7, viewed 18 Mar 2021, http://nla.gov.au/nla.news-article260720507

1927 'WILLSON'S DOWNFALL.', The Sydney Morning Herald (NSW : 1842 - 1954), 31 August, p. 10. , viewed 19 June 2025, http://nla.gov.au/nla.news-article28053854

1928 'COUNTRY ROADS,' Queensland Times (Ipswich, Qld.: 1909 - 1954), 22 December, p. 10 (Daily), viewed 2 Oct 2020, http://nla.gov.au/nla.news-article115338940

1928 'COUNTRY ROADS—WEEK-END TRIPS. Information for Motorists,' The Brisbane Courier (Qld.: 1864 - 1933), 22 December, p. 17, http://nla.gov.au/nla.news-article21340517

1928 'MEMORIES OF COBB AND CO.,' The Kyogle Examiner (NSW: 1912; 1914 - 1915; 1917 - 1954), 13 July, p. 3, viewed 19 Mar 2021, http://nla.gov.au/nla.news-article234664725

1928 'TENTERFIELD.', The Brisbane Courier (Qld. : 1864 - 1933), 27 April, p. 18. , viewed 18 June 2025, http://nla.gov.au/nla.news-article21247055

1929 'COBB AND CO.'S COACHING DAYS: COLOURFUL PAGE OF HISTORY CLOSED,' Sunday Mail (Brisbane, Qld.: 1926 - 1954), 30 Jun, p. 3, http://nla.gov.au/nla.news-article97696763

1929 'EARLY SCHOOL DAYS,' The Brisbane Courier (Qld.: 1864 - 1933), 11 September, p. 20, viewed 1 Feb 2023, http://nla.gov.au/nla.news-article21476078

1930 'AUSTRALIAN ELECTORAL ROLLS,' 1903-1980, Ancestry.com (Australian Electoral Rolls, 1930)

1930 'EARLY HISTORY—THE STANTHORPE LINE,' Warwick Daily News (Qld.: 1919 - 1954), 2 April, viewed 22 Mar 2021, https://trove.nla.gov.au/newspaper/article/177441547

1931 'LINKS WITH THE LONG AGO.' (1931). Queenslander (Brisbane, Qld. : 1866 - 1939), [online] 3 Dec., p.9. https://trove.nla.gov.au/newspaper/article/23144481?searchTerm=conveyance%20of%20mail%20tenterfield%20Maryland%201871 [Accessed 7 Nov. 2020]

1931 'COBB & CO.—THE ROARING DAYS,' The World's News (Sydney, NSW: 1901 - 1955), 14 January, p. 9, viewed 09 Apr 2021, http://nla.gov.au/nla.news-article136309064

1931 'COBB AND CO.,' The Brisbane Courier (Qld.: 1864 - 1933), 23 October, p. 10, viewed 19 Mar 2021, http://nla.gov.au/nla.news-article21737029

1931 'IN THE DAYS OF COBB AND CO.,' Northern Star (Lismore, NSW: 1876 - 1954), 18 November, p. 4, viewed 2 Feb 2023, http://nla.gov.au/nla.news-article94258607

1931 'LINKS WITH THE LONG AGO,' The Queenslander (Brisbane, Qld.: 1866 - 1939), 3 December, p. 9, viewed 7 Nov 2020, https://trove.nla.gov.au/newspaper/article/23144481

1931 'LIQUIDATOR'S REPORT and statement of receipts and payments with regard to Cobb & Co.,' [online] Record no. 99183797666802061. Available at: http://onesearch.slq.qld.gov.au [Accessed 6 Dec 2020]. State Library of Qld.

1931 'THUNDERBOLT SCENE', The Inverell Times (NSW : 1899 - 1907, 1909 - 1954), 9 January, p. 7. , viewed 18 May 2025, http://nla.gov.au/nla.news-article183308401

1932 'AUSTRALIANITIES,' Macleay Argus (Kempsey, NSW: 1885 - 1907; 1909 - 1910; 1912 - 1913; 1915 - 1916; 1918 - 1954), 6 May, p. 9, viewed 10 Dec 2020, http://nla.gov.au/nla.news-article234242364

1932 'KNEW THUNDERBOLT' The Cumberland Argus and Fruitgrowers Advocate (Parramatta, NSW: 1888 - 1950), 15 December, p. 7, viewed 1 Feb 2023, http://nla.gov.au/nla.news-article105937786

1932 'LINKS WITH THE LONG AGO,' The Queenslander (Brisbane, Qld.: 1866 - 1939), 8 December, p. 9, viewed 12 Apr 2021, http://nla.gov.au/nla.news-article23154196

1932 'LISMORE TO BRISBANE,' Northern Star (Lismore, NSW: 1876 - 1954), 8 October, p. 10, viewed 19 Mar 2021, http://nla.gov.au/nla.news-article94304441

1932 'PHAR LAP', Yass Tribune-Courier (NSW : 1929 - 1954), 27 October, p. 5. , viewed 08 June 2025, http://nla.gov.au/nla.news-article249519896

1932 'WEEK-END TOURING—R.A.C.Q. ROAD BULLETIN,' The Telegraph (Brisbane, Qld.: 1872 - 1947), 31 December, p. 2 (First Edition), viewed 8 Apr 2021, http://nla.gov.au/nla.news-article179219080

1933 'ECHOES OF THE PAST,' Warwick Daily News (Qld.: 1919 - 1954), 24 June, p. 7, viewed 7 Nov 2020, http://nla.gov.au/nla.news-article189762342

1933 'TRANSPORT THROUGH THE YEARS,' The West Australian (Perth, WA.: 1879 - 1954), 5 January, p. 32, viewed 13 Apr 2021, http://nla.gov.au/nla.news-page2816155

1934 'HOW TENTERFIELD GOT ITS NAME', Guyra Argus (NSW : 1902 - 1954), 8 March, p. 1. , viewed 05 June 2025, http://nla.gov.au/nla.news-article173622324

1934 'IT HAPPENED TO-DAY—Sept. 13 THEY HARNESSED 6,000 HORSES EACH DAY', The Argus (Melbourne, Vic. : 1848 - 1957), 13 September, p. 10. , viewed 29 May 2025, http://nla.gov.au/nla.news-article10957035

1934 'REMEMBERED "THUNDERBOLT "', The Sydney Morning Herald (NSW : 1842 - 1954), 16 May, p. 14. , viewed 18 June 2025, http://nla.gov.au/nla.news-article17053458

1934 'SIXTY YEARS AGO—Gleanings from The Queenslander Files,' The Queenslander (Brisbane, Qld.: 1866 - 1939), 25 January, p. 14, viewed 18 Mar 2021, http://nla.gov.au/nla.news-article23332061

1934 'THE COACH DAYS.', Western Star and Roma Advertiser (Qld. : 1875 - 1948), 10 November, p. 8. , viewed 03 June 2025, http://nla.gov.au/nla.news-article98153237

1935 'ECHOES OF THE PAST", Warwick Daily News (Qld. : 1919 -1954), 30 March, p. 9. , viewed 17 Jan 2023, http://nla.gov.au/nla.news- article177321285 The National Library of Australia acknowledges lenders & donors of collection material: State Library of Queensland. (Echoes of the Past, 30 Mar 1935, p.9)

1935 'THE LIGHTS OF COBB & CO.,' The Gundagai Independent (NSW.: 1928 - 1954), 5 September, p. 6, viewed 3 Feb 2023, http://nla.gov.au/nla.news-article225002753

1937 'A [?] DRIVE', The Australasian (Melbourne, Vic. : 1864 - 1946), 31 July, p. 7. , viewed 18 June 2025, http://nla.gov.au/nla.news-article141807670

1937 'ECHOES OF THE PAST—SOME BORDER MEMOIRS,' Warwick Daily News (Qld.: 1919 - 1954), 23 September, p. 3, viewed 10 Dec 2020, http://nla.gov.au/nla.news-article189299294

1937 'GOOD OLD DAYS,' 30 Jan 1937, p.8 – Source no longer accessible

1938 'LOCAL AND GENERAL,' The Richmond River Herald and Northern Districts Advertiser (NSW: 1886 - 1942), 27 September, p. 2, viewed 18 Mar 2021, http://nla.gov.au/nla.news-article126097052

1938 'THE DAYS OF COBB AND CO.', Daily Examiner (Grafton, NSW : 1915 - 1954), 4 May, p. 2. , viewed 20 May 2025, http://nla.gov.au/nla.news-article192642484

1938 'WHEN COBB AND CO. STABLED IN THE CITY,' Sunday Mail (Brisbane, Qld.: 1926 - 1954), 16 January, p. 38, viewed 8 Apr 2021, http://nla.gov.au/nla.news-article97864857

1938 'WILLSON'S DOWNFALL', The Courier-Mail (Brisbane, Qld. : 1933 - 1954), 6 June, p. 6. , viewed 05 June 2025, http://nla.gov.au/nla.news-article40985666

1940 'LINK WITH THE PAST,' The Age (Melbourne, Vic.: 1854 - 1954), 22 May, p. 6, viewed 26 Mar 2021, http://nla.gov.au/nla.news-page19415268

1942 'COBB & CO.', Daily Advertiser (Wagga Wagga, NSW : 1911 - 1954), 27 March, p. 3. , viewed 04 June 2025, http://nla.gov.au/nla.news-article144186821

1944 'ON THE TRACK', The Townsville Daily Bulletin (Qld. : 1907 - 1909 ; 1912 - 1966), 17 April, p. 3. , viewed 27 May 2025, http://nla.gov.au/nla.news-article63156368

1946 'MEET THE SHOW JUDGES', Glen Innes Examiner (NSW : 1908 - 1954), 21 February, p. 2. , viewed 07 June 2025, http://nla.gov.au/nla.news-article184629789

1947 'COBB AND CO.', Kalgoorlie Miner (WA : 1895 - 1954), 16 January, p. 3. , viewed 07 June 2025, http://nla.gov.au/nla.news-article95602314

1949 'TENTERFIELD', Tenterfield District Historical Society—Back to Tenterfield Week [online] p. 6 https://nla.gov.au/nla.obj-52861299/view?partId=nla.obj-105346111#page/n13/mode/1up [Accessed 8 Nov. 2020]

1951 'GOOD OLD DAYS' OF STANTHORPE', Warwick Daily News (Qld. : 1919 -1954), 30 January, p. 8. , viewed 19 June 2025, http://nla.gov.au/nla.news-article190770743

1954 'FINNEY'S DRAPERY STORE', Warwick Daily News (Qld. : 1919 -1954), 4 February, p. 3. (Warwick Daily News STANTHORPE Show Supplement), viewed 08 June 2025, http://nla.gov.au/nla.news-article189255285

1955 'COBB AND CO. COACH ON NEW STAMPS,' The Broadcaster (Fairfield, NSW: 1935 - 1978), 29 June, p. 5, viewed 19 Mar 2021, http://nla.gov.au/nla.news-article144075717

1968 'THE STANTHORPE BORDER POST,' Issue unknown

1971 'COMMUNICATIONS ACROSS THE GENERATIONS : an Australian post office history of Queensland.', Rea, Malcolm .M. (Read at a meeting of the Society on 22 July 1971).Journal of the Royal Historical Society of Queensland 9 (2) 168-226 [online] pp.168–226., viewed 08 Feb 2021, https://espace.library.uq.edu.au The University of Queensland. (Communications Across the Generations, Read 1971)

1975 'GUESS WHO POPPED UP AMONG THE PAINTINGS?', The Australian Women's Weekly (1933 - 1982), 1 October, p. 29. , viewed 07 June 2025, http://nla.gov.au/nla.news-article55186111

2003 'ERIC REMEMBERED,' Letters to the Editor, Education: Journal of the N.S.W. Public School Teachers Federation, v.84, no.09, 1 Sep, p.10. Call number NcF 331.8809944 EDU. https://trove.nla.gov.au/work/233799311?keyword=amosfield [Accessed 1 Oct 2020]

2004 'A THEMATIC HISTORY OF TENTERFIELD SHIRE—2004 Located in the New England region of New South Wales,' Halliday, K. [online] https://www.tenterfield.nsw.gov.au/content/uploads/2020/02/Shire-Wide-Heritage-Study-Thematic-History.pdf

2010 'AUSTRALIAN MARRIAGE INDEX, 1788-1950,' Ancestry.com Operations, Inc. Registration number 001966, p. 4972. [online] https://www.ancestry.com.au/family-tree/person/tree/42808744/person/19838110961/facts [Accessed 6 Dec 2020]

2015 'GEORGE FRANCIS TRAIN, One of the Few Sane Men in a Mad, Mad World,' New

England Historical Society. https://www.newenglandhistoricalsociety.com/george-francis-train-one-of-few-sane-men-mad-mad-world

2019 'OUR HISTORY QANTAS AU,' Qantas.com, viewed 11 Apr 2021, https://www.qantas.com/au/en/about-us/our-company/our-history.html

2021 'AIR TRAVEL IN QUEENSLAND,' Queensland Historical Atlas. https://www.qhatlas.com.au/content/air-travel-queensland

2021 'LISTON – AMOSFIELD WAR MEMORIAL,' Monument Australia, viewed 30 Mar 2021, https://www.monumentaustralia.org.au/themes/conflict/ww1/display/21890-liston---amosfield-war-memorial.

2025 'TENTERFIELD SADDLER' | NSW Government www.nsw.gov.au/visiting-and-exploring-nsw/locations-and-attractions/tenterfield-saddler

n.d. 'REPORT OF THE P.M. GENERAL,' Murray-Prior, Hon.T.M.L. (Report of the P.M. General, no date)

Index

Aberdeen Company 28

Acacia 53, 71, 74, 84, 86-88, 103, 104, 122

Accidents 12, 29, 54, 55, 71, 162

Adams and Co. 37

Aerial Mail 90

A. J. S. Bank 28

Alfred 43, 86, 122-124, 162

Allora 8, 53, 62, 104, 145, 166

American Telegraph Line of Coaches 5, 36

Amosfield 7, 54, 57, 74, 81, 86, 89, 94, 103, 104, 122, 124, 125-128, 136, 142-145, 147, 148, 150, 152, 154, 155, 157-159, 161, 162, 166, 167

Amosfield War Memorial 125

ANZAC DAY 30

Armidale 7, 13, 28, 29, 45, 47, 48, 53, 54, 56, 71, 75, 86, 116, 117, 126, 170-173

Barney Downs 43

Bathurst 4, 38, 44, 49, 51, 59, 73

Belgian Relief Fund 125

Bendigo 37,

'Billy' the Ram 28

Bolivia 43, 120, 161

Bond 46

Bookookoorara 9, 43, 48, 53, 54, 57, 65, 89, 116, 120, 161, 162

Boonoo Boonoo 7, 9, 43, 54-57, 71, 72, 74-78, 83-85, 89, 90, 104, 114, 116, 117, 122, 126, 130, 131, 153, 161

Bowers 55

Braeside 104

Brisbane 4-8, 10, 12, 13, 21-23, 25-27, 31, 36, 38, 43-46, 52-54, 59, 60, 62, 67-74, 88, 89, 99, 101, 104, 105, 107, 108, 111, 113, 114, 119, 125, 127, 161, 166

Bryan's Gap 74, 126

Burrenbilla 44

Bushrangers 42, 45, 46, 74

Canning Downs 27, 28, 34, 39-41, 53

Casino 12, 30, 81, 82, 104

Castlemaine 44

Catholic Churches 150

Charleville 4, 44, 61, 69, 73, 88, 89, 90

Cheviot Hills 43

Chinese 12, 59, 114-117, 121, 150

Circus 9, 57, 116

Clarence 8, 30, 38, 74, 85, 87, 103, 117, 162

Claverton 44

Clifton 27, 30, 43, 53, 60, 74, 81, 122

Cloncurry 69, 89, 90

Coach and Horses Hotel 57, 72, 78, 85

Cobb's Box 37

Commission Stores 26

Condamine 8, 45, 53, 62

Convict Barracks 26

Cooktown 69, 115

Cootamundra 90

County of Buller 7, 166, 168, 169

County of Ruby 7

Creeks 8, 11, 54, 55, 58, 73, 84, 113, 114, 117-121

Cricket 85

Currawillinghi 47

Dalby 8, 27, 45, 52, 53, 62, 74

Dalveen 11, 28, 69, 71, 103, 104

Darling Downs 27, 28, 39, 105, 118

Deepwater 43, 53, 81, 105

Deuchar 28, 39, 60, 104

Dirranbandi 105

Doctor's Nose 116

Drayton 7, 28, 43

Driver 2, 10, 38, 46, 47, 54, 55, 57, 58, 60, 61, 72, 85, 88, 90, 91, 105, 106, 123, 124, 160

Drought 88, 89

Eagle Farm 25

East Warwick 28, 127

Eaton Vale 27

Edenglassie 25

Edmonton's Paddock 26

Empire Day 125

England 9, 12, 13, 25, 26, 30, 40, 46, 48, 54, 57, 60, 70, 71, 76, 82, 86, 103, 109, 115, 117, 122-125, 127, 140, 149, 150, 161, 166

Examiner 28, 70, 129

Factories 44

Farley's Hotel 58, 70, 79, 90, 115, 119

Farm Creek 54, 76

Female convicts 25

Fire 88, 91, 126

Fireworks 83

Floods 82

Folkestone Station 114

Folkstone 60

Forest Creek 37

Four Mile Creek 10

Fox, James Benjamin 75

frogs 81, 181

Frogs 36

Gardiner 46, 47, 91

Gatton 43

Glen Aplin 104

Glenelg Station 118

Glenn Innes 7

Goulburn 44, 46, 74, 75, 90

Government Gardens 26

Governor Brisbane 25

Grandchester 45

Great Northern Road 1, 2, 4-8, 12, 13, 55, 72, 86, 103, 104, 112, 161, 166

Groom's Hotel 58-60, 119

Gympie 8, 38, 45-47, 52, 53, 62, 69

Handel 26

Hannon 103, 124

Hart 11, 47, 54

Herding Yard 7, 57, 113, 118, 120, 126, 128, 133, 161, 162, 166, 168, 169

Hewetson's Mill 104

Hotel 7, 9, 10, 11, 57, 58, 60, 61, 64, 70-72, 78, 84, 85, 88, 104, 119, 122, 132

Ipswich 8, 10, 13, 20, 27-29, 38, 43-46, 52, 53, 60, 62, 114, 118, 166

Jimbour 27

Jondaryan 27

Juergen's Store 9, 84, 123

Killarney 53, 54, 104, 124

Kyoomba 89

Last Cobb and Co. Coach 88, 90

Lawson, Henry 87, 88

Leech's Gully 89, 123

Limestone 27, 28

Lionsville 74

Lismore 16, 82, 90, 104, 178

Liston 2, 5, 7, 57, 74, 77, 78, 86, 87, 89, 94-97, 101, 103, 104, 109, 110, 112, 124-129, 133, 134, 136, 137, 139, 140-145, 147, 148, 149-154, 157, 159-162, 165, 166, 168, 169

Lord John's Swamp 118

Mail 2, 8, 12, 15, 16, 44, 45, 46, 52-54, 69, 70, 74, 88-90, 104, 106, 109, 111, 166, 168

Mail Robberies 45

Map 7, 38, 74, 124, 166-169

Maryland 7-13, 17, 28, 29, 31, 39, 43, 45, 47, 52-54, 57, 59, 60-62, 69, 71, 72, 74, 75, 85-88, 103, 110, 113, 114, 116, 118-120, 124, 127, 128, 161, 162, 166

Maryland Hotel 7, 87

Melbourne 37, 43, 56, 58, 72, 90, 105, 119
Methodist Church 125, 127, 150
Midkin 44
Millers' Quarry 125
Mineral Discoveries 113
Moreton Bay 25, 26, 38, 117, 166
Morpeth 12
Morton Bay 25, 38
Motor Buggy 90
Motor car 90, 91, 103, 108, 160
Mount Marlay 12, 58, 119
Murrurundi 7, 52, 53
Myall Creek 27
Norfolk Island 25
Old Koreelah 104
Pastoral Runs 27
Perricoota 44
Port Augusta 90
Post and Telegraph Office 10
Post Offices 9, 10, 25-33, 44, 52- 54, 57, 67, 74, 77, 87-89, 111, 124
Presbyterian Church 92
Proclamation of the State of Queensland 38
Qantas 90, 179
Quart Pot 10, 11, 29, 52, 57-59, 75, 112-116, 118-120
Queen's Wharf 26
Ragh 103, 124
Rathdowney 104
Redcliffe 25
Robertson & Wagner 37
Roma 4, 8, 45, 47, 53, 62, 69, 158
Rosenthal 28, 39, 41, 53
Rouse-Street 83
Ruby Creek 8, 52, 53, 113, 118, 120, 162
Rutherford 38, 43, 44, 46, 47, 50, 51, 62, 104
Saddlers 82
School 28
School of Arts 28, 81, 87, 103, 123, 126
Seven Mile Lane 161
Severn River 74
Silver Mines 118
Slade's Post Office 26
Squatters 27
Stannum 57, 58, 98, 113, 115, 118, 119, 121, 159

Stannum Miner 58, 115, 159
Stanthorpe 9-13, 17-19, 29, 31, 51-62, 65, 66, 69, 70-73, 79, 86-90, 92, 98-100, 103, 104, 110, 112-115, 118-120, 121, 124, 125, 127-129, 131-133, 135, 136, 138, 151, 155, 156, 158, 159, 161, 162, 166
St. John's Church 124
Storm 43, 73, 81
Sugarloaf 8, 10, 12, 57, 61, 72, 88, 89, 113, 117, 120, 121, 126, 129, 161
Surat 69, 90, 105
Sydney 2, 5-10, 12, 14, 25, 30, 32, 38, 44, 46, 51, 55, 56, 61, 70, 71, 86, 90, 114, 116, 117, 122, 127, 161, 166
Tabulam 8, 12, 81, 82, 104
Teacher 126, 127
Telegraphic Communication 9, 166
Tennis 86, 87, 140
Tenterfield 2, 4, 7,-10, 12-16, 27, 29, 30, 32, 43-46, 48, 52-57, 61-63, 69-74, 77, 78, 81-90, 93, 94, 103-105, 109, 113-118, 121-123, 125, 126, 130, 131, 141, 146, 154, 159, 161, 162, 166
Tenterfield Saddler 83
Tent Hill 114
The Boat House 26
The Gaol 26
The Rocky 117
The Roll Up Tree 59
The Swamp 28
Thirteen Mile Creek 10, 53, 92
Thulimbah 103
Thunderbolt 11, 46-48, 74, 75
Thunderbolt's Tree 48
Thunderbolt's wife 47
Timbarra 56, 74, 161
Tin Mining 52, 113, 115, 133
Toolburra 53
Toowoomba 4, 8, 10, 28, 33, 38, 43, 45, 52, 53, 58, 62, 66, 74, 89, 104, 125, 166
Train, George Francis 37, 40
Tread and Windmill 26
Undercliff Station 76
Verse: THE GOOD OLD DAYS. 24
Verse: GLENGALLAN. 36
Verse: COBB & CO. 68
Verse: JAMES RUTHERFORD. 50
Verse: MARSUPIAL BILL. 112
Verse: PHAR LAP. 102

Verse: THE BUSHRANGER. 42
Verse: THE DAYS OF COBB AND CO. 80
Verse: THE DAYS OF COBB & CO. 6, 160
Victoria Bridge 60, 62
Wallangarra 16, 73, 104
Ward 46-48, 74, 75, 120, 124
Warwick 2, 4, 7-10, 12, 13, 19, 20, 27-30, 33, 34, 39-41, 43, 45, 47, 52-55, 57, 58, 60, 61, 62, 68, 69, 70-74, 100, 103, 104, 114, 116, 118, 119, 124, 127, 129, 138, 150, 156, 161, 162, 166, 168, 169
Wedding 124
Westbrook 27
White Swamp 74
Willson's Downfall 53, 54, 57, 71, 72, 74, 86, 89, 104, 118, 125
Wilson's Downfall 7, 10, 12, 48, 55, 57, 71, 72, 74, 78, 84-90, 104, 113, 120, 124-126, 137, 161, 162
Windaroo 103
Windeyer 43, 47, 56
Woodenbong 81, 104
Woolshed Hill 103
Wylie Creek 87, 89, 95, 103, 118, 120, 124, 127, 150, 151, 153, 161
Yeulba 69, 74, 90, 105
Young 84, 124, 127